Testimonials for *The People First Effect*

"This superb book provides helpful insights for leaders to identify gaps in both their personal and organization's leadership. It provides readers practical and powerful ways to invest in and develop their people resulting in a culture of trust, engagement, and sustainable business results."

–Mike Hoseus, Co-author of Shingo Award Winning *Toyota Culture* and Executive Director of The Center for Quality People and Organizations

"This is an inspiring must-read for anyone who needs to build trust with others to achieve results—no matter what the field. How wonderful it would be if all CEOs were imbued with the People First Effect. And even better, how wonderful if this philosophy infected our politicians."

–L. Craig Johnstone, Former US Ambassador, Director for Resources Plans and Policy at the Department of State, Deputy UN High Commissioner for Refugees, Vice President of the Boeing Company, President of Cabot Plastics, and International; Board Executive at Vital Voices Global Partnership, Refugees International, and USA for UNHCR

"Jack Lannom's book *The People First Effect* provides every business leader with a proven roadmap to transform their business with his 7 Keys of Mastering High Trust in a Low Trust World. The reason that I was successful in my career is because I diligently applied these keys of trust to every business that I led. I highly recommend this book for any leader that is serious about creating a trust-based culture."

–Gerald Greenwald is the former chairman and CEO of United Airlines, the former Chrysler Corporation vice-chairman, and the Founding Partner of Greenbrier Equity Group

"Jack Lannom's empowering philosophy is a joyous affirmation for a way of life in business and personal relationships to grow the human spirit in a positive and productive manner."

–Thad Strom, Former Chief Counsel and Staff Director of the US Senate Committee on the Judiciary

"Unethical, disloyal people of egocentric greed are already mainstream, now suddenly embroidered in a world imploding with post truth, fake news and conspiracy theories. *Time* magazine covering its entire front page with 'Is Truth Dead?'

Jack Lannom's *The People First Effect* could not arrive at a more opportune moment, demonstrating how to build Trust both personally and professionally, reinforcing the fundamentals of ethics, loyalty, virtue, and truth.

A must and a light read for everybody in a disrupted world; a fast-flowing book weaving pragmatic wisdom into a suspenseful thriller.

A fascinating self-help book for managers and the general public alike, destined for the bestseller lists. A book I would have put into the Ethics and Worker Relations courses at MIT and every other university."

–Dr. Jan Hedberg, PhD '77 MIT

"The corporate world has changed significantly in recent years with the implementation of social media into the daily life of a generation of society to the changing world of communication. The reality of the emergence of new technologies and new media is that trust, communication, and integrity are a lost art. Business leaders underestimate the quantity and quality of communication necessary to build a successful team to navigate through an evolving business landscape. Jack Lannom captures the essential elements to successfully communicate, and more importantly, provides the tools needed to master the communications challenge. The seven Cs. Please enjoy and share with everyone you encounter every day."

–Jeffrey Dane Oetting, Chief Executive Officer of Featherwood Group of Companies

"The stories and insights shared behind this cover emphasize the most important facts of the way it should be, but in the real operating world it unfortunately doesn't happen enough. It isn't only about money. It is, in fact, all about people. Jack Lannom's life pursuit jumps out in what is shared in People First. The words resonate in importance. This book is about proselytizing people in the way they think and act and to reorient behavior. This is a must-read if you want to be dimensionally successful and make a difference. Bravo Jack, it is an honor to know you."

–Jeffrey Meshel, Author of *One Phone Call Away, Secrets of a Master Networker* and *The Opportunity Magnet*; Chairman/Co-Founder of DivorceForce; Chairman of Paradigm Capital Corporation; and Chairman and Founder of The Strategic Forum

—THE—
PEOPLE FIRST™
EFFECT

THE
PEOPLE FIRST™
EFFECT

Keys
for
Mastering
High Trust
in a
Low Trust
World

Jack Lannom

Foreword by Sir Olaf Halvorssen

A SAVIO REPUBLIC BOOK
An Imprint of Post Hill Press

The People First Effect:
7 Keys for Mastering High Trust in a Low Trust World
© 2017 by Jack Lannom
All Rights Reserved

ISBN: 978-1-68261-435-8
ISBN (eBook): 978-1-68261-436-5

Cover Design by Jorge Rendon
Interior Design and Composition by Greg Johnson/Textbook Perfect

posthillpress.com
New York • Nashville
Published in the United States of America

Table of Contents

Dedication

IT IS WITH GREAT JOY and heartfelt appreciation that I dedicate this book to my good friend and an exemplar of the People First philosophy, Tom Manenti. Even as I was in the process of writing *The People First Effect*, I knew without any doubt that I wanted to dedicate this book to Tom.

I met Tom in January 2010 at a retreat that I was conducting for the senior leadership team of Tom's company, MiTek Industries, Inc. At the end of my day of training, Tom approached me and asked if I would become his personal coach. I was deeply honored that he would consider me to be his trusted advisor and I gladly accepted.

However, I also told Tom that I wanted to do something very special for him and for MiTek Industries: I explained that I hoped that MiTek would become a People First Certified Organization during the time I was coaching him. I assured Tom that the certification process would fully meet Tom's personal growth needs and help MiTek to grow and develop as well.

Tom graciously accepted my offer, and MiTek became a People First Certified Organization in 2012. My relationship with Tom Manenti and his tremendous company has continued for more than seven years. Tom and I have engaged in several one-on-one "deep-dive" sessions, lasting eight hours at a time, and I truly know the depths and virtues of the heart, soul, and mind of this great man. It didn't take long at all to see how Tom Manenti's personal and professional life aligns with the timeless and transformational seven keys of trust that I lay out in *The People First Effect*: Character, Competence, Confidence, Caring, Communication, Consistency, and Commitment.

Let me briefly explain:

Character: Tom is a man of the highest integrity. His word is his bond.

Competence: Tom's vast knowledge and world-class skills in his industry led Warren Buffett—chairman, president, and CEO of Berkshire Hathaway, which owns MiTek Industries—to promote Tom to the role of MiTek's Chief Executive Officer in 2011. Mr. Buffett's trust has been richly rewarded; MiTek has doubled in size under Tom's competent leadership.

Confidence: Tom is a bold and determined leader because his life is grounded in his faith, his unshakable values, and his pursuit of personal and professional excellence. However, Tom's strong, unwavering deportment is characterized by genuine humility, not arrogance.

Caring: Tom Manenti genuinely loves people. His great care for his Purpose Partners is demonstrated through any number of kind, sincere interactions with them, including sending each one of MiTek's more than four thousand Purpose Partners a personalized birthday card.

Communication: Tom truly understands what great communication looks like and sounds like. His communication is always clear, concise, coherent, and compelling. But what really sets Tom apart is that he speaks the truth in love. Moreover, he has mastered the art of inspiring storytelling, which he uses to make his messages that much more engaging.

Consistency: As long as I've known Tom, I've seen him to be self-consistent in his words, beliefs, and behaviors. There is no integrity gap with this man; he is as trustworthy as the rising and setting of the sun.

Commitment: There is one thing that everyone knows about Tom Manenti: whatever he sets out to do, he is 100 percent committed to fulfilling his responsibility to the values, mission, and vision of the MiTek organization. If you are one of those who is blessed to have Tom Manenti lead you, you will witness his unassailable, unconquerable commitment to achieving the best results for MiTek.

I love Tom, his wife, Kathy, their children, and their grandchildren. Over the last seven years, Tom has become a faithful, caring friend to me and my wife, Debbie. I trust Tom because I know him. And I know that I am dedicating this book to a man who lives every moment of his life in harmony with the seven keys of trust that you will encounter in *The People First Effect*.

My life is richer because of my dear, trustworthy friend, Tom Manenti.

Foreword

WHEN I HEARD THAT JACK Lannom had written a new book advancing the People First philosophy, I couldn't wait to read it. The reason for this is, now more than ever, the world needs Jack's People First message. *The People First Effect: 7 Keys for Mastering High Trust in a Low Trust World* is a life-changing book; I consider it a great honor to have been asked to write this foreword.

I have read many forewords to a great number of books, and I have always wondered how well the person writing the foreword really knows the author. Therefore, I wanted to assure you that that I have known Jack Lannom for more than ten years, and Jack truly believes and practices the principles of People First. The man walks the walk.

Jack Lannom is the founder and CEO of People First International, a company that is dedicated to changing organizations all over the world with the People First philosophy. In addition, Jack is my personal mentor, my good friend, and our families have become very close.

If you liked Jack's book, *People First: Achieving Balance in an Unbalanced World*, you will thoroughly enjoy reading *The People First Effect*. This second book in the People First series brings forward all the original ideas in the first book and adds a provocative dimension around the concept of trust.

If you are intrigued by the idea of learning everything you need to know about creating high trust in your personal and professional relationships, I highly recommend *The People First Effect*. I believed that I was really good at establishing trust in all my relationships; however, after reading this book, my ability to create trust-based relationships has increased dramatically. I have read other books on the subject of trust, but no one ever laid out such an easy, user-friendly system as Jack's *7 Keys for Mastering High Trust in a Low Trust World*.

What I find most intriguing about *The People First Effect* is that Jack has done something I have never seen another author attempt in a leadership development book. Jack reprised several of the fictional characters from the first *People First* book and masterfully blended them with seven real-life People First leaders, using their actual words in the story. Jack selected these seven men from companies that have completed his *People First Strategic Leadership* certification program. Each leader was selected for his exceptional expertise in one of the seven keys of trust.

Here is the great benefit for you, the reader: you will learn specific strategies for accelerating trust in your organization from seven of the finest People First leaders in America, men who are currently leading multimillion- and multibillion-dollar companies.

If I were to recommend only one business book for you to read this year, one full of practical advice which you can immediately put to use in your organization today, I would not hesitate to encourage you to read *The People First Effect*. You are in for an intellectual feast and a personal development deep-dive unlike anything you have ever experienced.

There is nothing more fundamental and more vitally important to learn than how to create trust by putting other people first and treating everyone with the utmost dignity, respect, and honor. I only wish a course like this had been taught when I studied for my MBA at the Wharton School of Finance. Next time I visit Philadelphia, I plan to personally present a copy to the dean of the business school. I am quite sure he will love it as much as I did.

Enjoy!

Sir Olaf Leonard Halvorssen
Knight Commander to His Majesty King Harald V of Norway

Introduction

I HAVE BEEN TELLING AUDIENCES and individual clients for more than forty-five years that the two most important pillars in both our personal and professional relationships are trust and respect. But the load-bearing pillar of those two is *trust*; without trust, respect is not likely to last long or run very deep.

In truth, the life-giving taproot of every philosophy, every home, every business, and every community is trust. So no matter what you do during the day—whether you are a student, a job-seeker, someone who works in the home, or the leader of a business enterprise—building strong, trust-based relationships is probably the most important life skill that you can ever develop. But can you identify the seven keys of trust that are found in all credible people? Can you explain how each of those seven keys is lived out in the home, the workplace, and the community?

The People First Effect is the second book in the People First series. The response to the first book, *People First: Achieving Balance in an Unbalanced World*, which is now in its fourth printing, has been so overwhelmingly positive that I have been giving serious thought to how I might best serve the tens of thousands of men and women who have derived such great value from the wisdom that Sifu Li imparted to Dan Burton. I retained the main characters in order to maintain continuity of the People First message, but this new book contains all the elements of a great novel, with several new characters added to give the reader greater insight and depth into the common struggles that all of us face. You will see a clear contrast between the healthy outcomes that the People First philosophy produces, as opposed to the crippling outcomes for those who are subjected to living and working in a "People Last" environment.

I wanted to do something truly distinctive with *The People First Effect*, so in addition to incorporating all the compelling, fast-paced elements of a great novel, I'm going to introduce you to seven real-life CEOs and senior leaders of seven companies that are People First Certified. In the story, Dan Burton is facing challenges that are greater than any he has encountered, and he turns once again to his old friend Sifu Li for help. Sifu readily agrees to lead Dan into a deeper, more comprehensive understanding of the People First philosophy because of Dan's deeper need. The two friends embark on a new learning journey as Sifu builds on the foundation laid in *People First* by introducing Dan to seven business leaders who will mentor Dan in understanding how to create and sustain trust. And here is where a work of fiction steps into fact. Dan's conversations with these seven leaders are taken directly from extensive interviews conducted with each leader individually.

I have known all these men for years, and we have established strong, trust-based relationships. I wanted to share these men, whom I am proud to call my good friends, with all my other friends, with all my clients, and with all those who want to advance in the People First philosophy. These seven leaders have all experienced great success practicing the People First philosophy, and they all cheerfully agreed to contribute to this novel about personal and professional excellence. It is one of the greatest honors of my life that men of their caliber have freely given their time to share their insight about building trust in their respective industries.

- **Tom Manenti**—Chairman and CEO of MiTek Industries, Inc., a Berkshire Hathaway company—discusses Character.
- **James Donnelly**—President and CEO of the Castle Group, a full-service property management group—discusses Competence.
- **Ray Aschenbach**—Senior Vice President of North American Operations for Iron Mountain, the world's largest data storage firm—discusses Confidence.
- **Keith Guller**—CEO of Essex Industries, a leading supplier to the aerospace, defense, first response, and medical markets—discusses Caring.
- **Noel Fogarty**—Former Vice President of Operations for Boston Scientific, a leading innovator of medical solutions—discusses Communication.
- **Richard Thorne**—Leader of North American Business for Kimberly-Clark Professional—discusses Consistency.
- **Keith Koenig**—President of City Furniture, one of South Florida's leading retailers—discusses Commitment.

Introduction

Each one of these business leaders graciously consented to engage in extended interviews for this project, and I have reproduced their comments, using their own words, in *The People First Effect*. These men have far more than a classroom understanding of the keys to building trust; they have amassed decades of priceless experience successfully applying their knowledge and skills to real-world challenges and creating sustainable success.

I do not feel that I am exaggerating in the slightest when I say that you could not possibly get a better education in creating trust than the one you will receive from the seven men you will meet in this book. To have the opportunity to sit down with just one of them would be immensely profitable; to read the accumulated wisdom of all seven of these men will be like getting your PhD in building strong, trust-based relationships. I like to think that *The People First Effect* lifts the priceless diamond that is Trust into the light, and each of these leaders takes that diamond and turns it slightly so that you can see the incredible, intricate beauty of each of the seven facets of that diamond called Trust.

I am confident that *The People First Effect* will resonate with millions of leaders at a great many levels. Anyone who is in a leadership position, whether in the business world, the military, or a voluntary association, will greatly benefit from the knowledge that is laid out in a clear, conversational style; they'll also enjoy a darn good story!

I further believe this book will grip the hearts of anyone who is looking to increase trust and decrease tension in every aspect of their lives. Most of us have experienced the pain of professional difficulties, marital tension, a loved one's addiction, or a tragic death. We have felt ourselves shut down emotionally, even as our grief, anger, and confusion threaten to consume us. In that sense, Dan Burton represents every man and every woman who has ever struggled to maintain a relationship that has been damaged by distrust. He is every person who has struggled with doubt and grief and pain and come out of the crucible better for the experience.

But there are lots of good stories available to read; why should you invest in this one? Let me answer that question with one of my own: *Can you teach the people who are most important to you how to assess their level of trustworthiness in all their relationships?* And if you are a business leader, here is a second question: *How would it improve performance and profitability if everyone in your organization knew how to create and accelerate trust-based relationships?*

I have been studying this subject for more than forty years; I've been struck by the fact that all the schools of thought on trust—all the books and scholarly papers—do not come to a common definition of trust. Clearly, there is no consensus on the subject of trust. *The People First Effect* provides a comprehensive definition of trust, coupled with empirical data from some of the most trusted leaders and organizations in America. The seven keys of trust you will learn in this book—practical, time-tested strategies to establish trustworthiness—have transformed their companies, both in terms of employee engagement and improving sustainable profitability.

What will reading this book do for you? Learning from Sifu Li, Dan Burton, and these seven business leaders, all of them advancing the People First philosophy, will teach you how to build a home, a workforce, and a leadership team that consistently: (1) cultivates character, (2) develops competence, (3) instills confidence, (4) enhances caring, (5) improves communication, (6) unleashes consistency, and (7) inspires commitment.

No human being will reach his or her full potential without the ability to build trust-based relationships. Men and women who lack high levels of trustworthiness in their interactions with others live impoverished lives—in both their personal relationships and their careers. And, as you'll see in this book, the worst aspect of the lives of untrustworthy people is not just how their own lives are negatively impacted, but the devastating consequences on the lives of others.

I want *The People First Effect* to be a wake-up call to everyone who reads it. I sincerely hope you will realize that so many of the relational problems that we all experience can be traced back to a trust issue. Trust is not merely "a" factor concerning human connection and human betterment; it is *the* factor! And unless we all begin to take more responsibility to evaluate our own trustworthiness we will all suffer the outcomes of broken homes, failing businesses, and a dysfunctional society…all because of the trust deficits that you and I have created.

Now I invite you to turn to the first chapter and join Dan Burton on his learning journey. When you've learned how to apply the 7 Keys of Trust in all your relationships, you will begin to reap tremendous benefits from advancing in the People First philosophy. And if we all do this together, we will contribute to creating a safer, happier, and more profitable world for all of us.

CHAPTER 1

Profits First

DAN BURTON KEEPS HIS FACE carefully expressionless. He has fought in the ring several times, competing in top-level Kung Fu competitions, and has trained himself to keep his face neutral so that an opponent will not see overconfidence or confusion in his eyes. He is not in the arena today, but he can feel eyes on his face, and his insides are churning more violently than they were before his first major tournament. And there is another ugly sensation: despair.

John Kwan is a small man, Asian, impeccably dressed, and all business. He has been speaking for several minutes, and he has yet to flash even the slightest smile or communicate warmth of any kind. *He's communicating plenty, though,* Dan thinks sourly.

"Tough times demand tough leadership," Mr. Kwan says in clipped, precise tones. "Your new parent company has directed me to step in and make the difficult decisions these times require."

Dan has served as the CEO for Prestigious Products for twenty years and has been with the company almost twice that long. There have been moments of great joy and tremendous stress...*but I don't remember feeling quite so lost as I do right now.*

After enjoying seven consecutive years of growth and prosperity, Prestigious Products struggled mightily in the great recession of the late 2000s. As the name suggests, Prestigious Products' target market is the upper-middle-class

1

buyer and up. As consumers' fears about the economy deepened, customers became increasingly cost-conscious; they either cut back on their buying or switched to retailers whose pricing was significantly lower…or both.

"You struggled to adjust to the economic downturn in the previous decade," Kwan is saying.

"While there has been modest improvement in recent years, I will bring a fresh perspective and introduce austerity measures."

Dan glances down at his hands, folded in his lap. *"Struggling?" The whole country was struggling!* Dan muses bitterly. *I don't expect Kwan's "fresh perspective" will involve hiring more staff.* As he raises his eyes back to Kwan, he sees Claudia Barnes, a member of his Executive Committee, staring at him wide-eyed.

Kwan gestures toward a tanned, silver-haired man who is seated on the stage behind him. "The outgoing chairman of the board, William Newell, has agreed to stay on to help us with this transition."

A small spark of hope: *Bill Newell is a good man,* Dan thinks. *Perhaps he'll be able to give Kwan a clearer idea of what we've been doing here.*

Dan did not sit idle when it became clear in 2007 that the recession was deepening. He assembled a committee of executives and middle managers to examine expenses and make every cut possible. Product offerings and inventory were reexamined and cost savings were discovered. Advertising and pricing strategies were reexamined and adjusted. Dan ordered a freeze on all wage increases and canceled all executive bonuses.

But as quickly as Prestigious Products could cut costs, revenues dipped even faster. Then the really painful moves began. Stores were closed; staffers—or Purpose Partners, as Dan always refers to them—were released. With staff reduced by 30 percent, a severely weakened Prestige Products managed to stem the financial bleeding and even paid dividends for the first time in two years. For the next two years, Dan and his leadership team worked to adjust systems and processes for the organization's reduced sales force and outlets. Prestigious Products' share price increased steadily…if unspectacularly. Dan worked hard to communicate to all Purpose Partners what the plans were for the future and to assure them that the company was committed to long-term stability and growth.

And then, just two weeks ago, it was announced that the retail chain—which in 2006 had been showcased in *Businessweek* because of the dramatic success of the People First philosophy—had been sold to a large holding company based in China. Dan was instructed to assemble corporate staff and all senior managers at corporate headquarters, where they would meet John Kwan, the American-based representative of the new ownership.

Over the past five years, Dan has mentally reviewed his actions again and again. He can honestly say he would not have done anything differently. *Not that that makes me feel any better about what's happening here today,* he thinks grimly.

As if reading his mind, Mr. Kwan nods curtly in Dan's direction. "We know that Dan Burton has been working hard to try to manage the changes here. I'll be meeting with Mr. Burton this afternoon to outline our plans moving forward."

I'll be most interested to hear what those plans are. Dan can't seem to curb the sarcastic tone of his thoughts. Other than a curt email from Kwan announcing his appointment as chairman of the board and assuring Dan that "we plan to retain you as Chief Executive Officer," Dan has no clue what the "plans moving forward" might be. In fact, this public announcement is the first he's heard about a one-on-one with Mr. Kwan.

Kwan's black eyes are opaque. He slows his measured rate of speech even further, giving emphasis to each word. "But do not think that these familiar faces mean that we will be promoting the same old practices; it will not be 'business as usual.'

"I have been made aware of a phrase you use here: 'People First.' I have seen signs on the walls proclaiming this idea. I do not know what this means, but let me tell you that I am here to maximize profits, and that is what I intend to do."

Sounds like it's going to get ugly quick, Dan thinks, shaking his head inadvertently. *Bill Newell and I are here to put a friendly face on the bloodletting. Then, when we're down to a skeleton crew, Bill will quietly fade away, and I...well, I think I'd better update my resume!*

One-On-One with John Kwan

Dan leaves the conference room quickly, deliberately avoiding the anxious looks from many of his Purpose Partners. He expects that Kwan will be coming to his office very quickly, and Dan wants to prepare himself to receive the new chairman.

Dan sits at his desk and automatically opens his email inbox. He clicks on two messages before he realizes that he has not read a single word. His mind is racing. *Be courteous; be positive!* Dan takes a deep breath and releases it slowly. *Kwan is clearly a man who wants to intimidate. Don't let him get you backpedaling.*

Dan glances at a small, plastic pyramid sitting on his desk and reviews the words stamped into the pyramid:

Yes

Thank You

I Need You

I Believe in You

I Am Proud of You

These words are the outward expression of the People First philosophy that Dan introduced to Prestigious Products. Every business day for twelve years, Dan has used these words with his Purpose Partners and encouraged them to use the words at home and at work.

Not just to use them, but to use them sincerely, Dan thinks. *I can't think of a single one of them to use with John Kwan…not sincerely.*

"Dan?" His assistant's voice on the intercom interrupts his thoughts. "Mr. Kwan is here to see you."

Dan has not even had a chance to rise from his desk when Kwan appears in his doorway. Clearly, he had not waited to be invited to enter Dan's office. Dan hopes the smile on his face looks genuine. Inside he feels just as cold as the look in Kwan's eyes. "Mr. Kwan!" Dan says, trying to put warmth into his voice. "I am very glad to meet you in person!"

Dan extends his hand to shake. Kwan's grip is textbook: quick, firm, perfunctory, and quickly released. Dan gestures to a table and chairs at one end of the office. He tries another smile. "I'm sorry, Mr. Kwan, I don't know much about your background. Have you just relocated from overseas?"

If anything, Kwan is even more brusque than in his presentation to the staff. "My specialty is turning around underperforming businesses. I've been doing that here in the United States for a number of years."

Dan feels his smile slip at the "underperforming" barb. "Oh? That must be a rewarding job. Do you have family here?"

"Mr. Burton. I am not here to discuss my personal life or make small talk. I am here to inform you of the actions of the board moving forward."

Dan's smile vanishes. "Very well," he says levelly. "We've had no communication here about your plans."

"I am tasked with improving the meager dividends that Prestigious Products has been paying its shareholders. We believe that you can do a much better job of reducing costs in order to provide a better ROI. I have reviewed your financials and am prepared to provide direction."

"Mr. Kwan, may I give you some ground-level input?"

"That will not be necessary. I am perfectly capable of reading financial statements and drawing the appropriate conclusions."

Dan matches Kwan's crisp, even tone. "As am I. But your statements in today's meeting indicate that you have focused exclusively on the financials and not investigated the culture that allowed Prestigious Products to be so successful before the economy turned."

Kwan looks bored. "I made no effort to 'investigate,' as you say, because I view it as a culture of failure. My focus is on creating financial success."

"Mr. Kwan, with respect, if you believe we had a culture of failure here, then you haven't had a chance to review our financials from 2000-2006. We increased profits and our capital assets as much in those seven years as we had in the previous fifteen."

Kwan pushes back from the table. "And it all imploded two years later. Clearly, this culture you speak of was not one that bred success."

Dan struggles to maintain a polite tone. "I'd like to explain my thinking on that. This culture is what allowed us to rebound from the recession. We have paid dividends every quarter since the fourth quarter of 2010."

"Yes, I've seen all that. Frankly, I have no interest in your thoughts." Kwan rises to his feet. Dan rises also, struggling to conceal his astonishment at the man's discourtesy. "Mr. Burton, we will meet in one week. Instruct your CFO, Mrs. Lundgren, Mr. Clinton from Sales, and your Human Resources director to attend, prepared to discuss staff cuts and other cost-cutting measures."

"Staff cuts?" Dan is aghast. "Mr. Kwan, we've cut our staffing by 30 percent!"

"And we will cut it 15 percent more in one week."

Dan's mind is whirling. "If we're going to be discussing more staff cuts"—Dan emphasizes the word *more*—"then you'll want to talk to Claudia Barnes, our Director of Customer Service. She will have valuable input on the locations that are already struggling due to short staffing."

Kwan is already headed for the door. "That will not be necessary. Nine o'clock, one week from today."

"Mr. Kwan!" Now Dan's voice reveals his stress. "I have *serious* reservations about what you're planning."

Kwan turns and looks coldly at Dan. "How you feel and what you think is not important to me."

And he is gone.

Dan collapses back into his chair and sits motionless for several minutes. Then he sits up abruptly, reaches for his cell phone, and taps the voice dial application. "Bill Newell," he intones into the phone.

Dan waits a moment, and then: "Bill, I just had a very short meeting with John Kwan. He's planning to cut staff an additional 15 percent."

Bill Newell is normally a jovial man; now his voice sounds lackluster and distant. "I know. Dan, I'm sorry you had to find out this way. I was hoping to prep you after the meeting today."

"Don't worry about that, Bill. It's not like it comes as a complete surprise. But he's unpleasant! This is what the board wants?"

"It's what the *new* board wants, Dan. Seven of our members have resigned. I had written my resignation also, but I decided to stay on and try to slow Kwan down…to reason with him and urge some moderation. After today, I think I'm going to hit the 'Print' button on that letter."

"Bill, is there nothing you can do to get this man to *listen*? We've adjusted our systems to the last round of layoffs, but our customer satisfaction scores are still low. He wouldn't listen to a word I had to say, Bill!"

"Dan, I am truly sorry. I've had such great admiration for what you've done with the company, particularly in these last few years." There is a long pause. When Bill Newell speaks again, his voice is so low that Dan strains to hear. "I wish I could help you. My hands are tied."

"OK, Bill," Dan says softly. "You've been a great friend over the years."

Dan hears a beep; Bill Newell has hung up.

CHAPTER 2

Talking It Through

DAN DRIVES SLOWLY HOME, mentally replaying the scene in his office. The last few years have been very difficult, but he finds himself searching his memory for the last time he felt so discouraged. *I think it was that day I asked Sifu to meet me for breakfast,* he muses. *Twelve years ago! I thought I was going to lose it all—my marriage, my job...*

He pulls down the lane to where his four-bedroom home stands, and his expression brightens. *It's good to be home,* he thinks. *I don't like to dump my problems on Cheryl, but...I need a hug.* His lips move in a ghost of a smile.

Cheryl Burton is fifty-two years old and could easily pass for forty. She is busy making one of Dan's favorite dinners. Dan had told her this morning what lay ahead of him at the office. She expects her husband may be feeling badly, and she wants to greet him with a bright home and a hot meal. She looks at the clock again and smiles.

Twelve years ago, Cheryl's face seemed to be etched into indelible lines of anxiety and doubt, until the marvelous metamorphosis called "People First" began in the Burton home. Throughout the 1990s, Dan Burton had been the model of "the absentee husband." His executive position had provided plenty of money for their large home, a swimming pool, luxury cars, and exclusive schools for their two children. The Burtons enjoyed all the physical comforts a family could want, but their home had become cold and joyless. Dan worked a grinding schedule, rarely returning home in time for dinner with the family.

Cheryl had felt like a single mother, raising Marcy and David as best she could, and she could sense that the resentment of her two teenagers was building. Whenever she tried to speak to Dan about his absence from the home, he would harshly interrupt, "Cheryl, this is what it *takes* to live the way we do. Do you like this house? Do you *like* having a Saks Fifth Avenue account? Do you want to send Marcy and David to public school? You want me home all the time? Get ready for a major life-change!"

And before she could retort that she would gladly trade the Saks card for a Sears card if it meant having a husband and father at home at night, Dan would stalk off. Cheryl reluctantly began to consider divorce, an idea that clashed with her spiritual convictions.

It has been twelve years, but Cheryl's eyes still widen with wonder when she recalls the day Dan took her to lunch and told her that he had just come from a breakfast with Sifu Li, Dan's Kung Fu instructor. She chuckles as she recalls her astonishment when Dan said to her, "I feel like I just woke up from a very long, deep sleep. Sifu held up a mirror and made me look at my reflection…and I didn't like what I saw."

Dan promised that he would put her and the children first, and he never wavered from that commitment. Cheryl smiles a soft smile as she reflects on the many ways that Dan has demonstrated to her that he genuinely delights in her. Not that the past twelve years have been free of heartache; Cheryl heaves a deep sigh as she thinks of Marcy.

At that moment Cheryl hears the front door open and close. She offers a silent prayer that she will provide whatever Dan needs in the next moments. Dan walks slowly into the kitchen; one glance at his face causes Cheryl's eyes to narrow in sympathy. "It didn't go well," she says.

Dan shakes his head and reaches for her. Cheryl quickly goes to him and he takes her in his arms and holds her for a long minute. Cheryl waits, knowing Dan will speak when he is ready.

"It…was awful," Dan says heavily. "I wasn't expecting some happy pep talks, but that man is so unpleasant, Cheryl!" Dan releases from Cheryl's embrace but stays very close. He tries to smile.

"Dinner smells good."

They move into the living room and Dan plops down on the sofa with a deep sigh. Cheryl sits close to him and takes his hand. Dan turns to Cheryl, and his eyes are moist. "I think perhaps I should resign. It's everything I'd feared, and worse! 'Worse' because this man Kwan is so *incredibly* nasty."

Cheryl's eyes are dark with concern. "Nasty to you?"

"To me especially, but he's a pretty cold fish in general. But that's not the half of it, Cheryl. He's planning an additional 15 percent in staff cuts. Our customer service scores are *already* down, because our customers are unhappy that they're not getting the personal attention they've always expected from us."

"My goodness, Dan! Where will those cuts come from?"

"He's scheduled a meeting in one week to discuss it...although I don't think there will be much 'discussion'!" Dan's eyes narrow. "There's something odd there; I suggested that Claudia Barnes should be there to give her input. He said that wouldn't be necessary."

"He's not a People First kind of guy, huh?"

Dan's grip on Cheryl's hand tightens. "That was the worst of it. He told us, 'I don't know what this People First business is, but we're here to make a profit.' Looks like we're going to focus on profits first and people last."

At that memorable, life-changing breakfast twelve years ago, Sifu Li introduced Dan to the People First philosophy that Sifu used to build his vast network of Kung Fu schools. People First stands on the foundation of treating people with the utmost dignity, respect, and honor. Sifu challenged Dan to put people first at home and at work, and the results were nothing short of extraordinary. Prestigious Products enjoyed dramatic expansion for seven years...then the economy turned.

Dan spreads his hands in a hopeless gesture. "I don't want any part of what's about to happen.

Staff cuts will *not* make us more profitable. We looked at that long and hard and cut our levels as far as we dared. I'm quite sure that the only reason the new owners haven't dismissed me is to maintain some appearance of normalcy. And I don't want to give *any* appearance that I support this move."

"So Bill Newell is out completely?" Cheryl met the outgoing chairman of the board at several social functions. Of all the members of the old Prestigious Products board, Newell had been the most eager to adopt the principles of People First.

"Not yet," Dan says slowly. "Bill had agreed to stay on to assist with this transition. But he heard the same speech I did, and I believe he is just as distressed as I am. I spoke to him briefly just before I came home. I think he's going to resign."

Dan releases Cheryl's hand and stands, moving restlessly into the center of the room. "I believe in the People First philosophy with all my heart. I was totally imbalanced before—although not as badly as this man Kwan seems to be. I was all about profits. Then Sifu woke me up to the importance of people. And *that's* why I haven't resigned. If I really believe in this philosophy, shouldn't I stay and fight for it?"

Dan begins to pace. "When Kwan told me he was going to cut staff, my first thought was to say, 'Let's cut *me* right now!' We don't need the money, Cheryl. Our investments have taken a beating these last few years, and I'd have to figure out some new way to make money, but we'd be okay for a while."

"But I'd feel so *disloyal* leaving all my Purpose Partners after we've just taken this kick in the teeth. It would be like the *Titanic* hits the iceberg, and whoops! There goes the captain in a lifeboat!"

Dan looks directly at Cheryl, his eyes clouded with hurt. "If I abandon the people, doesn't that mean I've abandoned the People First philosophy? When we were making all these cuts the past three years, I tried harder than ever to recognize and celebrate all our Purpose Partners." Dan's shoulders slump. "But I can't think of a *thing* to celebrate today."

Cheryl smiles and pats the empty seat on the couch next to her. Dan nods and returns to his seat.

She takes his hand. "Dan."

Dan looks up and his eyes clear. "I'm sorry; it's just that you're the only one to tell it to."

"There *is* someone else, Dan."

Dan nods slowly. "Sifu? I was thinking about him on the way home. It's just that…Cheryl, I hate to bother him. I'm sure he's got his own issues with this economy."

Cheryl's voice can still assume the tone of disapproving mother. "Dan Burton!" she says with mock sternness. "Did Sifu seem like he was 'bothered' the last time you asked for help?"

Dan recognizes the tone. For the first time that evening a real smile flashes across his face. "No, ma'am," he replies meekly. "I'll call him in the morning."

CHAPTER 3

Breakfast
with a Champion

DAN HAS KNOWN SIFU LI for sixteen years, yet he still marvels that this remarkable man is his personal friend. Sifu (the name means "teacher" in Chinese and is pronounced "SEE foo") has earned international recognition as a Kung Fu Grandmaster. For twenty years he maintained an undefeated record as a world champion in international competitions. When knowledgeable devotees of Kung Fu discuss who might be the most accomplished living practitioner of Walu Kung Fu in the world, Sifu's name is always one of the first mentioned. Now in his sixties, Sifu no longer competes in the ring, but he still trains some of the top international competitors, and he makes four trips every year to Camp Lejeune, North Carolina, to train both instructors and recruits for the United States Marine Corps.

However, Sifu has enjoyed success in many more venues besides the arena. Throughout the 1990s he built a network of more than one hundred Kung Fu schools—Sifu uses the word *kwoon*, the Chinese word for "school" or "training room"—throughout the United States. At the peak of his prosperity in 2006, tens of thousands of students attended the Sifu Li Walu Kung Fu schools across the nation, plus more than one thousand more at two large facilities in Europe. Over the years, Dan learned that Sifu has made wise investments, purchased commercial property, and Dan and Cheryl have visited Sifu's palatial, ten thousand-square-foot home on several occasions.

One might well expect that a man who has met and mastered so many challenges—not the least of these being one of the world's deadliest forms of hand-to-hand combat—would be reserved and aloof, or perhaps overbearing and harsh. And this, Dan reflects as he drives to a meeting with the Grandmaster, may be the most remarkable thing about Sifu Li: he is the most gracious, kind, and genuinely warm man Dan has ever met. He is a voracious reader, a student of people and of philosophy, and Dan learned long ago that when the Grandmaster talks, Dan should immediately begin taking notes.

Twelve years ago, Sifu taught Dan his People First philosophy, which completely rejuvenated

Dan's marriage and his career. *I'm hoping Sifu can catch lightning in a bottle again,* Dan admits to himself as he maneuvers his car into the parking lot of his favorite breakfast café. Dan had arrived fifteen minutes early for his breakfast appointment with Sifu. His face splits into a wry grin as he sees his friend and teacher walking across the parking lot toward the door. *You gotta get up early in the morning to get ahead of Sifu,* he chuckles to himself.

As Dan walks through the front door of the restaurant, Sifu is shaking hands with a young Hispanic man and saying, "My old ears are getting dim; you pronounce your first name 'Yo-har-ee'?"

Dan chuckles again as he sees the quizzical look in the server's eyes. Clearly, most customers do not express such concern about the correct pronunciation of his name! The young man nods politely. "Yes, sir, that's correct. My name is Johari."

Sifu smiles. "I am very pleased to meet you, Johari. Please call me Sifu. It's just like 'seafood,' without the 'D.' I am waiting for a good friend of mine, who should be here any moment."

Dan feels a warm flush of pleasure to hear the Grandmaster refer to him as his "good friend." He takes a step closer to Sifu, and the Grandmaster swings smoothly toward him as he senses someone entering his space. Sifu's smile grows even wider and his eyes light with pleasure.

"Ah! My friend!" Sifu says brightly. He turns back to Johari. "I'd like you to meet my very good friend. This is Dan."

Dan quickly smiles and reaches out to shake hands with Johari. "I'm happy to meet you, Johari. I don't believe I've seen you before. Have you been working here long?"

Johari smiles shyly. "Yes, sir, but I was on the afternoon shift until recently."

"It's Dan," Dan replies warmly. He can see Sifu beaming at him from the corner of his eye. "Is this a better schedule for you, Johari?"

"Yes, sir—Dan. I take classes at the university, and this does work out for me. May I show you to a table?"

"A booth please, Johari, if you have one." Dan gestures to Sifu to proceed ahead of him. "What are you studying?"

"I want to be a builder, sir. I'm studying architecture."

"Ah, architectural design?" Sifu rejoins the conversation.

"Yes, sir."

"This country was made great by men and women who had a passion to build," Sifu nods approvingly. "It is exciting to meet someone like yourself."

Johari seems to stand a little straighter, and his wide smile matches Sifu's. "Thank you, sir. Will this be good for you both?" Johari gestures to a spacious booth.

"Thank you, Johari," Dan replies, "and we'll both have coffee."

Dan and Sifu sit across from each other. They see each other every week at the Kung Fu classes that Dan attends, but it has been months since they have met socially. Dan automatically bows his head and offers the two-handed salute that all of Sifu's students give the Grandmaster at the beginning and the end of class.

Sifu solemnly returns the salute, and then that dazzling smile lights his face. He grabs Dan's hand and shakes it with a firm grip. "My good friend," he says warmly. "I am so glad to have this chance to see you!"

"I'm so grateful to you for making time for me," Dan says humbly. "I wish I was here to tell you how great my life is going."

Sifu's eyes narrow with concern. "Not troubles at home, I hope?"

Dan shakes his head. "No, no, Cheryl and I are fine. She's busier than ever with her volunteer work. In fact, it was Cheryl who suggested that I ask your advice."

"And your children?"

Dan smiles. "David graduated from UM with his MA in psychology last June. He's working as a counselor at a rehab facility here in Miami. He's very happy."

Sifu's voice is very soft. "And Marcy?"

Dan's face clouds. "No change," Dan sighs. "It's…awful, Sifu. Drugs. Prostitution. David tries to keep track of her. He saw her about six months ago. He said she looked dreadful. I don't think David tells us how bad it really is. But he did say she was living in a crack house."

Sifu winces.

"David told her, 'Marcy, you're my sister, I love you; it kills me to see you like this.' He told her again that Cheryl and I will pay for her to go into any recovery facility in the country she chooses. She told him to mind his own business." Dan turns to look out the window and heaves a deep sigh. "David went back a week later and she was gone. We don't know where she is."

"I'm so sorry, Dan."

Dan shakes his head as if to clear it and looks at his friend. "I was pretty much of an absentee father when she was young. When you first taught me People First, I thought I had…reinvested in her in time. You know how well Cheryl and David responded. I made every effort with Marcy. I don't think any of us realized how bad things had gotten with her until it was too late."

"She's still very young, Dan. Twenty-four?"

"She'll be twenty-five next month." Dan's eyes are narrowed in pain. "Cheryl and I joined a support group. We've reached out to two families who are in a similar situation. We hope." He looks frankly at Sifu. "We pray."

Sifu is watching Dan closely. "You go to the meetings with your wife?"

"Oh, yes. Cheryl and I lean on each other." Dan tries to grin. "Hopefully not too much on David."

Sifu's warm smile reappears. "So you are still putting People First at home. I was so pleased to see your interaction with Johari."

"Thank you, Grandmaster. But that brings me to the reason I asked you to meet me today. Thank you so much for seeing me."

Sifu waves a dismissive hand. "Tell me how I may be of service to you, my friend."

Johari arrives with coffee. Dan is glad for an opportunity to gather his thoughts while he and Sifu place their breakfast orders. His stomach actually aches whenever he thinks of his daughter, and he wants to describe the situation at Prestige Products without succumbing to the despair he feels about Marcy's self-destruction. When Johari departs, Dan busies himself with flavoring his coffee. Sifu waits patiently.

Dan raises his eyes to Sifu. "I haven't wanted to burden you with what's going on at work. It's been pretty bad these past few years. When you taught me the People First philosophy twelve years ago, we really got on a roll. We opened new locations and brought in new product lines. I thought we managed our growth wisely. We were reinvesting profits into expansion and still paying healthy dividends. And I was careful to install managers who believed in People First and would communicate the philosophy throughout their locations. Our debt-to-equity ratios were good, profit margins stayed high, and our customer service scores were steadily improving."

Dan sips his coffee. "In early 2007, revenues started to slide. By the end of the year, just about everyone was using the 'R-word'…recession." He sighs. "We started closing locations early in 2008. Then we began layoffs at the remaining stores. We've had two waves of layoffs. Some really outstanding people were let go."

Sifu nods sympathetically. "They were very difficult times."

"They just got a lot more difficult for us," Dan says grimly. "We've been purchased by an overseas investor called the Chang Tao Group. A number of our board members have resigned, and we have a new chairman, a man named John Kwan." Dan shakes his head slowly. "Sifu, I think he may be the most unpleasant man I've ever met in my life."

Sifu nods. "He is tasked with representing the interests of the investors. Just as your board hired you to maximize profits for the shareholders, so this man Kwan is tasked with doing whatever is necessary to provide the investors with a good return on their purchase." Sifu stirs his coffee thoughtfully. "I have heard of the Chang Tao Group."

"You have?" Dan is surprised.

Sifu's eyes sparkle with gentle humor. "I *am* Chinese, Dan, even if I have lived in the United States for many years." He is serious again. "I have business interests in China and I still have friends and family there."

Dan smiles. "Sifu, is there anything you *don't* know?"

Sifu shakes his head apologetically. "I'm not sure I know how to give you advice that will cause you to walk out of here with a smile. For what it's worth, Dan, I have never heard a whisper suggesting that the Chang Tao Group is connected to any kind of illegality. They are a legitimate venture capital group. But they *do* have a reputation for doing whatever it takes to maximize ROI. No one has ever characterized them as a People First organization."

"Mr. Kwan made that *very* clear," Dan says sourly. "He told the entire corporate staff, 'I don't know what this People First business is, but from now on we're going to be focused on profits.' I'm to attend a meeting where he will explain his plan to cut 15 percent of our staff. That would amount to about one hundred and twenty jobs. Sifu, that's going to be *disastrous* for our organization."

Sifu looks at Dan carefully. "I need to ask you a difficult question, my friend."

"By all means."

"One of the hardest things, Dan, for men like you and me who place such a great premium on the dignity and worth of people is to cut staff. When you say 'disastrous,' do you mean it will harm your company's ability to do business? Or it will hurt morale?"

"Both," Dan replies promptly. "It's a fair question, Sifu, and it's one I've been asking myself for months. I told you we've been through two rounds of layoffs in the past two years. I worked on that personally. Yes, it hurt! It hurt me personally, and there's no question it hurt our morale.

"We did everything we could to soften the blow for everyone involved. The board was willing to provide generous severance packages for all Purpose Partners who lost a position. I met with every manager, some individually and some in groups, and explained why we'd made the cuts and what the path was for the future. I instructed each manager to meet with his or her Purpose Partners and carefully explain exactly what the situation was at Prestigious Products. We created an intranet site so that any employee could monitor our financial situation and compare costs to revenue."

Sifu is clearly impressed. He nods approvingly. "That is very good, Dan! You did everything you could to keep your Purpose Partners engaged."

"I did, Sifu. Yes, I lost some sleep over it, but I would do it all again if I was confronted with the same circumstances. Honestly, if I knew then what I know now, I probably would have conducted the layoffs sooner.

"But it hasn't been without fallout. The good news is that we did balance our books and we did pay dividends again for the first time in two years. But in addition to the layoffs, we had some resignations from folks who were, quite naturally, concerned for the company's longevity. There weren't many of those; I like to think that the emphasis we placed on communicating to our Purpose Partners helped to keep that at a minimum, but we lost some. What's worse, though, is that our market share has remained at 2009 levels, and our customer satisfaction scores are continuing to fall."

Sifu's eyes narrow thoughtfully. "Do you think your Purpose Partners are dispirited?"

"I think they're dispirited that they can't provide the personal service our customers were accustomed to. For years, our marketing theme was 'Prestigious Products and Unparalleled Service.' That's why we paid such close attention to our customer satisfaction surveys. Our ads spoke of 'A Shopping Experience Second to None.' After we cut our staff by nearly one-third, we changed the emphasis in our ad copy. We were afraid our service wouldn't match our promise!"

"And how are your customers responding to the changes?"

"They're feeling neglected. And I'm not going with my gut on that. I've talked to managers; I've visited a number of stores and talked to clerks and sales associates. They're getting negative feedback from customers. They say things like, 'You used to take care of me here. What happened?'"

"And what did your Mr. Kwan say when you shared this information with him?"

Dan looks levelly at Sifu. "That's just it, Sifu. That's why I asked you to meet me this morning.

When I told him I had serious concerns about his plans to cut staff, he said, 'How you feel and what you think is not important to me.' I asked him to let me explain about our People First culture and he wasn't interested. He called it a culture of failure."

"Oh." Sifu's voice is very soft. He leans back from the table and looks up at the ceiling for a moment, then looks sadly back at Dan. "That is the mind-set of one who values profits and profits alone…which is precisely why he has been placed in his current position. He is merely echoing the opinions of his employers in China. There is no thought given to building lives and passing on a legacy—only to building the bottom line."

Sifu's eyes are warm with sympathy. "What are you planning to do, Dan?"

"My very first thought was to resign."

Sifu nods silently, watching Dan's face.

"I have absolutely *no* desire to call more people into my office and tell them that their lives are being turned upside down. I can't see myself going out and giving pep talks to our Purpose Partners when I don't believe in what we're doing!" Dan looks at Sifu, his face almost defiant.

"I'm *not* going to lie to them, Sifu!"

"So you're going to resign?" Sifu is looking closely at Dan.

Dan shakes his head angrily. "I don't know what to do! I don't feel right at *all* about resigning. I *care* about my Purpose Partners!" He frowns down at the table. "I don't like Kwan. I don't trust him and I totally disagree with what he's doing. I don't want to lend my name or my word to this plan to strip the company down. And yet…"

Dan looks up, and is surprised to see one of Sifu's brightest smiles. Dan doesn't understand, and he cocks his head at Sifu in a questioning gesture. "What?"

Sifu's deep affection for Dan shines through his eyes. "My dear friend, I don't believe you have any intention of resigning."

Dan scowls at Sifu good-naturedly. "I guess I was hoping against hope you might tell me I should."

Sifu throws back his head and laughs. "I'm afraid not. The greatest confidence a leader can possess is manifested in the courage to stand for the truth of his convictions, regardless of the consequences. I know you to be a man of courage and conviction. I believe you are going to stand.

"Dan, there is a proverb that my Sifu taught me when I was very young. It is one which I have kept very close to me. You have heard me say it before."

Dan holds up his hand. He reaches for the iPad he has brought with him and sets it before him. He taps a button for the keyboard function, then waits with his hands poised over the tablet. "I'd like to take notes, Grandmaster."

Once again, Dan is rewarded with Sifu's warmest, smile; it is the look of a proud father. "My good student," Sifu says kindly. "How you honor me!" He nods toward the iPad, indicating that it is time to begin typing. "The proverb is: *Let no one seek his own, but each one the other's well-being.*

"Dan, the reason I am pleased to see you wrestling with thoughts of tendering your resignation is that it tells me that you have truly become a People First leader. You are not reacting emotionally; you are doing what you know to be right and true. Yes, you could walk away. One could argue that you *should* resign, so as to send a clear signal that there is a completely new management philosophy in place. Yet you are reluctant to leave, because you feel an obligation to continue to serve the men and women you lead."

"I feel like it would be wrong to bail out on them, Sifu, if that's what you mean."

Sifu's eyes are twinkling. "Less elegantly put, Dan, but you have captured my sentiments."

"Sifu, how *do* I serve my Purpose Partners? And for that matter, how do I serve John Kwan?

Right now, I don't even want to look at him. And I've gotta meet with him first thing tomorrow to talk about more layoffs!"

"It will not be easy, Dan. I suspect that Kwan believes the best way to accomplish his work is to intentionally avoid any type of relationship with the members of the organizations he is assigned to manage. If there are no relationships, he has no trouble sleeping at night when he has to dismiss them. It is a defense mechanism."

Dan nods thoughtfully. "Sifu, I hadn't given one moment's thought to Kwan's feelings; only to my own. What you say makes sense. But how does that knowledge help me work with him?"

"Dan, you know from your years in the ring that if your opponent is concentrating on protecting one area of his body, he makes himself vulnerable in another."

"Yes, Grandmaster," Dan replies slowly. "But how…"

"Dan, before I address your question, I'd like to expand the definition that you and I have for People First. May I do that?"

Dan's eyes light. "Please do!" His hands are poised over the iPad, ready to resume typing. "Just listening to you talk makes me feel more confident."

Sifu returns his friend's smile. "My friend, you should trust your instincts. Your heart is good.

You are operating according to the best philosophy. And you are using solid business practices. But let me broaden the foundation on which to stand."

Sifu seems to hesitate, as if searching for the right words. "Dan…I appreciate the struggle you are facing more than you may realize."

Dan misses the significance of what was just said. "You've always been very gracious to walk a mile in my shoes with me."

Sifu shakes his head and smiles his gentlest of smiles. "Many of us were hit hard by the recession. Businesses all over the world had to cut costs and close outlets." Again, Sifu hesitates.

"I had to do that myself."

Dan's eyes widen. "*You*, Sifu?"

"Oh, yes," Sifu says softly. "I closed thirty *kwoons* around the country in 2008 and 2009. I've only reopened seven of them."

Dan is stricken with guilt. "Sifu, I had no idea! I've been so consumed with my own issues...I never thought to ask you..." Dan scowls and shakes his head angrily. "I have *not* been a good friend to you."

There is nothing but gracious reassurance in the Grandmaster's eyes. "My friend, I never mentioned it to you or anyone else at our *kwoon*. Like you, I did not want to burden others. There is no way you could have known. And Dan, did *I* ask *you* about the state of *your* business during these past six years? We are both stewards who are trying to guide our organizations through this new, whitewater world. It keeps us busy, yes?"

Dan looks gratefully at his teacher. "It sure does!"

"So let us purpose to meet together more often," Sifu replies, "and spend more time asking each other how we may bear one other's burdens. Agreed?"

Dan's voice is suddenly husky. "Sifu, I'd be honored to be of service to you any way I can, any time."

Sifu smiles kindly. "My friend, you pour into me by being such an eager student. You give *me* energy by the energy you put into your learning. Now," Sifu's voice reverts to the brisk tone of the instructor, "let us return our attention to expanding our understanding of People First."

Dan grins. "We'd better ask Johari to heat up our coffee!"

CHAPTER 4

The 7 Keys of Trust

"DAN, SEVERAL YEARS AGO I suggested that you needed to humanize your company. You recall?"

"I'll never forget it!" Dan says warmly.

"And I told you that the people in your organization are your most valuable asset and your greatest competitive advantage, yes? I said that business leaders must focus their energy and attention on people first—not profits first."

Dan nods his emphatic agreement.

"People First has one fundamental purpose, Dan: to teach leaders about human value and how sustainable profitability is unalterably related to that value. People First gives us one purpose—one passion—with unlimited possibilities for success!"

Dan nods again. "And we did enjoy tremendous success for several years."

"Dan, I have been giving this a lot of thought in the last few years. As I was forced to downsize my own business and lose some very fine Purpose Partners—some of whom had been with me for years—I found myself reexamining the People First philosophy."

Dan is familiar with the intense, focused expression that comes over the Grandmaster's face when he is introducing his advanced students to a complicated new technique. There is excitement there, but also a burning desire to present the new skill clearly and well. That light is in Sifu's eyes now.

"Dan, after subjecting the People First philosophy to the fire of sustained adversity, I am more convinced than ever that this is the *right* way to lead; putting people first is leading the right way and for the right reasons. But as I dug down to the bedrock of the philosophy, I realized that there was an important aspect to putting People First that I knew intuitively but had not fully developed."

Sifu nods toward Dan's iPad. "Let me give you a purpose statement which will be the foundation for everything we discuss today: *The People First Effect is the result of a leader learning how to treat people exceptionally well—which will create trust capital, which in turn creates a harvest of wealth, both socially and financially.*"

Sifu repeats the definition and waits for Dan to get it typed into the tablet. "Let us begin by defining the word *trust*, shall we? *Trust is an unwavering, secure belief in the character, competence, confidence, caring, communication, consistency, and commitment of another person.* I refer to these seven attributes—character, competence, confidence, caring, communication, consistency, and commitment—as *the seven keys of trust*. There comes a point, Dan, in every interpersonal interaction in which people decide whether they can trust you or not. If you are acutely aware of each of these seven keys, you will be much more intentional in your attitude and actions so that you will not create distrust."

Dan looks up from his typing, his head tilted in a questioning gesture.

Sifu smiles, anticipating Dan's question. "How is the definition of trust related to the People First philosophy?"

Dan shakes his head admiringly. "Sifu, you're always one step ahead of me."

"No, my friend, it's just that I have been pondering these issues for several months now. I have asked myself these questions and been forced to answer them." Sifu smiles. "Dan, it's time for you to grow in the People First philosophy. We agreed on the foundation of the philosophy years ago; now we will build a superstructure on top of that."

Dan grins, rubbing his hands together like a man sitting down to a great meal. "I'm ready!"

"Very good!" Sifu beams. "Dan, as you know, *the basis of the People First philosophy is the definition of who people are*: men and women, boys and girls, each one of them made in the image of God, possessing exalted dignity, exalted worth, and exalted potential. Every human being you meet is a living marvel, a walking miracle, and a masterpiece of creation. These things you know; you demonstrated that knowledge in your interaction with Johari this morning.

"Now, Dan, I want to build on that foundation and help you become a more mature practitioner of the People First philosophy."

"*A People First practitioner*," Dan murmurs happily; his fingers are flying over the iPad's keyboard. "I like that!"

"Dan, a People First practitioner who has achieved mastery in building high trust will produce *The People First Effect* at home and at work." Sifu looks curiously at Dan. "Would you like to hear more?"

"*Please* tell me more!"

"Let me begin with a question: What is your biggest issue with Kwan? Is it his abrasive personality?"

Dan hesitates, then shakes his head. "No. Kwan is *very* rude and unpleasant, but I've maintained productive relationships with some very difficult people. But I don't trust him, Sifu. And he is breeding mistrust in our company."

Sifu nods. "Can you tell me specifically why you distrust him?"

"I can't put my finger on it, Sifu. I just don't believe he cares about anything other than making a profit."

"Dan, let me help you develop a more mature understanding of the concept of trust. Do you trust me?"

"Of course!" Dan answers promptly.

"Have you ever thought about *why* you trust me?" Sifu asks.

"I guess not," Dan says slowly. "You've never given me any reason to distrust you."

Sifu grins. "I am very glad of that!" He is serious again. "Dan, I do not believe that people think deeply enough about why we trust certain people and distrust others. And this is because most of us were never taught to identify specific reasons why we place our trust in someone.

"Many of my students have come to me under circumstances similar to yours—they are struggling with a difficult relationship. I ask them why the relationship is strained, and they reply that they do not trust the other party. I always ask the same question I asked you a moment ago: 'Can you tell me specifically why you have this feeling?' They usually respond as you did, Dan; they say, 'There's just something about him.' No one has ever given a structured response as to why they have this mistrust."

Dan nods his understanding. "We'll say, 'I've just got a bad feeling about that person.'"

"Yes. We have vague feelings of mistrust, Dan, but we cannot identify the root cause of the problem. I have developed a system that identifies seven specific points—the seven keys of trust—that equip us to articulate exactly why we distrust another human being.

"When you take your car to a mechanic, Dan, he plugs a diagnostic device into the electronic control system in your car, and the computer checks several different elements. The mechanic runs through a specific checklist; then he tells you, 'Your car is functioning well in *these* areas, but we should address these areas.' In the same way, I have developed a systemic checklist for evaluating our trustworthiness."

Dan is typing rapidly on the iPad. "So you're not going with your gut," he says. "You have a well-designed system for diagnosing the problem."

"Yes, Dan, that's very good! You are able to state with specificity where the breach of trust is. Instead of a vague feeling of unease, you can identify why you distrust an individual. Now you are able to sit down with that individual and say, 'This is what I need from you in order to regain trust.' Your conversation becomes solution-centered, rather than accusatory.

"And this system is not only for evaluating others, Dan. More importantly, you can evaluate yourself to see if *you* are sending signals that you are untrustworthy. I need this system of thought, Dan; you need this system. None of us will ever 'arrive' at the point where we no longer need to evaluate ourselves. We must consistently and intelligently challenge ourselves; we must weigh our words and our behavior to be sure we are communicating the right message. These seven keys help us do that."

Dan's eyes are very bright. "Sifu, I've never given the quality of trust this kind of thought. It's always been a 'vague feeling,' like you said. I would love to have a system like you're describing! And I'm excited to learn that there's more room to grow in People First."

Sifu nods approvingly. "Truth is eternal, truth is timeless, and truth is bottomless, which is why I am still a student among students and a learner among learners, just as you are." Sifu glances up at Dan with a warm smile. "And I am delighted to see that you bring the same joy to growing in People First as you do to growing in the martial arts.

"Dan, let me give you an acronym that will help to amplify the definition of trust I gave you a moment ago. Think of TRUST as…

Total
Reliance
Upon
Someone's
Truthfulness

"Dan, you've already written this down: Trust is an unwavering belief in the character, competence, confidence, caring, communication, consistency, and commitment of another person. To put it more simply, trust is Total Reliance Upon Someone's Truthfulness. And that truthfulness is characterized by these seven keys. These seven keys tell others that they can totally rely upon your truthfulness.

"When someone tells me they have a 'gut feeling' that someone cannot be trusted, one of these seven keys is missing from the totality of that individual's life. And the power of these seven keys, Dan, is not in their individual nature, but in their interconnectedness and interdependency. Truth is a system of thought, and I have discovered that trust is also.

"Dan, when so many very bright men and women cannot tell me why they had this vague feeling of mistrust, I realized that I needed to develop a framework that would define what trust is and what it is not. Then I could take a student through a process of elimination. I could say, 'You distrust this person. Is it their character?'

"'No,' the student would say, 'he has good character.'

"'Well,' I ask, 'do you doubt his competence?'

"'No,' the student replies. 'He is highly competent.'

"So I continue through my list. 'Does he lack confidence?'

"'No,' the student says, 'he exudes confidence.'

"'Do you believe that he is caring?' Perhaps the student's eyes widen in realization at this point.

'That's it!' the student says. 'I don't believe he cares about me at all!' I developed these seven keys so my students could identify specifically why trust was being violated. It is a systemic approach to trust; until you develop a system of thought, you will not truly understand a concept or grow in it. How can I become more trustworthy if I do not know the keys to trust?

"In the science of systems thinking, until you have developed a proper problem statement you cannot devise a solution, because you have not rightly identified the problem. Until you can discuss the problem intelligently, you cannot solve it. You must utilize a structured approach to help you isolate the root cause of mistrust and articulate solutions for rebuilding trust."

"Otherwise, you're simply grasping at straws," Dan agrees.

Sifu nods. "Grasping at straws and wrestling with half-defined concepts. We hear a great deal of talk in the business world about Return on Investment, but how often do we hear business leaders talk about Return on Trust? When the seven keys of trust—character, competence, confidence, caring, communication, consistency, and commitment—are solid and strong in our homes, our businesses, and our community associations, the People First Effect is at work. Individuals and organizations flourish when you have a strong Return on Trust."

Sifu pauses for a moment, allowing Dan to finish typing his notes. When Dan looks up, Sifu asks,

"Do you see now how the two philosophies—trust and putting People First—are related?"

Dan shakes his head slowly. "I'm sorry, Sifu, I understand why being able to clearly define trust is important, but I haven't made the link with the People First philosophy."

"Dan, please write this down: the ideological bridge that connects the two philosophies is truth. Truth exists, Dan, and knowledge is possible. Let me give you two maxims which are the foundation for everything I'm going to teach you today: I gave you the first a moment ago: Let no one seek his own, but each one the other's well-being. The second is: Speak the truth in love."

Dan is nodding as he types. "I've heard you say these things for years in the kwoon."

"It follows then, Dan, that if I have caused a person to mistrust me, then likely I have not spoken the truth in love or I have not been considerate of their well-being. So if I really believe in the People First philosophy and I genuinely value others more highly than I value myself, I will always strive to speak the truth in love and I will be consistently careful to consider the well-being of others. As a People First leader, I strive not to create a trust deficit in any of my relationships. Rather, I will use all seven keys to build trust capital at every opportunity.

"Let us broaden our focus for a moment, Dan; can we expect to be successful in any area of life if we're operating on a trust deficit?"

Dan shakes his head. "No. You've said many times that the two most important pillars in every relationship are trust and respect."

"Precisely right. And if I do not trust you, I will not have much respect for you. So nothing is more important to our personal and professional relationships than constantly growing in trustworthiness. Dan, when I first introduced you to People First, I said the entire philosophy rests on the triad of truth in all things, wisdom in all things, and excellence in all things. Do you recall?"

"I certainly do! I've been striving to live by those principles ever since."

"Very good! If you practice these timeless, transcendent principles, you will put people first and they will of necessity trust you. The only logical foundation for trust is truth, wisdom, and excellence in all things."

Sifu looks at Dan thoughtfully. "My friend, you honored me greatly a moment ago. I asked you if you trust me and you responded without hesitation. I thank you for that."

Dan shrugs. "You're welcome, Sifu, but I wasn't being kind; it's just a fact. I trust you implicitly."

Sifu beams his wide, white smile. "Thank you, my dear friend. Now I will ask you a question and I want you to give it serious thought before you reply. Who is the one person in your life whom you trust the most?"

Dan's eyebrows furrow. "Sifu, no one ever asked me that question."

"If you could name only one person, Dan, who would you trust with your life?"

"That certainly narrows it down." Dan grins. "It's a small list, and you're on it!" He is serious again. "If I could only name one person, it would be Cheryl."

"Very good!" Sifu nods approvingly. "Why would you trust Cheryl with your life?"

"She's always been truthful to me, Sifu," Dan says slowly. "You said we must speak the truth in love; I thought of Cheryl when you said it. She always speaks the truth to me, but she always does it in love. She's never been spiteful or hurtful, not once during our marriage. It's not just her love, though, as important as that is. Cheryl has never been untrue. I trust her with the fidelity of our marriage, I trust her to be a rock of love and strength in our home. Cheryl is a person of the utmost integrity, Sifu; she's the most trustworthy person I know."

"Dan, can you boil down what you've just said into just a few words?"

Dan looks off into the distance for a moment. "When I ask her a question, I can rely on her to tell me the truth, no matter how difficult it might be."

Sifu beams at Dan with delight. "I don't know if you did it intentionally, but you just used the TRUST acronym I gave you a moment ago."

Dan blinks. "I did?"

"Yes! TRUST is Total Reliance Upon Someone's Truthfulness. That's what you just said about your wife."

Dan smiles softly, nodding his head. "I'd never thought of it that way before, but your acronym is spot-on, Sifu. That's how I feel about Cheryl."

Sifu nods. "And how important it is to have that level of trust in your life's partner! Our American courts have provided a wonderful visual aid for trust in cities and towns all across the country with the swearing in of the witness in a courtroom. Our whole jurisprudence system—the right to a trial before a jury of your peers—hinges on the truthfulness of the witnesses who testify. If the truthfulness of a witness can be impugned before the jury, the whole case is likely to fall apart. And so, in many courts all across America, the witness will place his or her hand on a Bible and an officer of the court will ask, 'Do you swear to tell the truth, the whole truth, and nothing but the truth, so help you God?'"

Dan is paying close attention. "I've seen that scene dozens of times on TV."

"It's easy to miss the significance of the Bible in that ceremony, Dan. The laying of the hand on the Bible indicates that there is a foundation for truth, an unwavering standard of right and wrong. Trust must have a foundation of truth. Trust is a necessary outcome of truth."

Sifu is warming to the subject, and he begins speaking rapidly. "More and more people keep their trust locked up these days, Dan. We have become cynical; we're living in a low trust world.

We've seen too many politicians, too many business leaders, even many spiritual leaders lie.

And because we've seen so many people break trust, many people have no desire to give away their trust.

"There was a time, not so long ago, Dan, when the greatest commodity was not gold or silver, but trust! People lived by the proverb that a good name is more to be desired than great riches. You could shake a man's hand and he would say, 'My word is my bond.' And he meant it!

"Dan, the greatest commodity we have in these perilous times is trust. I would encourage you to explain to John Kwan that, although his greatest concern is building the bottom line, if your company makes no investment in building trust capital with the people who work for it, the bottom line will be negatively impacted. When trust is lost, your Purpose Partners no longer show up to work because they want to, but because they have to…because they are afraid not to. There is no joy, no passion, no discretionary effort in an environment that suffers from a trust deficit, only malicious obedience.

"Then the snowball gathers momentum. If our internal customers do not trust us, neither will our external customers. I believe this is the primary reason your market share is not recovering as you would like, Dan. The foundation for loyalty is trust. And loyalty must be earned. People freely give their loyalty when they trust you, when they are convinced that their good is your first concern.

"These are the simple economics of trust, Dan. If our employees—our Purpose Partners—don't trust their leaders, they're not engaged. If there is no trust capital, there can be no return on trust, because there is no trust! And our customers are sensitive to the environment they enter, Dan, as you well know. After a few close encounters of the impersonal, non-trusting kind, customers pick up on the Purpose Partners' lack of trust, and they start looking for a place where they sense a connection, rather than dysfunction."

Dan is nodding as he types. He looks up at Sifu, and there is a clear light of understanding in his eyes. "Our customer service scores haven't returned to prerecession levels because the uncertainty—the lack of trust—that our Purpose Partners are feeling is communicating itself to our customers. The customers are saying to us, 'You're not serving me like you once did,' but what they really mean is, 'You don't care about me like you once did!'"

"That's it, Dan!" Sifu's eyes are very bright. "If you don't care about me, why should I trust you? If there is a deficit of caring, there will inevitably be a deficit of trust, and that deficit affects our internal and our external customers!"

Dan looks at Sifu thoughtfully. "So if I perceive that you don't care, I'm not going to trust you. But you said there are six other keys to building trust. Where do they come in?"

Sifu nods, grinning. "I apologize, my friend. You are such a quick study, and I am passionate about this subject; I started to run ahead of myself! Caring is vitally important, but as you say, it is still just one of seven keys to unlocking trust. When you've grown in all seven of these keys in your own life, Dan, you will be able to explain these keys to John Kwan. You will be able to help Kwan to see trust in this holistic sense—as a system of trustworthiness."

Sifu turns away from Dan and gazes out the window for a long moment. Then he nods to himself and swings back to Dan. "Would you excuse me for a moment?"

Dan's eyes follow Sifu as he strides toward the front door of the restaurant. Dan notices that Sifu has pulled out his cell phone. Dan is curious; he has never known Sifu to interrupt a personal conversation to take or make a call. That's OK, Dan, he tells himself. Sifu has given you plenty to think about. He looks back down at the seven keys of trust on his iPad. I don't know how I missed this! Our Purpose Partners' trust in us was badly shaken during the recession, and we've done very little to reestablish that trust. And if Kwan announces that we're going to cut staff by another 15 percent, what trust remains will be destroyed.

Dan mentally reviews the seven keys of trust. They will question our character…they will wonder about our competence and confidence if we cut staff when the company's financial position is improving…they will have no reason to believe we are caring…in fact, our communication will be that we don't care about people at all, only profits…we will show no consistency, because we talk about People First but we're acting like it's profits first…and it will be very clear that we have no commitment to our Purpose Partners. Dan heaves a deep sigh. He is so engrossed in his thoughts that he is startled when Sifu slides back into the booth.

"Dan, do you have time to go for a drive?"

"Okay, Sifu, if you'd like." Dan sounds uncertain.

"Dan, rather than sit here and talk to you about the seven keys of trust, I'd like to show you how some friends of mine are living them out in their personal and professional lives. You would have some case studies to share with Kwan. What do you think?"

Dan doesn't even look up at Sifu; he is busy slipping the iPad back into its carry case. "Let's go!"

CHAPTER 5

Put Principles First; Profits Follow!

DAN AND SIFU ARE ZIPPING along the interstate in the quiet comfort of Sifu's Lexus. They ride in a companionable silence; Dan is mentally reviewing what he has learned this morning.

Sifu looks over at Dan and smiles his gentle smile. "You are very patient, Dan."

Dan's eyebrows shoot up. "Me, patient? Sifu, I'm grateful that you would give me such a big chunk of your morning."

"Dan, what I have in mind will take several mornings. I want to introduce you to some business leaders who are making the People First Effect a reality and who exemplify each of the seven keys of trust." Sifu glances over at Dan again. "You know I have schools all over the country; I have friends all over the country, and some of them are among the finest business leaders in the nation. Would you like to meet them?"

"I certainly would!"

"Good!" Sifu eases the Lexus into an exit lane. "We are going on the first of those visits today. I had planned to have lunch with a very good friend who is visiting from Missouri. *Character* is the foundation of the keys of trust. When the idea struck me to show you what these keys of trust look like in the flesh, rather than simply describe them, I immediately thought of Tom Manenti. So I called him and asked if you could join us."

Dan is troubled. "I feel badly about interrupting your time with a friend whom you don't see often."

"Rubbish!" Sifu replies briskly. "It will be my pleasure to introduce you, and Tom's delight to meet you. More importantly, Tom will have marvelous insights on the subject of character. He is the chairman of MiTek Industries, and he has worked very hard to model character to all of his Purpose Partners and instill a strong sense of character in MiTek's senior leaders."

"Sifu, if he's a good friend of yours, I know I'll enjoy meeting him."

Sifu chuckles. "Tom said the very same thing about you when I suggested that you join us." His tone changes slightly. "Dan, let's talk about character for just a few moments."

Dan smiles. "I'd like that."

"This first key of trust that we'll be talking with Tom about—character—is vitally important, Dan, because the other six keys that follow are all dependent on it. Trust begins and ends with character. If a person reads you as having bad character, the other six keys simply don't matter, because there is already a trust deficit.

"When people talk about character, Dan, they frequently start by talking about *integrity*. The Greek word *integra* means *whole*; integrity means you have wholeness; you behave consistently with your professed values at home, at work, and in your interaction with your community.

"Integrity is an extremely important part of a leader's character. You can't build trust equity without it. However, Dan, I must add that integrity is a subjective foundation for character, because it is based on you keeping your word. Here is the critical question: Integrity is important; it is important to be consistent and whole; but consistent to *what? There's a difference between subjective integrity and objective truth.* We must dig down to bedrock; there must be an objective philosophical foundation for integrity."

Dan looks at Sifu thoughtfully. "So you're saying that what we have integrity *to*—what we are being consistent *to*—is the deeper question?"

"Precisely. *The only premise for trust is the truth.* Trust is inextricably related to truth. If there is no truth, there is no trust. It's not enough to ask a leader, 'Do you tell the truth?' I'm asking the antecedent to that question: '*Is your integrity built on truth?*' Theory precedes practice, Dan. Philosophy precedes performance."

Dan nods thoughtfully. "What we believe determines how we behave."

"Yes. Someone might ask, 'Is there something more fundamental than practice?' The answer is yes; the *truth* on which that practice is based. *Theory without practice is dead; however, practice without theory is blind.* And theory without truth is a flimsy reed that will collapse under the slightest pressure.

"So..." Dan says slowly, "the only premise for trust is the truth."

Sifu glances at Dan with an approving smile. "Precisely. Truth is the bedrock of character, Dan. If there is no truth, there is no trust. So the concept of character is not a simple question of integrity. The primary question is, on what truth is the leader's integrity built? I wanted you to meet Tom Manenti because he has developed his foundation of truth as well as anyone I know."

Sifu's eyes narrow slightly. "Dan, we must recognize that *character* is a neutral word, just like the word *culture*. Culture simply refers to the environment that people operate in; it does not carry any connotation of moral quality. The same is true of the word *character*; the word does not communicate good or bad in and of itself. There is good and bad character; there are men and women of strong character and those of weak character.

"Something I have noticed over the years, Dan, is that it can be very easy to confuse *personality* with *character*. A great many people confuse the two words because they do not understand that distinction between them. Personality describes the way we interact with others. Some people are extroverts; they are very outgoing and fun-loving. Others are more soft-spoken and reserved.

These are *personality* traits, not character traits.

"To keep these two words distinct in our thoughts, we should remember that personality is not a choice; personality is inherited from our parents. Of course, you can choose to adjust your personality in order to bond with others; you and I do that in business every day. But that does not mean that we are *changing* our personalities; we are simply adjusting our behavior in order to relate to others more effectively and make them feel comfortable."

Dan nods. "Our customer service trainers use the phrase *behavioral flexibility.*"

Sifu nods. "I like that phrase. Character, on the other hand, unlike personality, is based *solely* on choice, particularly with regard to whether we display good or bad character. A person who is dishonest has *chosen* to behave in a dishonest manner. If you or I display bad character, Dan, we have *allowed* it to happen!

"There is no moral value judgment attached to one's personality. No one would say, 'That man should be more outgoing; it is immoral that he is reserved.' But the person who has embraced a bad philosophy will inevitably choose bad character traits. He has chosen a bad path for his life, and he is responsible for making that choice."

Dan has been listening closely. "I never thought of that before, Sifu! It didn't occur to me that *choice* separates personality from character."

"And it is so easy to confuse the two, Dan! When I was young, and I was opening my first few Kung Fu schools, I hired a teacher who was highly animated and clearly loved interacting with people. I mistook those personality traits for good character. Today I know better; you see someone's personality very quickly, but *character* takes much longer to reveal itself. You must wait patiently and watch carefully for a person's character to reveal itself.

"Many men and women have admitted to me that they've made this same mistake. They trusted someone because of their personality, only to discover much later that the person in question had questionable character. We all tend to gravitate toward those people who exhibit similar personality traits to ours. We like someone immediately because their personality style meshes with ours, and our defenses go down. We are drawn to the other person's *personality*, which is perfectly fine and normal, but the most important thing to discern is the *character* of the other person."

Dan nods vigorously. "Sifu, I've made that mistake myself!"

"We all have, Dan. And there are people who are very skillful at hiding their character behind a winning personality. That is why, in any relationship, we must take time to test a person's character. Their character must be *proven* character. Is there an integrity gap between someone's lips and their life? Do they consistently tell the truth, even when it may hurt them to do so? How do they treat people? Again, I am not talking about personality; people who are very shy or highly extroverted can treat people very well or very poorly; the way they treat people reveals their *character*.

"Character is also revealed in our associations. It is very interesting to note, Dan, that if someone knew the five people who are closest to you, it would not be necessary to examine you to discern your character. One would need only to observe the behavior of those five people; their character would reveal your own character, Dan. And so, if you want to develop good character, associate with those who have the best character traits and ask them to speak truth into your life."

Dan is deeply impressed. "Sifu, what you're saying is so important! I'm so grateful I have you to speak truth to me."

Sifu bows his head slightly, acknowledging Dan's compliment. "The true value and worth of a person's life is based entirely on his or her character. A person with bad character cannot be trusted. It does not matter how 'nice' or 'serious-minded' they may appear. So you and I must learn to read character well. We must work to become skillful at reading the mark that people are carrying around—the image of the philosophy that has imprinted itself upon their being. We do that by observing *character traits*—the elements that make up someone's character. We look for good, positive character traits, such as integrity, humility, and kindness. When we see that a person is dishonest, arrogant, or rude, that raises an enormous red flag."

Sifu turns the Lexus onto a narrow lane shaded by tall palm trees. "Dan, I've discovered that far too many people in our society are *never* taught these things. Character is not an issue today; all too often people are looking for flash and flamboyance, not for faithfulness and fruitfulness. We must develop our *character*, Dan. We must be faithful to live lives of truth, wisdom, and excellence; we must bear good fruit and live profitable lives that are worth modeling.

"And we do not do these things only for our lives and our homes, as important as that is. Our character is vitally important for the success of the organizations we lead! How do leaders make an organization strong? By building a positive debt-to-equity ratio? *The strength of an organization is based on the strength of the character of all the people in that organization.*

An organization will never exhibit sustainable strength if its members' lives are marked by weak character.

"As leaders in our homes, our businesses, and our communities, Dan, you and I must *build bridges of truth that will bear the weight of trust.* When the foundation of truth has been laid down, it forms that highway of trustworthiness."

Sifu has parked the car and killed the motor. He looks over at Dan and smiles. "Now, Dan, let us see what the People First Effect looks like in the flesh!"

CHAPTER 6

"Paper Holds Everything"

By Tom Manenti, MiTek Industries

"ONE OF THE THINGS I'M most proud of is that, shortly after I became CEO of MiTek, a team of thirty-five Purpose Partners unanimously chose 'Integrity' to be our Number One Core Value." Tom Manenti's bright brown eyes twinkle with humor. "Of course, it's easy to *say* integrity is our Number One value; sometimes I'll say that 'paper holds everything.'" He is serious again. "But it's another thing altogether when four thousand-plus people really *believe* that and they know that integrity is the basis of how you build trust in an organization. You can't *say* you're one thing and then *be* another and expect a long-term, positive outcome. It just doesn't work that way. So Sifu, when you ask me how important character is to our success at MiTek, I'd say it's paramount. Everything else builds on valuing character and living in integrity."

Tom Manenti is a lean, compact man with an air of relaxed confidence that Dan has seen in both the arena and in the boardroom. Tom is one of those people who is completely comfortable in his own skin. The fact that this man is the chairman and CEO of an organization that employs more than 4,000 people on six continents makes that confidence that much more impressive. *If Tom ever had doubts about his ability to lead MiTek,* Dan muses, *he answered those internal questions long ago.* And yet there is a humility that is very much present in Tom's warm personality. The laugh lines around his eyes bear silent witness to the fact that this is a man who smiles often and enjoys a good joke.

"And you've had good success building your organization on a set of values, Tom?" Dan asks.

Tom nods. "We tell our customers that MiTek is the industry leader in every market we serve worldwide, and that's a statement of fact. We set very aggressive performance indicators for ourselves every year, both financial and production goals, and we've reached or exceeded those goals every year. We've got a fabulous group of people at MiTek who are dedicated to our success. I consider myself blessed to work at such an organization."

Despite his own internal stress, Dan finds himself liking this man almost instantly, and he is genuinely happy to hear of his new friend's success in putting people first. "I'm sure your board of directors considers themselves blessed to have someone like you to lead at MiTek."

For the first time, Tom Manenti looks uncomfortable. Dan will learn during the visit that Tom is perfectly happy to heap praise on anyone who deserves it...except himself. "Well, I report directly to Warren Buffett. So far he seems pleased."

Impressed, Dan gives a low whistle, and then laughter bubbles up in his throat and he grins at Sifu.

"A Berkshire Hathaway company! Sifu, I must confess that it never occurred to me that you were bringing me to meet the owner of Joe's Hardware store!"

Sifu grins back at Dan and nods at Tom. "If I knew such a man and thought he could tell us more about the importance of being a person of character, I would have introduced you. But when I think of words like 'character' and 'integrity,' I think of Tom Manenti. And here we are."

Tom shifts in his chair, obviously eager to change the subject. "Dan, Sifu told me you're having some difficulty with the new ownership at your company. I'm happy to help you any way I can, but I'm not quite sure how."

Sifu clears his throat. "I have been telling Dan that one of the most important elements of the People First philosophy is creating trust capital with the people in our organization. I have laid out seven keys to building trust within an organization, and the first one of those keys is character. As I said a moment ago, I simply can't think of anyone I know who exemplifies character as well as you do, Tom. So here we are."

Tom smiles and nods, acknowledging the compliment. "Well, thank you, Sifu, I'd say Dan was already sitting with *the* exemplar of character when you got this idea. But please tell me how I can help you."

"Tom," Dan begins, "as Sifu and I were driving here, Sifu said that you have worked very hard to instill a sense of character in your leadership team. Why do you feel that's so important?"

"Dan, I've already said that character is vital to our ongoing success at MiTek; that character must start with me and my senior leaders. If you're going to begin to build a relationship of trust, it must begin with character! I instill character by emphasizing our core values; I talk about them at every opportunity. Our fourth core value is 'Empowered Purpose Partners.' I always qualify that by saying that 'Empowered Purpose Partners' starts with empowered leadership.

"Sifu, you were the one who said to me that 'fish rots from the head down.' You have a thought, and that thought—whether good or bad—as you entertain it, that thought turns into a belief. That belief motivates our behaviors, and once those behaviors are acted out for a long enough period of time, they become strongholds. Those strongholds become extremely difficult to break. So if we have the right belief system about doing the right thing and empowering others to live and work in integrity, we'll do the right things, and over time those correct behaviors become strongholds."

Tom looks steadily at Dan. "On the other hand, I can take an axe to those beliefs and behaviors in an instant."

Dan looks at Tom curiously. "But if you say that they've become strongholds...?"

Tom nods and smiles, anticipating the question. "I was chatting with my sister, Mary Ellen, at a wedding recently. At one point she leaned over to me and smiled and said, 'Your kids will find you out.' Now, if our children can see through any false faces we might put on, how about our Purpose Partners? I spend a great many more hours at MiTek than I do at home, so when you think about character from a senior leadership standpoint, your Purpose Partners will find you out.

"My senior leaders must be confident that I will act in a way that is consistent with what I believe and what I say about being a values-driven organization. If they see that my character is based on nothing more than on what's expedient, I undermine their own character. If I have no foundation for character greater than what works in the moment, our leaders will learn to do the same thing.

And then the folks who report to *them* will learn the same thing, and I've created an ugly avalanche of bad beliefs and bad behavior."

Dan has been typing notes on his iPad. Now he looks up at Tom thoughtfully. "So you agree with Sifu that character is essential to establishing trust with your Purpose Partners?"

Tom grins. "You and I have the same mentor, Dan, so you probably know what I'm going to say. It's most certainly essential! You can't fake sincerity. I once heard an executive from another organization say, 'My staff is way too busy working on their projects to watch what I do.' I couldn't disagree more! People see everything, much more than we realize, and our actions completely overshadow anything we say."

Tom leans forward in his chair, his eyes narrowed in concentration. "What we say not only has the *possibility* but the distinct *tendency* to become our promise. And we all know that a broken promise destroys trust immediately. You spend a lifetime building this thing we call trust, you put your character on the line, and all it takes is just one broken promise…and it's gone immediately! I recently read an article in which the author said, 'Credibility is far easier to maintain than to repair.' That's it exactly."

Dan shakes his head sadly. "My goodness, yes! But Tom, if you don't mind, I'd like to pursue this a little further. As I listen to you talk, I've been evaluating my own behavior as a model for the senior leaders at Prestigious Products. I've been very conscious of my example, but I think I'd always assumed that character would take care of itself if I made good hiring decisions. It sounds like you're not leaving anything to chance."

"Dan, I once read an author who said that the *culture in an organization is the out-living of the in-living beliefs of leadership*.[1] It's almost genetic; an organization takes on the complexion of its leadership. You have someone at the top who is leading the organization. He or she could be leading well or leading the company off a cliff, but that individual at the top is creating expectations among the rest of the senior leadership team. You and I both do that, Dan. And that's important, because the senior leaders will take on the complexion of that top person and the rest of the organization takes on the complexion of their leadership.

---

[1] Jack Lannom, *People First Leadership: How to Develop World-Class Leadership and Pass On an Enduring Legacy* (Pembroke, Pines, FL: Lannom Inc. © 2017-2000), p. 217

"So if the way leadership in an organization goes about getting results is by deceit and conniving, eventually the good people—the people of integrity—will leave, because they're just not going to stay around for that. But the ones who don't care, and the ones who feel trapped and don't see any way out, they'll just adopt that sort of behavior, because they think that's what is required. The organization has taken on the complexion of its leadership."

Tom's warm smile flashes again. "I loved how you said it, Dan; you thought character would take care of itself if you made good hiring decisions. You may have heard that old saying, 'The harder I work, the luckier I get.' So the harder I work, or the harder our VP of HR works to make sure we find the right candidate, the more blessed we are to get the right people on the bus, as Jim Collins says. I always say that it's far better to take more time than you'd planned when hiring; it's so much easier than firing somebody."

Sifu and Dan both nod their emphatic agreement.

"So I work hard at hiring the right people," Tom continues, "but I also work hard at developing the folks who are here. Skills can be taught, so we invest in skills training. A lot of leaders don't give it any thought, but character can be built, so we invest in building character also."

Sifu graces Tom with one of his brightest smiles. "So you are not merely investing in human doings, Tom; you are investing in the human beings."

Tom nods emphatically. "That's right. Look, people will make mistakes; that's going to happen.

But tarnishing our reputation…that should never happen. There's one directive that all Berkshire

Hathaway managers have, and it comes directly from Warren Buffett. Every year at the annual meeting, Warren tells us, 'Lose money for the corporation, and I will be forgiving. Lose one *shred* of our reputation, and I will be ruthless.'

"So yes, Dan, it's *very* important to make those good hiring decisions, but it doesn't end there. You've got to work at pouring into your Purpose Partners. Left to their own devices, people will be influenced by someone or something. So you want to develop the men and women who will become the dominant shapers in your organization."

Dan has been typing rapidly. "Wow! Tom, I really want to get that last sentence: *Develop the men and women who will become the dominant shapers in your organization.*" He looks up at Sifu, and his eyes are wide with understanding. "Sifu, now I really see what you meant about digging down to the bedrock of the People First philosophy. There's a lot more to being a People First practitioner than I'd realized!"

Dan looks back at Tom with a grateful smile. "Tom, I'm so glad to have had this chance to meet you! This has been a real eye-opener!"

Tom smiles. "I've been fortunate to work for an outstanding organization with a leader who believes in me and empowers me. From what little Sifu has told me, Dan, you're dealing with a situation that's quite different."

"Yes, but I *must* get better at this!" Now it is Dan who is frowning with concentration. "Tom, can you tell me some of the things you've done to encourage and develop character at MiTek?"

Tom does not hesitate. "It all begins with our senior executive team. Everybody in that group knows my motto, which is, 'It doesn't matter who's right; just get it right!'"

"Hmm," Sifu says softly. "You and I discussed this not so long ago, Tom. You said, 'It's vital that I get this right. It doesn't matter if I'm right or someone else on the team is right, but we've got to get this right!'"

"I believe that very strongly," Tom nods. "So I spend a lot of time investing in my senior leaders. I'm very aware of our seven core values, and I understand that if I'm not modeling these core values, what's the use? If I'm not living the values, then who will? I have to live them, and I insist that my senior leadership team exhibit core value behaviors also.

"Now, we give permission to fail." Tom looks at Sifu. "I learned that from you, Sifu, and I've never forgotten it. We're not waiting for someone to stumble so that we can squash them and make an example of them. We're looking to catch people doing things right, and if they need some coaching so that they can do the right thing, we're there to help.

"I write about character and integrity frequently in the CEO updates I send out company-wide. I speak about it. If someone asks me to speak—whether it's to a group of our Purpose Partners or an organization outside of MiTek—it's very easy for me to start talking about our core values.

"I even talk about our values with companies that we're looking to acquire. At first, I wasn't sure how a business owner would embrace my talking about our values, but I've found that people are starving for this kind of leadership."

Again, Tom looks over at Sifu. Dan is learning that this is a habit with Tom Manenti, one of the many little things that sets this man apart. He has been very careful throughout this conversation to include Sifu with his eyes and with his words, so that Sifu is not ignored. It is a way of showing honor, and Tom does it so unconsciously that Dan is quite sure that if the third person in the room was the newest member of MiTek's facilities staff, Tom would show him the very same courtesy.

"Sifu, you once told me that people are over-managed and under-led in business and in so many areas of life. That was another truism that I've seen borne out time and time again. So I set the tone right up front when we begin talking to a company about a potential acquisition. I tell them, 'If you don't want to be associated with this kind of values-driven organization, just let us know. We may not be the right fit for everyone.'"

Dan raises an eyebrow. "And have there been many like that, Tom?"

"Actually, we've had at least three acquisitions who didn't want to join our family of companies at first, *until* they learned about our culture. I recall one in particular that really wasn't for sale.

They had gone to the eleventh hour with a potential buyer, but it fell apart at the end because the other company couldn't come up with the financing. So they were extremely skeptical when we approached them. But when one of our senior leaders met with them and started talking about our values and our culture, the other company's executives looked at each other and said, 'You know what? This sounds like something we want to sign up for.' And they did!"

"How about internally, Tom?" Dan asks. "Have you had to overcome any restraining forces within your company as you've worked to build the character of your team?"

"Sure," Tom admits frankly, "there are always skeptics and there are always detractors…but not many. Most people *want* this kind of leadership. This is the way they want to live and it's the way they want to be led." Tom nods at Sifu. "Dan, I'm sure you've heard the Grandmaster say, *'This is a philosophy fit to live by, a life fit to live with, and a legacy fit to live for.'*" Tom grins. "Sifu, if you knew how often I quote you to other people, you might start charging me royalties!"

The three men laugh. "You and me both, Tom," Dan says with feeling. "For the first few years I tried to give Sifu credit for the things I was saying, but as time went by—" Dan shakes his head—"not so much." He chuckles again. "And now, Tom, I may very well start stealing great quotes from you too!"

Sifu beams at his two prized students, who are so clearly enjoying each other's company. "Do you really think I developed this philosophy myself? I learned this from my teacher and from the great thinkers of past centuries. I thought about it and thought about it, and over the years it became my own. We are all standing on the shoulders of giants."

That warm smile, always so quick to surface, lights Tom's face again. "I sure have enjoyed the view from your shoulders, Sifu. Thank you! Anyway, Dan, you asked about restraining forces. We clearly and consistently state our expectations; everyone knows our key business imperatives. I insist that our leaders and Purpose Partners embrace the core values of our company and strive to accomplish those key business imperatives. And then we base all performance reviews—not just mine or those for the senior executives, but everyone's—on the same core values and criteria. That creates harmony, and that harmony helps to eliminate the dissonance. And when all else fails, you prune."

Dan nods and glances at Sifu, then back at Tom. "I've found that in most cases it's a self-pruning culture, just like the palm trees here in Florida that shed their lower branches as they continue to grow. A People First culture consistently attracts the best performers, but it also repels those who are content with average. Those people who are just there to pick up a paycheck or get some kind of psychological kick from acquiring power usually leave for a place where they aren't expected to give or to serve."

"You're absolutely right, Dan," Tom says emphatically. "I found that to be particularly true when we first began to instill the People First philosophy at MiTek. The vast majority of our team embraced People First from the outset. But there were a few who resisted or grew resentful because their old way of doing things was changing. And they retired or resigned. A friend of mine who is also a CEO calls it 'opting out.'"

"When you put it that way, Dan, it's true, I had very little pruning to do." Tom grins at Dan. "'A self-pruning culture'! That's a phrase I'm likely to appropriate from you!"

Dan shakes his head ruefully. "I've been listening to you talk for the better part of an hour, and I've taken all these notes, and I've given you one phrase in return. It doesn't seem like a fair trade! Tom, tell me some of your success stories. Tell me how your focus on developing character among your team has benefited your Purpose Partners and your customers."

Tom leans back in his chair and smiles up at the ceiling. "There are so many stories!" He thinks for a moment and leans back toward Dan. "Well, since it starts with leadership, let's talk about the character and trust that's grown among our executive team, which has made them so much more productive. When I took over as CEO of MiTek, I spent most of the first year observing, and then eventually getting involved with the internal relationships on our senior team. I actually placed more emphasis on relationships than results at first, because I knew that the results would come more readily if they could trust one another and work together as a team. I've seen that cohesion grow over the last five years, to the point where our senior leaders are now focused almost 100 percent on results and not on any kind of internal politics. I see so many leaders who get it backwards; they focus exclusively on results and think relationships will just happen. It doesn't work that way!

"As Sifu says, you can't impart what you don't possess. When we have those solid, trusting internal relationships, we see how building trust with our customers has impacted the growth of our business." Tom's eyes glimmer with humor again. "A very wise man once told me that whatever you want your external customers to feel, your internal customers must feel first."

Tom and Dan both grin, knowing full well that "the very wise man" Tom is referring to is seated there with them. Sifu looks on innocently. "One of our sales reps was recently in town with one of our customers," Tom continues, "and he asked me if he could bring the client by. Now, this customer isn't one of our top-billing accounts, but Sifu, you know me, I came up in sales. I *love* customers! I said 'Sure!' But this guy just couldn't believe that he was sitting in the CEO's office. He kept talking about the high principles of our company and our Purpose Partners, and then he said this: 'MiTek always makes me feel like I'm the biggest and most important customer they have.'

"I told him that's actually a goal we set for ourselves. We never say, 'Don't worry about that guy; he doesn't buy that much from us.' Then I asked him, 'What does that mean to you, to be treated that way?'

"He said, 'It gives me confidence in the marketplace, confidence that I can go up against the big boys.' Now, he's competing for market share against other organizations that are bigger and probably have a bit more capital to employ. But he knows he's going to get the same service from us that we provide to the bigger companies."

"Confidence in the marketplace," Dan murmurs as he types the phrase. "That's a happy customer!"

Tom nods. "There's a phrase we use internally: 'Outrageously engaged Purpose Partners serving incredibly delighted customers.' That's the goal we shoot for. And that brings me to one last success story, Dan, and that is the comment

I get from so many of our Purpose Partners about the concept of *permission to succeed and permission to fail.*

"I remember something I heard years ago at a Weight Watchers meeting. They said, 'It's not failure; it's feedback.' So when you have a setback—you ate that piece of cake you shouldn't have, or you didn't call the customer right away because you didn't think he was going to be upset, and later you realize you should have moved heaven and earth to call that customer before you went home that night—OK, so you failed at that. Here's the feedback: next time, you do whatever you have to do to call that customer. You just learned something that didn't work. Great! What have we learned from that and how are we going to improve because of it?

"As that concept has taken hold at MiTek, I've had dozens of people tell me, 'I'm not tentative in what I do. I'm not afraid that if I make one little mistake that someone's going to hit me over the head with a hammer.' I am certain that this is what allows us to be more innovative than our competitors. We regularly encourage our team to *challenge the known and defend the unknown.* They have to know they can do that without fear of criticism or retribution.

"One of our key business imperatives, Dan, is 'Competitor Irrelevance.' When our Purpose Partners are confident that they can challenge the way we've always done things and get outside the box and be more innovative, we will deliver better products and offer better service. And if we keep doing all of *that* right, we won't keep looking back over our shoulder at our competitors, because they will have become irrelevant in the process."

"My goodness, Tom, this is *great* stuff!" Dan is grinning as he types on the iPad. Then he glances over at Sifu. "Sifu, I'm sorry; I've really been monopolizing the conversation. How about if I sit quietly for a while and you and Tom talk?"

"Dan, Tom and I invited you here so you could ask questions and listen, which is exactly what you've been doing. There is no need to apologize. But I would like to pursue a subject with Tom that you and I touched on during our drive here, and that is the idea of *character clues.* Tom, how would you profile a leader who displays character?"

Tom considers the question for a few seconds, then answers, "Leaders display character by not being easily rattled. Their values are immutable. Now, I'm not saying that a leader who displays character will never explode. That will happen, but you can do it without compromising your character."

Tom looks back at Dan. "I've been a huge baseball fan all my life and my hometown team is the St. Louis Cardinals. I'm friends with Mike Matheny, the Cardinals' manager. He's that kind of leader, one who's not easily rattled. I've seen Mike barking at an umpire and get thrown out of the game; the next day he'll come to the park and go up to that umpire and apologize. He'll say, 'I'm sorry, I let my emotions get the best of me.' And they'll usually say, 'Mike, I understand. You're a gentleman.' It's a consistency that men and women of character have that people come to trust. Mike exemplifies that quality."

Sifu nods thoughtfully. "Consistency is actually one of the seven keys of trust that I've identified. Let me ask you this, Tom. Dan has been asking you about developing character in your organization; how about the individual? What should a leader like Dan who wants to continue to grow do to continue to develop character?"

Tom does not need to ponder this question. "You need accountability," he replies firmly. "You need at least one person, or preferably a group of people in your life that you can count on to tell you where your blind spots are. We all have them. But, of course, a great many people won't tell you about them!

"I remember hearing someone say that we need three different kinds of mentors. You need someone who has arrived at the point of wisdom and experience that you'd like to attain. They are likely to be older than you, but more importantly, it must be someone you trust and respect. I'm so very fortunate to have you, Sifu, and some other men in my life who are pouring into me. Then you should have someone you're mentoring; you're pouring into them. And then you need someone who's at your peer level, someone who you're not overly impressed by and they're not overly impressed by you. What I mean by that is that you're not worried about being too polite with one another. The trust and respect are there, but you get in the trenches with each other and just let it rip about the areas you see for growth. Iron is sharpening iron, and when the sparks fly, you're both OK with that. For me, accountability is the key to developing character."

Sifu has that bright gleam in his eyes that communicates his full engagement. "Tom, what you've said is so true and so important! And yet I would be willing to guess that 90 percent of the leaders I know don't have those relationships that you just mentioned. They are so busy with the demands of business that they simply don't make those relationships a priority!"

"I'd have to be the first one to plead guilty to that charge," Dan says humbly. "Especially since the recession hit. I had a *lot* of years of ignoring my family to make up for, and I didn't lose that focus, but after that, trying to keep our company solvent was my only other thought." His eyes turn to Sifu. "I have the best mentor a man could possibly ask for, and I didn't reach out for help until I'd just about hit the rocks."

Tom looks at Dan with genuine warmth, but that sparkle of mischief is glimmering in his eyes.

"You and about 10,000 other husbands and fathers and business leaders, Dan. Including me! Do you think during difficult times that I don't get caught up in keeping my nose to the grindstone? To the point where I can't see anything but grindstone? And it comes right back to accountability; I need someone to tell me that I'm letting myself get out of balance.

"Someone asked me just a few weeks ago how many hours I sleep each day. What he really meant was, 'How do you do everything you do each day?' The leading, the learning, the accountability, the communication, the physical exercise, the travel, *and* family time. He couldn't understand how I get seven hours' sleep and still do what I do. And my answer is that it's a matter of scheduling priorities. I make those mentoring relationships a priority, just as I make time with my wife a priority. So the grindstone is a priority, but I also discipline myself to do the other things that make me more effective at working on the grindstone."

"Discipline myself to schedule priorities," Dan murmurs as he taps on the iPad.

"Tom," Sifu asks, "if you're agreeable, I'd like to throw out a few of these character clues I've been considering. What I mean by 'clues' is the attitudes and actions which reveal the trustworthy character of a leader. I'd love to hear what you think of them and if you give any thought to living out these clues in your own life."

Tom chuckles and glances at Dan. "And if I *don't* live out these character clues, I'd better schedule some new priorities!"

Sifu laughs aloud. "No, my friend, I'm really asking you to help me develop my own thinking on this subject."

Still smiling, Tom nods his head. "I'll be happy to."

Sifu is thoughtful again. "Tom, I think that the foundation for character is *ethics*. In other words, a man or woman of character possesses *a thoroughly developed moral sense of what is right and wrong, based on truth.* In other words, there is an objective foundation for truth which underlies the sense of ethics."

Tom nods. "You need that foundation. Sifu, I believe that most people *want* to do the right thing.

You're always going to find the bipolar, nefarious person, but again, if you've done a good job in vetting and on-boarding a person during the hiring process, your Purpose Partners will want to do the right thing. Many times when someone *isn't* doing the right thing, it's because they lack guidance: they don't know what's expected or they haven't learned to judge their actions according to our values.

"My point is, most people know right from wrong, so that means we *choose* to act rightly or wrongly. I was fortunate to have parents who taught me the right thing to do. My wife reminds me and our children regularly! Something will come up, and one of us will say, 'Gee, I don't know what to do in this situation,' and Kathy will say, 'Do the *right* thing. You know what's right, so there's some other reason you're having a tough time with this.'

"I believe I send character clues by doing the right thing, even when it's not the popular thing to do. That's like a litmus test. Someone is observing and says, 'Hmm, he did the right thing, even though he knew he was going to take some fire over that decision.' And a big part of that is that when I make a mistake, even though I thought I was doing what was right, I take ownership of my mistakes. People will forgive your mistakes, but they will not forgive your cover-up."

Sifu nods approvingly. "As you say, Tom, your Purpose Partners will find you out."

Tom nods. "Exactly. Admitting my errors is not always a comfortable experience, but it is always the right thing to do."

Sifu waits a moment to be sure Tom has finished speaking before he says, "The second clue I'd suggest is that *a person of character always walks with integrity. Their behavior matches their beliefs, and there is no contradiction between what they say and what they do.*"

"You're speaking my language, Sifu," Tom grins. "We have posters up in our corporate office for each of our core values, and there's a little explanation for each one. The explanation for *Integrity* simply says, "Walk the Talk." Actions speak louder than words; if our behavior doesn't match our beliefs, or what we *say* we believe, then there's dissonance. And that creates internal conflict—and that 'internal' can be within the organization or within yourself. And what does *that* do? It creates stress; you can't possibly be as effective when you're under that stress as you would be if you were walking in integrity, where you don't have that stress.

"I look at some of our politicians and I just can't relate to the way they live. I can't imagine what it's like going through life maintaining a cover-up. Warren Buffett will ask us, 'If the behavior that you're contemplating was going to be printed in the newspaper the next day, where your wife and children would see it, would you still do it?' I'll actually apply that when I'm considering something. It's not difficult, when you're in a position like mine, to be tempted with power and recognition and things like that. Power simply magnifies our character. I'm sure you've heard the great quote from the Englishman, Lord Acton, who said that 'power tends to corrupt and absolute power corrupts absolutely.' Now, I don't have anything like 'absolute power,' but I have to stay on guard. I'll ask myself, 'Is this something that I'd want everyone to see?'

"Everyone's going to leave a legacy, every one of us. So we should ask ourselves, 'What's mine going to be?' Will it be a legacy based on integrity? Or one based on mistrust? Those are the kind of things I think about."

Dan looks at Tom curiously. "So…even before People First…you're thinking about integrity first?"

Tom nods slowly. "I'd never thought of it quite that way, Dan, but yes. Without integrity there's no trust, and without trust there are no relationships, and without relationships…it would be pretty tough to put people first!"

All three men laugh. Dan types a note, still chuckling. "That's a great point," he acknowledges.

Sifu ticks off a third point on his finger. "My third character clue is that *men and women of character recognize the exalted worth and dignity of all people, and that belief about people causes them to respect and honor others.*"

Again, Tom nods with certainty. "I was raised with this idea. My parents taught me that I'm not better than anyone else; I'm just different from them. I believe what was written by our founders, that it's 'self-evident that all men are created equal and that they are endowed by their Creator with certain unalienable rights, that among these are life, liberty, and the pursuit of happiness.' I believe that with all my heart.

"I hate injustice and unfairness and I'll do whatever I can to prevent it or mitigate it. Respect and honor are very important to me and my family. I was raised with these concepts. I was taught to have respect and show respect.

"Our Purpose Partners need to know that we, as leaders, care. I suppose that might sound trite to some people, but I've seen too many leaders make it painfully obvious that they don't care. They care about their image, but will they really go out on a skinny branch for an individual who might seem to be insignificant when compared to the overall scope of a company? Would they throw a person under the bus in order to save their image? I've seen it happen too many times, and heard even more stories about that happening. The old phrase is so true: people don't care how much you know until they know how much you care."

Sifu nods thoughtfully. "Those leaders who don't care are the reason I developed the People First philosophy. And that brings me directly to my fourth character clue, which is that *a man or woman of character will be a servant leader, not a despot.* I believe that concept of servant leadership springs directly from our vision for people."

"Sifu, you and I have talked in the past about humility versus hubris," Tom says. "I have a T-shirt that says, 'Givers gain; takers lose.' One of my very good friends is a coach for the St. Louis Cardinals and the St. Louis Blues. He serves two major professional sports franchises, and he never asks for a thing. He pours into people's lives, and he believes that his role is to put things in the light of eternity. I talked about legacy a moment ago, and he has that long-term view also. We've talked about what will mean the most when we're gone, and what we want that legacy to be.

"That man is a servant leader. He lives that sincere humility; it's really about giving and not expecting to receive anything in return. Sifu, you've said so many times that *real power is the power that makes other people powerful.* And I agree with you that it takes character to understand that what is given away multiplies and what is withheld diminishes."

"Mmm," Sifu murmurs, as if he has just tasted something especially delicious. "You've really given this thought, my friend! I like to say that servant leaders practice the universal law of sowing and reaping. They sow the seeds of self-sacrifice to reap a great harvest of good for others. And that harvest includes sustainable success for the organizations they serve."

Tom grins at Dan. "What do you say I stop talking, Dan, and you and I listen to the Grandmaster for a while?"

Sifu smiles. "To the contrary, Tom, you have helped me solidify my thinking on this subject. And you have already completely validated my final character clue, which is *complete transparency. Men and women of character have nothing to hide. They don't try to hide their flaws; they freely admit that they are still under construction.*"

Tom nods emphatically. "We're not perfect; we don't have all the answers. We learn from our mistakes. So why would we pretend to be anything else *but* under construction?! And guess what? Our loved ones and our Purpose Partners already *know* we're not perfect! They already know we don't have all the answers, so every time you try to make it look like you know everything, you can see the eyes roll. I am quite certain that it creates credibility when you're open and transparent, and that credibility is the basis for trust."

Later that afternoon, Sifu and Dan are driving back from their visit with Tom. Dan leans back in his seat and sighs. "Sifu, listening to you and Tom talk about character—which is just the first of seven keys of trust—I'm amazed that I had the success I did implementing the People First philosophy at my company! I hadn't given any concentrated thought to this idea of trust. I think I was cruising on autopilot!"

Sifu smiles, but shakes his head. "I disagree with your assessment, Dan. I believe that People First filled in the gaps for you. You have always been a man of character; clearly, you are a competent, confident businessman. Your actions after the recession took place prove that. You are consistent, and when you set your mind to something, no one can match your commitment. So what were you lacking? Before you adopted the People First philosophy, you were weak in two of the seven keys of trust. You were not *caring*. You cared more about profits than you did about people. And though you *did* care about your wife and children, you did not *communicate* your caring well. Your actions communicated something quite different than caring.

"But when you committed to putting People First, Dan, you reversed the order; you started caring about people first, then profits. You communicated to your family and your Purpose Partners that you truly *did* care, and the results—for your marriage and for your company—were dramatically positive."

Dan sighs and nods sadly. "That's true. And I'm grateful that that my marriage is still strong. I wish I could say the same for my company."

"Let's see what we can do to make improvements there," Sifu says briskly. "If you have time, I think we might be able to have lunch with James Donnelly of the Castle Group. I'd like to talk with him about competence, the second key of trust. Would that work for you?"

"I'll make it work!" Dan says eagerly.

"Give me a few days to set up the rest of our visits. Some of these men live in other parts of the country; we were fortunate to catch Tom here on vacation. We can use Skype for meetings that won't work in person. In the meantime, Dan, do everything you can to model character for your Purpose Partners and with Mr. Kwan. Remember what Tom said: no matter what comes your way in the next few days, don't let yourself get rattled."

Dan takes in a deep breath and then releases it in a long sigh. "I'll do my very best, Sifu. I'm afraid I've got a very difficult day coming up next week."

CHAPTER 7

Competence Based On An Unshakable Core

James Donnelly of the Castle Group

"IN THE GREEK LANGUAGE, Dan, *profit* conveys the idea of increase. And the first location of profit that a company should focus on is increase with respect to the development of their Purpose Partners."

Today Dan is driving and Sifu is seated comfortably in the passenger seat of Dan's Acura. It is a short drive from Dan's office to the corporate headquarters of the Castle Group, where Dan and Sifu will meet James Donnelly, Castle's founder and CEO. Dan will be meeting with John Kwan in two days to hear his plan to lay off 15 percent of Prestigious Products' workforce. He feels his whole body filling with tension.

Dan glances over at Sifu. "Sifu, I'd be willing to bet that most CEOs would say, 'Yes, training is important, but the first place we need to invest is in our equipment and systems.'"

Sifu chuckles and nods. "You're absolutely right. It wasn't that long ago that you would have been one of those CEOs!"

Dan grins at the truth of Sifu's statement. "That's why I know the script so well!"

"And the script is not false, Dan; it's a matter of primacy. You and I are going to talk with James Donnelly about Competence, the second key of trust. The Castle Group is a property management company, and I've come to know James and his team well due to some real estate ventures I'm involved with. This man *radiates* competence. I'm sure he will talk to us about the efficiency of his organization's technology and systems. But I'm also quite sure that he will tell us that the competence which marks the Castle Group is the result of the investment he has made in his Purpose Partners."

Dan sighs. "I'm afraid John Kwan is coming from a completely different mind-set. He seems to believe that profitability comes from cutting costs to the bone."

Sifu looks over at Dan. "Did you hear how you just phrased that, Dan? You didn't use the word 'sustainable.' Everyone knows you can boost short-term profits by cutting staff and slashing operating costs. A great many leaders, you and I included, were forced to do that during the recent economic downturn. And we must always be looking for ways to maximize our efficiency. But in order to create *sustainable* growth in your organization, it is imperative that you focus on the personal growth of people first!

"A wise leader is consumed with helping Purpose Partners grow and become all that they are designed and equipped to be. Then his company can grow and become all that it can possibly be."

Dan has pulled the car into the parking lot of the Castle Group's headquarters. He turns in his seat to give Sifu his full attention. "So..." Dan says thoughtfully, "when you speak of 'competence,' you're not speaking only of professional ability? There's more to it?"

"Yes," Sifu nods emphatically. "Let's go in and see what James has to say about it. You'll like him, Dan. I don't know of a better person we could speak to about this subject. He embodies the blend of high-tech and high-touch that is the hallmark of the People First Leader."

Dan kills the motor and swings his door open. "I'm looking forward to this!"

Like Tom Manenti, whom Dan met a few days ago, James Donnelly is a neat, trim man with bright eyes and a cheerful smile. He welcomes Dan and Sifu warmly and escorts them to his office. When the three men are seated, James smiles at Dan. "Dan, when Sifu called and asked if I'd be willing to help a friend of his, I was only too glad to say 'yes.' In addition to introducing us to a number of our current clients, Sifu, you've been one of our most effective sales representatives, and you probably don't even know it!" James grins at Sifu.

Sifu cocks his head and looks at James curiously. "Sales representative?" he asks.

James' smile broadens. "Without a doubt! Sifu, I take you with me on almost every sales presentation I make. I tell our prospects that we believe whatever we want them to feel, our Purpose Partners must feel first. And we want our clients to feel that when they walk into one of our offices, they are walking into a Ritz-Carlton. Sometimes I feel like I should be paying you royalties!"

Dan laughs aloud. "James, I was just talking to a man the other day who said the same thing!"

Dan gives Sifu a playful grin. "Don't be giving the Grandmaster ideas!"

Sifu smiles warmly at the two men. "To the contrary, I am delighted to hear that the People First philosophy is continuing to expand here in Florida and throughout the country. You may both quote me whenever you wish."

James is still grinning at Dan's remark. "I'm grateful, Sifu. You've made an impact on our organization. And, I must confess, I've been looking forward to this conversation ever since you called me. I'm fascinated by your concept of these seven keys of trust and the way you have Competence second in order of importance."

Sifu raises a cautionary finger. "James, I probably didn't explain myself very well. I believe all of these keys are equally important to a person's integrity. If you and I as leaders are weak in just one of those keys, we create mistrust and the profitability of our organizations will suffer for it."

James nods thoughtfully. "Thank you, that does help clarify it."

"James," Sifu continues, "let me start by asking you this question: *How important to the success of The Castle Group is the competence of your organization?*"

"You can't have success without organizational competence," James says matter-of-factly. "Two of our company's three founders are accountants. We started this property management business that leverages our competence in finance, and today we highlight that competence. We have a fiduciary responsibility to the owners of our properties to make sure that their monies are spent correctly and that investments are made wisely. If we're going to project that competence to our clients, we *must* make the requisite investments in developing our Purpose Partners. So, bottom line, if our internal and external customers are going to trust us, it begins and ends with competence."

Sifu gives James his brightest smile. "My friend, that is *so* well said! I told Dan that you were the best person I knew to speak to about this subject, and you have proven me right in the first five minutes of conversation."

James grins. "It certainly has been a long learning process! And what I've learned, now that we have more than one thousand Purpose Partners, is that I also need organizational clarity. I've never valued this as highly as I do today."

Dan has been typing notes on the iPad, but now he looks up at James curiously. "Organizational clarity?"

"I phrase it, 'Who does *what*, *when*, and *how*?'" James replies. "You see so many companies that *don't* have clarity, which results in a poor culture and all sorts of dysfunction. Competency is basically what we at the Castle Group sell. We are a property management company for residential real estate. So when I make a sales presentation to an owner or an association, I have two primary thrusts. Both points are all about establishing trust with the potential client.

"The first point is our philosophy. Perhaps I'm sitting with the board of directors for a high-rise condominium on Miami Beach, and they ask me, 'James, what's the difference between you and your competitors?'

"I'll say, 'We believe that to be great at what you do, you need incredible people.' And I lay out the People First philosophy, Sifu. I'll tell them, 'The extent to which I treat my team well will reflect almost exactly how your residents will be treated by my team.'"

Sifu smiles broadly and nods his agreement. "You cannot impart what you do not possess."

James nods emphatically. "It all begins and ends with the people. So I'll tell a prospective client, 'You need great people, and then you need the best systems, because even the best people are not perfect.' By the way, Dan, those systems represent an organizational competence for us, because they're created internally.

"Then I tell the prospective client that our 'secret sauce' is the technology that ties our people and our systems together. We manage ninety thousand units across the state of Florida, Dan, and we use technology to make sure that our people and our systems are doing what we've promised our clients. We've created a triad of people, systems, and technology."

Dan looks at James frankly. "That's an impressive presentation!"

"That's only the first *half* of my presentation," James smiles. "The second half is this: as I said before, we believe that every person who enters any of our buildings should feel like they're walking into a Ritz-Carlton. Ritz-Carlton sells their intellectual property, and I attended their university in Washington. I came back, and we created a program called Royal Service. The essence of Royal Service is that every time one of our Purpose Partners interacts with a resident of one of our buildings or one of their guests, it should be a special moment in that person's day.

We like to think that our competency in customer service is unequaled in our industry.

"When I've presented these two primary points to a prospective client, the next thing I'll say is, 'Let me give you ten reasons why we're different,' and I'll go through these ten distinctions one by one. Sifu, three of those ten points are competency-based: accounting, Royal Service, and our technology, which is another area where we believe we lead our industry."

Sifu nods. "*So your competency as an organization is central to your success and even to your sales presentations?*"

"It's fundamental," James replies promptly. "It's that important! When we're going for that new account, it is essential that our presentations are all about establishing trust with the property owners."

"OK," Sifu says, "if I may, James, I'd like to shift our focus slightly and ask you this: *How important to the success of The Castle Group is the competence of your senior leadership?*"

"We place a great deal of emphasis on developing our leaders," James replies. "And again, we have two areas of focus for leadership development at Castle. The first is competency in subject matter. Our leaders are required to be Subject Matter Experts—SMEs for short. That is, you are required to lead in our firm in a particular subject. The second area is developing competency as a leader. We've created our own seven-week leadership training course, which we offer annually to our top twenty leaders."

"Well done, James!" Sifu smiles brightly. "You're addressing leadership competence in a very comprehensive way!"

"Thank you, Sifu," James says warmly. "I define leadership as the ability to inspire a team. How can you inspire a team if you're not competent in what your company does?

"We're not in a high-margin industry, so we had to sit down and consider, 'How can we create the solid client-relationship requirements of our company *and* possess the competency that is required for what we do?' The answer was to hire Subject Matter Experts. So we have a regional director who owns ten account relationships. But that same director used to work with Ritz-Carlton, so he is also our Royal Service SME. The next regional director, who also has ten client relationships, is a licensed engineer. We select people who love customer service, and we make sure that each person we hire also has a competency area that can be leveraged throughout our firm.

"So if we have a client who has a physical plant problem, even though it's not our engineer's account, he'll go over and provide that expertise. And it might very well be that at the same time, the regional director who specializes in Royal Service is at the engineer's account working with the folks at the front desk. So the bottom line, Sifu, is that the competence of our senior leadership is *vitally* important to our success."

Dan is typing rapidly on the iPad. After a moment he looks up and grins at Sifu. "You said this was going to be a great interview, Sifu; you didn't exaggerate!" He shifts his attention back to James. "*James, from everything you've said, I'm thinking you would agree with Sifu that competence is essential to establishing trust.*"

"I certainly do," James nods. "I recently read a book titled *The Speed of Trust,* by Stephen M.R. Covey. My biggest takeaway was his assertion that there are two aspects of trust: character trust and capacity trust. They line up perfectly with your first two keys of trust, Sifu. Covey defined character trust as integrity and intent. Capacity trust was all about competence, which he defined as capability and results.

"I believe you and Covey are right on the money, Sifu; both character trust and capacity trust *must* be there. If you can't trust a leader's character, I don't think his or her competence matters.

"But you could have a leader with impeccable character who doesn't have the capacity to deliver results; people won't trust that leader either. They may *like* that person, but there won't be trust, because the leader isn't competent."

"Those are my thoughts exactly," Sifu says approvingly. "*James, how much of a role does leadership at the Castle Group play in instilling competence in your organization, and how much of it is simply the result of good recruiting and hiring decisions?*"

"That's a good question, Sifu," James says thoughtfully. "In one sense, leadership is essential to instilling competence; if you haven't developed a crystal clear strategy, you don't even know what competence to hire. So you need strong leadership to define what competencies you need for your company before you can make the best hiring decisions.

"Our leadership course explains the four levels of competency. You've both heard them: unconscious incompetence, conscious incompetence, conscious competence, and unconscious competence. And there's a fascinating dichotomy there. As I've said, we want leaders who are Subject Matter Experts. So in hiring for that, we're looking for that fourth level of competence, the unconscious competent. But when you come to the *leadership* piece, we've found that most people are unconscious incompetents. They don't even know that they don't know! They're just out there flying by the seat of their pants."

Dan and Sifu both chuckle at the truth of James' observation.

"So," James continues, "we thought that these four levels of competence are particularly relevant when it comes to leadership competence. But it can't all be trained. Knowledge learning is relatively easy; behavior learning is practically impossible! It's easy to teach someone how to utilize Excel, but when you try teaching them to change their behavior..." James' voice trails off and he makes wry face. "Try changing even one habit! So when it comes to leadership competence, you've got to select the right person. We focus on character a lot when it comes to leadership, because we can train anyone any skill, but you can't teach character."

Dan throws back his head and laughs with delight. "Wow! 'You can teach competence, but you must select for character.' James, I hope I can spend some more time with you on another day. I'll have somebody besides Sifu to steal my best quotes from!"

Sifu looks happily from Dan to James. "What a delight to listen to you interact with each other! James, one of the things you and I talked about on the phone was how one might profile a leader who displays competence. *What would you say are competence clues—those things which reveal the trustworthy competence of a leader?*"

"Sifu, when I got to thinking about that, I returned to the two categories that Stephen M.R. Covey used: character and capacity—or what we would call competence. I'd start with the capacity aspect. I see three clues there: *knowledge, skills,* and *experience.* These are the three elements of having the capacity to do the job. The leader has the know-how; he or she knows *what* to do.

"In addition, the leader has the ability to apply the knowledge; he or she knows *how* to do it. And finally, the leader has done it before; he or she has applied that knowledge and skill enough times to be at least a conscious competent.

"But as I say, all that can be taught; there is the second aspect to these competence clues, which is the message the leader sends through his or her *attitude* and *actions*. There are leaders who have all the ability and intelligence to do the work, but how is their *attitude*? This is the part that is so very difficult to teach. We've all seen people in leadership positions who are eminently qualified to perform the task at hand, but their attitude is awful! They may be impatient, bad-tempered, overbearing, prideful—any number of deep-seated traits that are *very* difficult to change. That's why we're so careful in our selection process. A person like that can really kill your culture."

"Tell me about it," Dan groans, thinking of John Kwan.

James grins wryly at Dan. "So you've had one of those too, huh? That last competence clue—*action*—might be the most important one. I've seen men and women with all the requisite knowledge, skills, and experience, who had a great attitude, but totally fell down when it came to taking *action*.

"I remember someone telling me about a senior executive who had been dismissed from his organization. This man had all the requisite knowledge, skill, and experience. He communicated a tremendous desire to advance the organization, and he was popular with the staff. Great attitude, in other words. Yet he was incapable of translating that ability and attitude into *action*. Initiatives that should have been implemented in weeks were delayed for months. There always seemed to be a need for more analysis, more meetings, and more caution. My friend said that this executive drew a great map, but he was unwilling to drive down the road! His inertia cost him his job, and the organization he was supposed to lead was badly hurt by it."

Dan nods thoughtfully as he types his notes. "A competent leader will act. Tell me, James, have you encountered any restraining forces? *Were there obstacles you've had to overcome in building competence at The Castle Group?*"

James nods. "The first thing we had to overcome was that we were the product of some acquisitions in the early '90s. As you both know, it's much harder to change a culture than to create a culture. So our biggest hurdle was that, even though we knew who we wanted to be, it was difficult to get from Point A to Point B. We were fighting legacy.

"The second hurdle was that we hadn't rightly appreciated the challenge of behavioral learning. We thought we could teach behavior the same way we taught knowledge. We learned pretty quickly that it doesn't work that way!

"People are often very impressed when they visit our offices. They'll ask me, 'How did you get to be this good in your operations?' I say, 'You learn a lot from twenty-five years of doing it wrong!'"

"I spent plenty of time in that school myself!" Dan chuckles ruefully.

"Yes, and it's time well spent, isn't it?" James says brightly. "Our experience is one of our selling points. When I got in this business, I was a kid, twenty-eight years old. I'll be fifty-three next month. And that's true of my partners; together, we have seventy-five years of experience. Experience—even the experience gained from the times we got it wrong—is a hugely important asset.

"There was a third bump in the road on the way to competence," James continues. "It took us some time to get the organizational clarity. We had people reporting to the wrong places in the organization. We had way too many dotted lines! Now we are organizationally clear. So I would say that legacy, culture, and clarity were the restraining forces we had to overcome."

"OK, now give me the good news, James," Dan says eagerly. "*Can you share your favorite success stories regarding how the competence of the leadership at The Castle Group has benefited your organization?*"

"Well…" James gathers his thoughts. "We defined our culture and we were relentless. It took us several years, but once we'd defined it, you either honored our culture or you didn't work here. And it's become so powerful now that when we miss on a hire, which we still do from time to time, those people resign before we have to terminate them. They quickly realize they're in the wrong company! I said a moment ago that culture was our biggest challenge, but it's probably also our biggest success story.

"Another great story is that we were determined to become technology leaders in our industry. That has led to the creation of a cutting-edge software company called The GRID Systems. Right now, twenty of our communities are using this software. This was the direct result of deciding to be good in a particular field and then hiring the right people to develop that competence and ultimately leverage it into a new business.

"So our first success story is the culture, the second one our technology, and the third is that we truly have created an outstanding customer service product—our Royal Service. As with technology, Royal Service was a direct result of starting with a particular competence, leadership developing a strategy to become the industry leader in this area, and then taking action."

"Those are tremendous successes, James," Dan says sincerely. "Let me ask you one last question: *When you have a leader who has the character and the capacity to lead well, what should that person do to continue to develop his or her competence?*"

"In order to develop our own personal leadership competence, we have to stay cutting-edge in leadership," James replies. "We keep reading the best books and staying up with the latest and greatest. Stephen Covey Sr. called it 'sharpening the saw,' and we use that phrase also.

"I like to think this is the reason why the Greater Miami Chamber of Commerce just awarded our company the Miami 'Good to Great' award, which is sponsored by the Collins 'Good to Great' organization. That doesn't happen by accident. Collins' group sent a team of people who came in and ripped our company apart! That's part of keeping the saw sharp—listening to those things that make you uncomfortable."

Dan smiles at Sifu, who has been sitting quietly, enjoying the conversation. "Grandmaster, that's the lesson you taught me so graciously and so well. I need someone to show me my blind spots. I must be able to hear what those blind spots are, no matter how uncomfortable that makes me!"

"That is one of life's most difficult lessons to learn, my friend," Sifu says softly. "When I was very young, my teacher told me that a man is tested by the praise he receives. I had no idea what he was talking about. I wanted to hear *more* praise!" Sifu grins. "But James is right. Those who speak the truth in love to us, no matter how painful that truth may be, are doing us a great service. When we hear only praise, we are being tested, because we may begin to believe we are above criticism."

James looks at Dan thoughtfully. "There's one other thing I'd say is essential to developing competence. Someone once told me to take agency over my own learning. I've never forgotten those words, and I've made it a rule to try to make sure that I'm the dumbest guy in every room I enter. That may not sound very inspirational to a young manager, but if I surround myself with bright, engaged men and women, I'm always learning from people who are smarter than I am. I try to remind myself every day that I've never arrived; I'm always learning."

Dan grins at James. "I'm afraid you broke your rule today, because *I'm* the dumbest guy in this room!"

James smiles and waves a deprecatory hand.

"Seriously, James, I can't thank you enough," Dan says warmly. "I really hadn't understood why competence is essential to building trust in relationships. You've really opened my eyes on this key. Thank you!"

CHAPTER 8

"Do You *Really* Believe that Man Can Change?"

TWO DAYS LATER, DAN IS preparing to meet with John Kwan in thirty minutes to discuss layoffs. Dan has been pulling data from financials and customer service scores that he hopes will convince Kwan that cutting more staff will be counterproductive.

He hears a soft voice at his office doorway. "Dan?"

Marcia Lundgren has been Prestigious Products' Chief Financial Officer for several years. She was the first woman to reach the executive level at the company, largely thanks to being championed by Dan, who sincerely believed Marcia was the best person for the position.

When Dan first introduced People First to the executive leadership team, he correctly assumed that Marcia might have difficulty adjusting to this new philosophy. But adjust she did, and she has been a trusted colleague and confidante for many years. And when Marcia celebrates one of her Purpose Partners—which she is faithful to do frequently—no one thinks that she is engaging in flattery. It is not Marcia's nature to be disingenuous.

Dan starts to ask Marcia if she can wait until after the meeting with Kwan—which she will be attending—but one look at her face causes Dan to change his mind. Marcia looks drawn and pale, and she has thick, dark circles under her eyes. Normally bold and confident, she now appears utterly dejected.

"Please come in, Marcia." Dan gestures toward the chair in front of him, but Marcia walks up to the desk and stands before him, her eyes roaming nervously around the office, never resting on Dan.

"Dan…" Her voice is raspy, as if she has a bad cold—or as if she has been shouting. Marcia is clutching a folded piece of paper in her left hand and repeatedly creasing the fold in the paper with her right hand. "Dan, I…"

"Marcia, please sit down and tell me what's wrong."

Marcia eases herself onto the edge of the chair. She is a tall, thin woman; her long fingers continue to flatten the fold in the paper. Finally, she looks at Dan, and to Dan's utter amazement her eyes fill with tears. The tears overflow and run down her cheeks, but it may be that she is unaware of them. She makes no move to brush the tears away.

If Marcia had walked into his office and slapped him, Dan would be no less surprised. Marcia is as tough-minded an executive as Dan has ever known. Throughout the recession and slow recovery, they shared the stress of falling revenues and the resulting layoffs, and Marcia's input has been dispassionate and insightful. Dan has found her to be as steady and resilient as any man he has ever worked with.

"Marcia?"

She abruptly tosses the folded paper onto Dan's desk. "It's my resignation. I wrote it early this morning. I haven't slept much." Marcia removes her glasses and looks at Dan, wide-eyed.

Dan tries not to let his deep concern show in his eyes. He makes a show of reaching into his desk drawer for a box of tissues for her. The confident, self-possessed woman he has relied on for so many years suddenly looks like a bewildered teenage girl. "Marcia, what has happened?"

"John Kwan has happened!" Her voice is several octaves lower than her usual prim tones. Dan hears smoldering anger in her voice and realizes that her tears are not tears of grief, but of rage.

"Dan, you know I had to deal with some pretty sexist good old boys as I worked my way up here." Marcia dabs at her eyes with a tissue. "I've been patronized, I've been shouted at. But I have *never* in my *life* met a man who is so unpleasant!" Her voice is practically a hiss.

Dan will not utter platitudes with this trusted Purpose Partner. "I think I said exactly the same thing to my wife," he says soberly.

"My *goodness*, Dan! You've told us so many times that humility is the key that unlocks the prison to our preoccupation with self-importance. That man is locked *tight* in self-importance!"

"Tell me," Dan invites again.

"He came into my office last night. I had all the financials ready for our meeting this morning. He asked me to explain last quarter's dividends, so I began to speak. I handed him a copy of the spreadsheets, and I'm looking at my copy, and I'm directing him to where I am in the financials. I look up, and he's *texting* someone! We're going to be talking about people's jobs at the meeting today, people's *lives*, and he's not even listening to me. He's *texting?!*

"'Mr. Kwan?' I said. "He kept right on texting.

"'Continue,' he said.

"I said, 'I'd prefer to wait until I have your attention.'

"This time he looked at me. 'Mrs. Lundgren, your job is to provide information in whatever format I require. If you are unhappy with your duties, feel free to submit your resignation.'

"I kept my voice level, but I said I'd give that option careful consideration.

"'Please reach your decision quickly,' he says. "'I'm confident I can find a replacement who will command a salary significantly lower than yours.' Dan, what do you *say* to someone like that? It's all about power and control; he has the power and he's in control."

Marcia springs from her chair and paces rapidly back and forth. "Kwan must have had a humility bypass," she fumes. "Everything I've done here marginalized in just a few *seconds*—who I am, what I've accomplished—all of it totally devalued." Marcia comes to a stop in front of Dan's desk and glares at him, her fists resting on her hips. "He missed the 'I Need You' part of the Pyramid; he doesn't need *anyone*! He is self-sufficient, self-satisfied, in need of nothing!"

Marcia snatches up the letter from Dan's desk and waves it back and forth. "I'm half a mind to tear this up. I don't want to give him the satisfaction of running me out!"

"I wish you *would* tear it up," Dan says softly. "I need you."

Marcia sits again in the chair. This time she leans back and expels a long sigh. When she speaks again, the edge is gone from her voice. "You taught us that it's not about power, it's about humility. It's not about control, it's about freedom. This man—" Marcia shakes her head "—is the antithesis of everything you've taught us about People First."

She leans forward, her hands gripping the arms of the chair, and the intensity returns to her voice. "Dan, you taught us a philosophy twelve years ago—a way to think and a way to live. It's an ennobling philosophy; it's a generous way to live. But once you've begun to think this way and live this way, there's no going back to a People Last way of living!"

Marcia's grip on the chair relaxes. She looks down at the floor and shakes her head. "I don't know what to do. All of us here know that People First is not just 'a way' to live, it is *the* way to live in excellence." She looks up at Dan, her eyes strained. "Even during these last few years, which have been *so* difficult, I always came to work with my head up, because I believe in you, I believe in our Purpose Partners, and I believed in what we were doing here. I didn't want to go *anywhere* else."

Her eyes flare into fire once again. "But *that man!* I don't trust him, Dan, *no one* here trusts him! His pride has blinded him to the importance of anyone besides himself. He is the most arrogant man I've ever met!

"*You* taught us how valuable we are as human beings, because of our God-given value. I've never forgotten it. You taught us never to devalue the human spirit of any person. How can you expect *any* of us to work in this terrible situation, under this high-command, high-control mentality? I don't know how *you* can stay, Dan, in light of all of the knowledge that you have about People First." She rests her chin on one fist and stares morosely at the resignation letter on Dan's desk.

"You gave me my break here, Dan," she says quietly. "I wouldn't be where I am if it wasn't for you. Tell me what to do."

"Marcia, I've told you before: I promoted you because you were the best person for the job. And you've done nothing but reward that decision ever since. You don't owe me or anyone else anything."

She flashes a ghost of a smile. "Thank you."

"Have you talked to Bob?"

"We sat up most of the night talking about it." Another small grin. "Well, *Bob* talked. I was ranting and raving mostly. Like I've just done with you. I'm sorry."

"No need to apologize. I've done some ranting at home myself. What did Bob say?"

"Bob is wonderful. He said he would probably quit, but he'll support me 100 percent in whatever I do. He encouraged me to talk to you before I decide. So here I am."

Dan glances at his watch. "Marcia, we're going to be meeting with Kwan in ten minutes. I'd be lying if I told you that I haven't thought about submitting my own resignation. It's not inconceivable that I may be dismissed after this meeting, because I'm planning to fight against more layoffs. And I do *not* want you to feel obligated to me for your professional success. You would be the CFO of Prestigious Products no matter who was in charge, I'm quite sure of that. You have to do what's best for you and Bob."

Marcia does not reply. She is staring at the letter again.

"Having said that, Marcia, I'd be most grateful if you choose to stay. I need someone I can trust who will give me a clear, accurate financial picture as we navigate these troubled times."

"*Troubled* times!" Marcia pushes out a sarcastic snort of laughter.

"I trust you and I respect you, Marcia," Dan continues. "If you leave, I don't know how much freedom I'll have in selecting your replacement. If Kwan makes the selection, I would struggle to develop the confidence in a new CFO that I have in you." Dan gives Marcia a wry smile. "I know I'm not making your decision easy, but as far as I'm concerned, you are irreplaceable."

Marcia looks at Dan curiously. "You're going to stay, Dan?"

"Yes," Dan says firmly. "It's like you said: I brought this philosophy to our team. I'm not going to bail on you and Roger and Claudia and Jerry and the others now that it's under attack." Dan looks steadily at Marcia. "And I'm going to continue to try to win John Kwan over to putting people first."

"Good luck!"

"It wasn't so long ago that I thought very much like he does. I was the hammer and you all were nails. But when crisis time came, I was willing to listen to someone who believed in the exalted dignity and worth of people. Perhaps that day will come for Kwan."

Marcia eyes search Dan's face. "Do you *really* believe that man can change?"

Dan shakes his head slowly. "I don't know. I'm not hopeful." His voice grows stronger. "But I'm not leaving."

Marcia looks steadily at Dan for a long moment. "I'm not hopeful either." A little grin tugs at the corner of her mouth. "But I'm betting on you." She takes her resignation letter off Dan's desk and looks at it. She sighs, but the grin blossoms into her first real smile of the morning. "This I've got to see." She tears the letter in half and places it in front of Dan. "Would you throw that away for me?"

Dan's voice is suddenly husky. "Thank you, Marcia. Thank you very much."

Marcia stands and casts a glance at the clock on the wall. "We don't want to be late for Mr. Kwan," she says briskly. She starts for the door, and Dan, deeply moved, begins to gather his papers.

"Dan?"

Dan looks up.

"Thank you for everything." Marcia says warmly. "I wouldn't have missed these last twelve years for anything." She lowers her eyes, as if checking her feelings, and nods thoughtfully. "It would be wrong for *me* to bail on *you* now. Thanks for being here this morning. I need you too, you know."

Dan is afraid his voice will break if he speaks. He can only nod and smile.

CHAPTER 9

Another Difficult Meeting

MOMENTS LATER, DAN STRIDES THROUGH the door to the Executive Conference Room. Three people are waiting there, all longtime executive leaders. Roger Clinton, VP of sales, is in his mid-fifties. Normally an outgoing, garrulous man, he merely nods a greeting at Dan and continues nervously rubbing his beard. Despite Dan's best efforts to encourage him, Roger seems to feel that the financial woes plaguing Prestigious Products are his fault. *I don't imagine Kwan will do anything to change Roger's thinking*, Dan thinks gloomily.

"Good morning, Dan." Sarah Woods is the director of Human Resources. The youngest member of the Executive Team, Sarah just turned forty, but still looks as if she should be coaching a university cheerleading squad. Her youthful good looks are normally matched by a sunny disposition, but today her eyes are clouded with worry.

Marcia is the third member of the group. She makes a wry face at Dan. "Once more, dear friends, into the breach…" she says softly.

Roger makes a weak attempt at a chuckle.

At that moment, John Kwan strides quickly into the room and there is a sudden hush. Dan's gloom deepens. Twelve years ago, Sifu Li had asked Dan, "Dan, are you the kind of leader that the room lights up, glows, radiates…when you walk *out* of the room?" Dan had not been able to look his teacher in the eye as he muttered, "Yes, Sifu, I expect that I am." *And John Kwan is too*, Dan thinks.

I had that same high-command, high-control mind-set. There's got to be a way I can reach him!

"Good morning, Mr. Kwan!" In trying to sound cheerful, Dan's voice seems forced and unnaturally loud in the stillness.

Kwan looks levelly at Dan and does not reply. He moves to the head of the conference table and remains standing. Dan can feel his temper rising. *This man never misses an opportunity to try and intimidate*, Dan thinks.

Kwan doesn't bother with any introductory remarks. "I've assembled you here to discuss cost-cutting measures. The bulk of that cost-cutting will come from a 15 percent staff reduction." Kwan's eyes swing to Dan for a moment. "Your previous attempts at cost containment nibbled around the edges of the problem. I have identified an entire department which will be closed immediately."

Kwan looks around the room. Everyone is frozen still. *I swear, he's pausing for effect, like he's on stage!* Dan's anger is simmering now. *Is he actually enjoying this?*

Dan's calm tone masks the turmoil within. "You're planning to eliminate a department." *Dan, you've been taught not to react to an opponent who taunts you in the ring. That's all this is, a battle for control. Keep your temper. What did Tom Manenti say? Don't get rattled.*

"I just said that." Kwan doesn't even look at Dan. Marcia forcefully expels a short breath. Dan knows the sound; Marcia is growing impatient. Roger lowers his head, looking like a man expecting to receive a blow.

"You will notify all members of the Customer Service Department that their services are no longer needed," Kwan says. Sarah gasps audibly. Roger's head snaps up, his eyes widening.

Marcia puts her head in her hands.

Again, Dan is conscious of his tone of voice. He speaks slowly, quietly: "Mr. Kwan, Prestigious Products has traditionally marketed our superior customer service—"

Kwan cuts him off. "Mr. Burton, you can be quite certain that I have no interest in hearing about tradition. The organization is underperforming. We must take strong measures to shake this company out of its lethargy."

Kwan's eyes swing to Sarah. She has not made another sound, but her eyes are brimming with tears. Kwan makes an impatient sound. "Please! Miss Woods, if you are incapable of discussing these issues..."

"Mr. Kwan," Dan interrupts, "everyone in this room is perfectly capable. Sarah is simply reflecting our surprise at your decision. You're talking about one hundred and twenty-five people."

"One hundred and thirty, counting their senior managers. And there should be no surprise." Kwan says coldly.

"We must cut costs or close the doors." He glances at Dan. "I told you four days ago that we would be reducing staff by 15 percent. Frankly, I am surprised that this team, which you claim is capable, would be unprepared for this news."

All color has drained from Roger's face. He is staring at Kwan in disbelief. Dan struggles to keep his face impassive. *That's why Claudia Barnes isn't here.* Cold realization washes over him.

He's eliminated her position!

Kwan swings back to Sarah. "These cuts are effective today." He glances at Marcia. "Payroll closes today, correct?" Marcia nods almost imperceptibly, her eyes blazing. "Miss Wood, inform these staffers that they will be paid until the close of business today, plus two weeks' severance. Those who have any unused vacation time will receive that as well."

"Two weeks?!" Marcia is aghast. "How can you…"

Dan quickly interrupts before Marcia can attack. "Mr. Kwan, there are people in that group who have been with this organization for a great many years. Claudia Barnes has been with this company as long as I have, and there are several with twenty-plus years. Surely you don't intend to dismiss these people, in this economy, with only two weeks' pay."

"I do. I am not here to act as some sort of unemployment office."

Roger shakes his head, like a man waking from a bad dream. "You heartless, unfeeling—"

"Roger!" Dan's anger at Kwan makes his voice ring sharply. "This is not the time or the place. You can be sure I will articulate your concerns at the appropriate time." He can feel his temples starting to throb, and he looks back at Kwan. "Forcefully."

"I am not interested in your concerns," Kwan says briefly. "Mr. Clinton, your department will assume the duties of customer service. I have some ideas on how that should be done, but I will wait to see how you perform. Have your plan on my desk Monday morning."

Roger is staring at Kwan in utter astonishment. His mouth moves but no sound comes.

Kwan's eyes scan the room. "Are there any questions?" No one moves or speaks. Kwan looks at Sarah. "All those staffers are to have vacated by the end of the day." And with that, Kwan walks out of the room.

"Oh my goodness!" Sarah's voice is choked. The tears are streaming down her cheeks now, and she fumbles in her bag for a tissue. Roger looks like a frightened child.

For a moment Dan looks straight ahead, then he turns to the group. He speaks slowly, precisely.

"I don't want any of you to do anything or say anything about this until I tell you. Sarah?" Dan's voice softens. "I doubt I'll be able to change his mind, but don't speak to anyone yet. If worse comes to worse, I'll make the initial phone calls myself. Please excuse me." Dan is up out of his chair, and he heads for Kwan's office.

As he strides down the hallway, Dan's thoughts are a blur. *Keep your temper!...Yeah, but I don't remember the last time I was this angry...You told Marcia you wouldn't resign. You owe it to the team to try to make a difference... What does Sifu always tell us?* "He who is slow to anger is better than a warrior; better to control your temper than to conquer a city."

Dan is approaching the entrance to Kwan's office, and his steps slow slightly. *What else does Sifu say?* "A fool shouts out his anger, but a wise man quietly holds it back." *Sifu tells us a day will come when we should recall these proverbs and repeat them.* Dan picks up his pace again. *Today is that day, but I'm not sure I want to hold back today! Kwan's not the only one who can play the intimidation game.*

Dan knocks on Kwan's door, two sharp taps, and opens the door without waiting for an invitation to enter.

Kwan glances up from his desk, and a look of distaste sweeps across his face. "Mr. Burton, you'll have to see my assistant."

"I'll see you now." Dan says firmly. "You're about to lose half of your executive leadership team, maybe more. When I resign, most of the team will go with me. You'll have to install an entirely new leadership team in a time of crisis. And you're doing a masterful job of creating a crisis! Is this the mandate you've received from the board?"

Kwan's eyes narrow. "You've come here to threaten me?"

"I've come to tell you that if you persist in your rudeness to me and to my Purpose Partners, I will resign immediately. If I do, a number of my key reports will follow. I can't imagine that the board is hoping to see the entire leadership team disappear."

Kwan shrugs. "I think they'd be pleased at the salary reduction."

Dan's voice rises. "And that is *precisely* why nobody wants to work for you. There is a way to address people without being rude, eroding trust, or crushing a person's spirit. But you don't care about that, do you? You have made it painfully clear that you care *nothing* about people. All you care about are your precious profits!"

Kwan looks back down at the work on his desk. "I am pleased that I have been unambiguous. Profits keep the doors open. People are easily replaced." He looks at Dan pointedly. "*You* are easily replaced."

"Very well, start looking for my replacement today." Dan takes two steps closer to Kwan's desk. "But before I leave, I intend to tell you exactly what I think of you."

Kwan looks bored. "I have told you I have no interest in what you think."

Dan is warming to the combat, just as he does in the ring with a top opponent. "Cracks like that are about to cost you your entire leadership team. I don't know if you are utterly insensitive or deliberately insulting, but unless you plan to ride herd on a number of junior executives, you'd better starting *listening* to what other people think!" Dan's voice is louder still. "I don't think you really want to train six or eight senior managers all at once."

"On the contrary, I would enjoy the opportunity to work with a team that is focused on turning a profit..."—here Kwan's voice becomes thick with contempt—"... and *not* on 'putting people first,' which has produced *disastrous* results."

Dan's eyes flare wide. "Let me tell you something, you smug little man. You are about to see the disastrous results of being rude and bullying. Just this morning I talked one of your key reports out of resigning. Watch what happens now! When my people hear that I'm gone, you'll see a *mass* exodus out of this place. And all your threats and insults will push them out the door that much faster."

Dan's peripheral vision has disappeared. All he can see is the man at the desk. He rests his hands on Kwan's desk and leans toward him. "You've got nothing I *want,* Kwan. You've got nothing I *need.* You've...got...*nothing.*" Dan punctuates each of the last three words with a *thunk* of his forefinger on Kwan's desk.

Kwan is unfazed. To Dan's amazement, his lips seem to move into a small smile. Kwan's eyes are still cold, but Dan imagines there is a softening in his demeanor. "What do you want?" Kwan says flatly.

Kwan's little smile ignites Dan's anger into rage. His brain is starting to shut down. "What do I *want?*" He stretches to his full height, towering over Kwan. "I want to give you some leadership lessons!"

Kwan nods. There is no mistaking the smile now. "So you intend to resign?"

"You bet!" Dan realizes he is shouting.

"I'd like you to stay."

"I'd like to win the lottery," Dan snarls. "Not much chance of either happening."

"And what do you hope to accomplish by quitting?"

Dan opens his mouth to slap out another retort...and hesitates. Kwan's question hits him like ice water. *Yeah, Dan. What* did *you hope to accomplish by coming in here and shouting like an angry child?*

Kwan looks at Dan shrewdly. "You have invested thirty years of your life in this company. You don't strike me as a quitter. Surely I am not the first person you've worked with who rubbed you the wrong way."

Dan is careful to lower his voice, but the intensity is still there. "You have a *genius* for rubbing people the wrong way."

Kwan nods, like a man acknowledging a compliment. "So what will it take to get you to stay?"

Dan steps back from Kwan's desk and takes a deep breath. He hears his own voice assuring Marcia, "I'm going to try to win John Kwan over to putting People First." Dan feels a sharp pang of conscience. He recalls Sifu talking about character during the drive to meet Tom Manenti. "Do you keep your word, even when it hurts?" Sifu had asked. "If a promise you've made suddenly becomes inconvenient or unprofitable, do you still keep your word?"

Dan swings back to Kwan. "I want to meet with you every morning before we begin business."

His voice is back to normal volume, but there is no mistaking the authority in his voice. "You are the chairman of the board and you will give instructions. You will listen *politely*"—Dan pauses for emphasis—"to my objections and suggestions. I will explain my thinking to you and you will listen. I will do the same for you. At the end of our conversation, I will be tasked with conveying your final instructions to the rest of the organization."

"That's it?"

"No," Dan says evenly. "We have a severance policy here."

"You *had* a severance policy," Kwan interrupts crisply. "The board has given me complete authority to arrange whatever terms of termination I see fit."

Terms of termination? Dan thinks incredulously. *Who* thinks *in language like that?* "Those terms are unforgivably meager," Dan says flatly. "We've already laid off about four hundred people, as you know. We announced the terms of the severance policy to the entire staff. Everyone with less than five years' service time received four weeks' pay, plus their health insurance ran for that time. Everyone with five years or more got one week's pay for every year of service, plus their insurance."

"My employers in China will never accept that."

Dan is unfazed. "Here is what you must convey to your employers: when word gets out—and it will spread like wildfire—that you have dismissed people with ten years' service, twenty years' service, *thirty* years' service, and given them only two week's severance, you can be certain that every one of our Purpose Partners will be scanning the want ads the following day. That is an absolute certainty."

Kwan hesitates, then shakes his head stubbornly. "They will not accept your proposal."

"What *will* they accept?"

Kwan reaches for a calculator and taps on it for several minutes. He looks back up at Dan. "I will follow your policy, but only to a maximum of twelve weeks."

"Sixteen weeks."

Kwan looks steadily at Dan. "Is *that* it?"

"I have prepared a plan for 10 percent staff reduction. It keeps Customer Service in place. I'd like to discuss it with you."

"No. This plan has already been approved by the board. However," Kwan quickly continues as Dan's lips tighten, "I will consult with you before we make any future moves. Remember, however, that I am the chairman of the board. You serve here at my pleasure."

Dan nods. "I understand." He draws a breath. There is no sense of triumph; he feels only a weight of great sadness. "Thank you." He turns for the door.

"Mr. Burton." Dan turns again. Kwan's face is utterly cold. "You may be congratulating yourself on winning some concessions. Do not make the mistake of thinking that I am a man who takes kindly to ultimatums. And do not come marching into my office uninvited again."

Dan nods and manages a tight smile. "I understand. Please tell your assistant that I have an appointment with you every morning at 8:15. If that is agreeable with you?"

"Not agreeable. But we will give this arrangement a try. In the meantime, I'll be taking a good, long look at those junior executives who are qualified for promotion. Good day, Mr. Burton."

CHAPTER 10

John Kwan at Home

IT IS NEARLY 10 P.M. when John Kwan's Mercedes glides up to the valet desk at an exclusive Miami Beach high-rise condominium. A young porter trots up as Kwan emerges from the car. He greets Kwan with a wary "Good evening, Mr. Kwan."

"Seven-fifteen tomorrow morning," Kwan says peremptorily.

"Yes, sir," the porter replies politely. "We'll have it ready."

Kwan swings toward the porter. "You had better be ready with more than mere words," he says sharply. "I had to wait several minutes this morning. Surely a residence such as this is not so inept as to be incapable of having my automobile ready at the time I specify?"

The porter's eyes are focused at a point just beyond Kwan's shoulder. "I'm very sorry you were inconvenienced, Mr...."

"You will be *very* sorry if it happens again," Kwan interrupts. "I'll be on the phone to the management company. When I say I want my car ready at 7:15, I mean *ready*, not that someone begins to search for the keys when I walk out here."

A muscle ripples along the porter's jaw. "Yes, sir."

Kwan turns on his heel and starts toward the building. Automatic glass doors slide noiselessly open before him, and he strides across thick carpeting toward the penthouse elevator. He holds a gold key fob to activate the elevator door, which is accessible only to residents of the 34th and 35th floors. He yawns once to relieve the pressure building in his ears as the express elevator rapidly ascends to Penthouse 1, on the top floor. In just a few seconds, the doors sigh open and Kwan steps out.

He is home. The large living room is tastefully and expensively put together, yet so impeccably neat as to give the impression that the room is prepared for a *Florida Living* photo shoot, not for a family to relax in. Kwan pauses, as if listening for activity.

He turns left and walks into a huge kitchen. Kwan flips a light switch and pokes around the gleaming kitchen for a moment, opening the dishwasher, glancing in the trash bin. Finally, he peers into the spacious refrigerator and extracts a small container. He pops the top and places the container into the microwave, sets the timer, and moves through the kitchen toward the back of the condominium. The hallway is dark, but as he moves toward the master bedroom, he sees a gleam of light from a television.

Peijing Kwan is sitting upright on their large double bed. She is dressed in traditional Chinese pajamas with a full robe. She has several pillows propped behind her back, and she is watching a game show with what appears to be great interest. She does not even glance at Kwan standing in the doorway.

Kwan's eyes narrow with disapproval at the sight of a large tumbler sitting on the nightstand next to his wife. Kwan takes two steps into the room and speaks in a low, commanding tone. "Peijing."

She turns her head slowly from the TV, as if reluctant to miss even a moment of her show. She looks at Kwan impassively for a moment, then turns back to the television. She had been a slender, demure girl when Kwan asked her hand in marriage thirty years ago. Her eyes had sparkled when he told her about coming to the United States to represent the Chang Tao Group. That sparkle has long since disappeared. Peijing is now fifty pounds heavier, and her eyes have the flat, resigned look of a woman sitting in a dentist's chair. Without taking her eyes off the television, she reaches for the tumbler and takes a deep swallow.

"Peijing, did you have dinner?"

She nods once. "Maria left a container for you in the refrigerator."

"I found it. But there are no dishes in the dishwasher, no trash." Kwan gestures at her glass. "Are you having vodka for dinner again tonight?"

Finally, she glances at him. Her eyes are large and dark and opaque. "It helps me forget how much I hate it here," she says listlessly.

"Aaah!" Kwan rolls his eyes and pushes out an impatient sigh. "You would hate it much more if I were to file for a divorce."

"You're never here anyway," she says dully. "What difference would it make?"

"It would make a dramatic difference in your ability to spend my money on paintings and furniture and alcohol."

She sounds bored. "And you, my husband, how will your life change when you have to write me an alimony check every month?" Her lips twitch in what might be a smile. "I expect you would no longer be able to afford the penthouse… darling." At last there is expression in her voice—bitter, biting sarcasm is packed into the pet name. She takes another long pull from her tumbler of vodka.

"You are married to your job and I am married to a stranger," she says, as if speaking to herself.

Exasperated, Kwan turns for the door. Peijing's voice stops him.

"Your son was here today."

Kwan swings back to look at her. "Johnny was here?"

"Yes." She mutes the television and finally turns to face her husband. The resigned look in her eyes has been replaced with cold anger. "He had a girl with him. She looked like a prostitute, the way she was dressed." Her eyes are boring into Kwan. "Perhaps she is. She had an enormous snake tattooed on her neck and shoulders. It was hideous."

"What did Johnny want?"

Again, the grinding sarcasm fills her voice. "He wanted us to meet his fiancée!"

"Fiancée?" Kwan is nonplussed.

"Yes." For the first time a tipsy slur intrudes on her speech. "Lessee, John, would that be fiancée number three? Or is this four? Wait—is it his fourth car and third fiancée? I can't keep track."

Kwan's voice is icy. "What a shame that alcohol has disrupted your focus."

Abruptly she springs off the bed and stands directly in front of Kwan, glaring up at him with blazing eyes. "No, *you* need to focus on something besides your work!" she says shrilly. "You care nothing about our marriage. Fine! Then pay some attention to our son while there is still time!"

Kwan, startled by her rapid transformation, takes a step back. "What are you *talking* about?"

"I'm talking about how our son is flushing his life down the toilet and you are making it worse!"

Kwan is back on balance. "We are not having this conversation again, Peijing."

"You *never* want to have conversation about *anything* that matters!" she says savagely. "You don't want to listen and you don't want to *see!* Your son is screaming at you for help and you don't care!"

"Peijing, get control of yourself!"

"Don't *talk* to me about control!" Her voice is now low and intense. "If a father left his son to die in a burning house, people would call him a monster. But *you,* who have no heart, are watching your son burn the house down around himself, and you do *nothing,* you *horrible,* inhuman man!"

Hot tears of rage are filling her eyes.

Kwan's face seems to have become thinner, sharper. "Really, Peijing, this melodrama is absurd."

"*Absurd!* What is absurd is a father who continues to *fund* his son's self-destruction. Johnny cries, 'Look at me! Take notice of me, Father!' And *you!*" Her voice is ugly with contempt. "You write him *checks!* You buy him *cars!* You talk to him about his *future!* He *has* no future, John, if you are so blind to see that he cares *nothing* for his future!"

"He needs to learn to work…"

"He's been working as hard to show you how much your indifference hurts him! And you see *nothing!* The first girl was actually nice, but you did not approve of her family. So he brings home these *whores,* trying to get a reaction from you. You ignore him. He gets drunk and destroys a Corvette, so you buy him a Porsche—and then another one after that! He says he has no plan for his life and you enroll him at the university. He fails all his classes and you berate him—and then you enroll him for another semester. He overdoses on cocaine. The doctors say his life was in grave danger, and you buy him a boat. A *boat!*" Her mouth trembles. "Did you ever ask him—just *once,* John—did you ask him what is wrong? Did you ask him what he is feeling? If you were this tone deaf with your businesses, we'd be living in a slum in China!"

Kwan's mouth is a thin slit. "You are a miserable lush. You blame your emptiness on me." He turns to go.

Desperately, she grabs at his arm. Her fingers dig into the flesh, like the grip of a drowning swimmer. She has never done this before. Kwan's eyes widen with anger, and for a moment they stand frozen. Peijing relaxes her grip on his arm, but there is no mistaking the desperate plea in her eyes and voice. "John, *please* talk to him. Tell him that you care about him! His eyes tonight…It was obvious he had been drinking, but he looked so unhappy! He looks like he's locked in a prison, John! It's like he is trapped inside himself and he can't get free!"

Kwan looks at her hand on his arm, and Peijing quickly lets her hand drop to her side. "Have another drink, Peijing," Kwan says contemptuously. "You do enough talking for both of us." He turns and walks out of the room.

Peijing stares at the empty doorway for a moment. Then her chin droops almost to her chest and she shakes her head back and forth despairingly. She reaches for the tumbler of vodka and drains its contents.

Out in the kitchen, John Kwan extracts his dinner from the microwave. He glances at the dish, then his lips tighten and he walks away, leaving the food untouched. He walks slowly through the living room, finally pushing open a heavy glass door that leads to the balcony.

Kwan moves out onto the balcony and leans his elbows on the railing, looking out over the Atlantic Ocean. It is a clear night, and a full moon creates a glittering, golden tapestry on the water far below. The view is spectacular, but if it gives Kwan any pleasure, there is no change in the hard lines of his face. And then, suddenly, his shoulders sag and his head drops down. Without knowing it, he mirrors his wife…shaking his head slowly back and forth.

CHAPTER 11

"I Blew It!"

"SIFU, THAT'S THE CLOSEST I'VE ever come to punching someone who wasn't a competitor in the ring. If it wasn't for those proverbs of yours…I might be sitting in jail."

Sifu's face is grave. "You did well not to give full vent to your anger."

The two men are talking alone after Dan's weekly Kung Fu class. Dan shakes his head vehemently.

"No, Sifu, I did *not* do well; I blew it! You've told me to speak the truth in love." Dan grimaces. "I didn't raise a hand to him, but I attacked him with my words. I spoke out of fury—to be honest,

I spoke out of hatred!" Dan looks at his friend miserably. "I'm ashamed."

"Ah, my friend." Sifu smiles warmly at Dan and grips his bicep. "Let us sit for a moment. Do you have time?"

"Sifu, I'm the one who's imposing on *your* time," Dan says gratefully, "dumping my problems on you, and you act as if I'm doing *you* a favor. You are very gracious."

The two men walk back to Sifu's office. "Failure can be a great teacher, Dan," Sifu says as they sink into the plush leather chairs at his desk. "Failure keeps us from becoming prideful. And it helps us empathize with others when *they* fail."

Dan purses his lips grimly. "For twelve years I've tried to pass on what you've taught me: truth in all things, wisdom in all things, and excellence in all things. And today I threw it all away. I wanted to make Kwan feel small. I wanted him to know how much I dislike him. I was trying to hurt him emotionally. I am no kind of ambassador for your philosophy."

To Dan's surprise, Sifu laughs gently. "My dear friend, I am pleased to see you so contrite about losing your temper. You should be! You abandoned your training. But Dan, these principles of truth, wisdom, and excellence are not 'mine.' They are timeless. You and I are responsible to live our lives in harmony with them. They are the perfect standard toward which we strive.

"Dan, I never want you or anyone else to think I believe I am perfect—or even *close* to perfect—in the practice of these principles. You have heard me say that I have considered printing T-shirts with the words 'Under Construction' on them and giving them to everyone I know. Wearing the shirt would be a reminder that we are all still learning and growing."

"I'm not so sure I *am* growing!" Dan says glumly. "In an instant, I changed back to my old self."

Sifu leans across the desk toward Dan. His voice is soft, but there is no mistaking his urgency.

"Yes, you changed! Everyone changes, especially when we are under great stress. We do not always speak and act in harmony with what we believe. But make no mistake, Dan, Kwan needs you to model those principles. He needs your example. He needs wisdom. He needs love!"

Dan recoils. "*Love?*"

Sifu nods slowly. "This man lives an impoverished life. Kwan *admitted* that he seeks to grow profits, not people. What a tragedy, Dan, for a wealthy person to believe he has gained the whole world, only to realize that he is the poorest of all human beings because he invested his life in worthless things. To realize when it is too late that you have forfeited your soul—the essence of who you are—in pursuit of a bank account! How shattering! And that day *will* come for John Kwan."

Realization is hitting Dan. "And instead of grieving for him, I got even angrier!"

Sifu nods. "You reacted according to your emotions rather than according to your knowledge." He smiles his gentle smile. "You reacted like a human being! But John Kwan needs more from you, Dan. He needs to see you living the truth. Sometimes you can win someone to your way of thinking by your manner of life more than by what you say. You must demonstrate that these principles of truth, wisdom, and excellence are right by living them out before this man, no matter what the trial or provocation."

Sifu hesitates. "Dan, may I have permission to wound you in love?"

"Please do!"

"I would like to remind you of another wise proverb that is one of the most important that I have learned for my own growth; it is, 'Faithful are the wounds of a friend, but deceitful are the kisses of an enemy.'

"When you speak the truth in love to someone, Dan, you run the risk of angering them or even losing their friendship. However, if they are willing to be humble and submit to a loving rebuke, that constructive guidance can provide one of life's greatest growth opportunities. One of the most powerful kings in history said, 'Let a righteous man strike me. It will be a kindness! If he reproves me, it is medicine. Don't let me refuse it.'

"The purpose of my rebuke is not to hurt you or diminish you, Dan, as you hoped to hurt Kwan; my intent is to lovingly build you up so that you will grow stronger and wiser."

Dan looks straight at Sifu. "What do you want me to learn, Grandmaster?"

"Dan, can you name the seven keys of trust?"

Dan does not hesitate. "Character, competence, confidence, caring, communication, commitment, and consistency."

Dan expects to receive the usual bright smile that Sifu lavishes on a student who performs well, but his mentor shakes his head sadly. "Dan, you violated *every one* of those keys with Kwan! Your *character* wasn't in harmony with the truth. You didn't put Kwan first; you put your feelings first. You demonstrated that you are not *competent* in this philosophy, because you let your emotions overrule your mind. Your *confidence* was misplaced, Dan. You were bold, but only in your self-righteous anger. You showed no *caring*. You cared nothing about serving Kwan or teaching him; you admitted that you wanted to make him feel small. Your *communication* was not edifying; you did not speak the truth in love."

Sifu's somber expression is broken by a flash of humor. "You may very well have spoken the truth...but not in love. There was no *consistency* in your actions, Dan. Instead of expecting truth, wisdom, and excellent behavior from you, Kwan now knows that he can prod you into being wholly reactive. And finally, my dear friend, you showed no *commitment* to your job, and you abandoned your commitment to the People First philosophy."

Sifu smiles at Dan to take the sting out of his words. "If Kwan is *ever* going to learn how to put People First, Dan, he must be able to listen to you—*really* listen to you. He will not listen to you until he knows he can trust you. You *must* create trust capital with him."

Dan has been sitting motionless, looking steadily at Sifu. Now he drops his eyes. "I've utterly failed." His voice is almost a whisper. "I got in the ring with him and tapped out in the first round."

"Against a very tough opponent." Sifu nods. "Dan." He waits for Dan to look up at him. "This is not the first time you have lost a match."

Dan cocks his head in a mute question.

"What do I tell all the students at the *kwoon* when they fail to master a new form?"

"Fall down seven times, get up eight," Dan replies promptly.

This time Dan is rewarded with Sifu's wide, approving smile. "In the past, Dan, when you lost a match, you have always bounced back with even greater determination to succeed."

The stricken look fades from Dan's face. He gives Sifu a crooked grin. "Sifu, I don't know that I ever got *thrashed* in a match like this."

"Dan, I met a man who was a champion rodeo rider. His specialty is what they call saddle bronc riding—staying on a wild horse for eight seconds. At one point he said to me"—here Sifu gives a very passable imitation of a Texas drawl—"'Never was a horse that couldn't be rode, and never was a rider who couldn't be throwed.'"

Dan chuckles, but the Grandmaster's eyes are intense. "There *never* was a horse, no matter how wild, that could not be ridden by a skillful, determined rider. What John Kwan needs from you more than anything else is to see you *determined* to live the People First philosophy.

"Dan, the men I've introduced you to—and the men you'll meet in the next few days—all possess true wealth. They are not necessarily the richest men in the world in terms of dollars, but they are *very* wealthy when it comes to possessing wisdom and moral excellence. Kwan needs to see that same excellence in you."

Dan purses his lips. "I want to be a man like that. Thank you for speaking the truth in love to me when I veer off course. And I can't thank you enough for being so kind to arrange these meetings. But I feel like I'm wasting your time. That man makes me so *angry*, Sifu!"

Sifu leans forward, and his eyes are boring into Dan's. "Dan, you are going through a test. Every truth you learn—at least the ones that matter—must be tested in the furnace of relentless adversity. When you come through such a trial, you will stand firm on that truth, regardless of any future temptation to abandon it. Moreover, when the furnace has finished its refining process, your spirit will emerge with unconquerable strength, humility, and courage. You will be like a tempered sword."

Dan makes a face. "Today I feel more like a flimsy reed than a sword."

"Which is why you are going through the test!" Sifu's eyes are very bright. "There is *no* growth without adversity, Dan! If you desire to mature as a man and as a leader, you must prepare your mind for the necessity—for the *inevitability*—of testing! And to the degree of severity of the test, to that same degree it affords the greatest growth potential! We should not shun testing, but welcome *every* test as an opportunity to prove to us and others that our philosophy is trustworthy in the midst of all trials."

A new light of understanding dawns in Dan's eyes. "So…I'm not going through this just for me?"

"Precisely!" Sifu raps his knuckles on the desk to emphasize his approval. "It is of the utmost importance to see the test as a *gift*, a gift marvelously masked as an impossible situation. Once we have been humbled and matured through suffering, we can confidently point others to the philosophy that enabled us to rise above our humanly impossible situation.

"John Kwan is a very *poor* wealthy man. I don't wish to demean him by saying these things, but I do want to paint an accurate picture of the condition of his soul. Dan, you may be the only visual aid for truth, wisdom, and excellence that he ever sees. Dan, how many men does Kwan know who live this philosophy? I am quite certain that his employers at the Chang Tao Group care nothing for putting People First."

"There's certainly no indication of that," Dan says dryly.

"Dan, there may be an even deeper element to what you are experiencing. I can tell you from my own experience that these tests often prepare us for even greater challenges that are yet to come. Every United States Marine goes through 'Boot Camp' when they begin their service, what other branches of the service call 'Basic Training.' I've worked with these young Marines, Dan, and many of them say that Boot Camp was the most grueling experience of their lives. But that arduous test prepares them for one of the most punishing tests of all: combat.

"It may be the same for you, Dan. Perhaps this trial at the office will prove to be the training ground which prepares you to endure even greater testing at some point in the future. If you can't take the charge of an ant, you won't meet the charge of an antelope. If you can't meet the charge of an antelope, you'll never withstand the charge of a lion. Adversity is a tremendous teacher, Dan. Allow it to strengthen you and help you grow."

"I'll do my best, Grandmaster. I must admit that this has been the greatest challenge I've faced in quite some time."

"There are greater challenges, Dan." Sifu's eyes grow distant for a moment. "I've known men for whom success was far more crushing than the worst defeat."

"I'm not sure I understand."

Sifu refocuses on Dan. "I was just thinking of one of the most powerful, wealthy men I have ever known. One of my students referred him to me. He was incapable of manifesting any kind of warmth. This man had everything that money could buy: an enormous home, vacation homes, luxury automobiles, even a yacht."

Sifu shakes his head sorrowfully. "But he was an empty soul, Dan. He had a lovely wife and two fine children, but made no secret that he kept a mistress. The women were possessions to him. The children were little more than trophies in a case. Six months after he'd joined us, I told him he was no longer welcome at our *kwoon*. It was clear that he wanted to learn the art so that he could take pride in establishing physical dominance over others."

"How did he react?" Dan asks curiously.

"He was furious! I think it was the first time in his life that someone had told him there was a closed door that he could not buy open." Sifu sighs. "Pride is the devaluation of all that is good, Dan. Pride blinds the mind from seeing the amazing gifts, talents, and potential of others."

Dan scowls. "That's John Kwan. He says he cares nothing for what anyone else thinks or says."

"Those who are consumed with pride cannot listen to the ideas of others because they are so impressed with their own inner dialogue." Sifu smiles at Dan. "Humility goes before honor, Dan.

When a person's thoughts and actions are clothed in genuine humility, it is one of the most attractive and ennobling character traits a human being can possess. It is the only lens that enables you to see the exalted dignity, worth, and the incredible God-given abilities of others.

"As you've heard me tell students, Dan, meekness is not weakness, but strength under control. Humility gives us the desire and freedom to genuinely celebrate the gifts and the successes of others. Without humility, our lives become empty.

"You've heard it said, Dan, that 'pride goes before a fall.' That wealthy man came to see me several years after I barred him from the *kwoon*. He told me he came home from work one night and the house was empty. His wife left a note saying that she and the children had moved to California. Two weeks later he discovered that his mistress had embezzled half a million dollars from him. He had also suffered severe reversals in some of his investments. He was a broken man. Everything he had relied on to give him a sense of significance had been stripped away."

Dan is fascinated. "He asked you for help *after* you'd barred him from the *kwoon*?"

"He said I was the only person he could trust," Sifu says simply, "the only person who didn't want to take something from him. And he was just beginning to realize that he had an impoverished view of wealth."

Dan squints at Sifu. "Wait. 'An impoverished view of wealth'? That seems like a contradiction of terms."

Sifu smiles at his friend. "That is an excellent question, Dan. I say 'impoverished' because he believed his bank balance was all he needed to earn trust and respect. Then he discovered that the people who were closest to him did not trust him, did not even want to remain in his life.

"I meet many young people, Dan, who have graduated from the top universities, but they have only been introduced to one dimension of wealth—financial wealth. They've heard a great deal about that, and they expect to amass wealth in just a few years. But they were *never* introduced to the second dimension: building trust-worth—establishing a name that is trustworthy. Are those young people truly educated? I would suggest that their professors are guilty of gross educational malpractice!

"Dan, my Sifu used to tell us over and over, 'Wisdom is the principal thing; therefore, get wisdom.' For years I didn't fully understand. But throughout history, when a society begins to disintegrate, people look to wise leaders to turn things around. They don't look for a wealthy man; they want someone who is rich in wisdom and strong in their spirit."

Dan nods slowly. "I'll certainly need to exercise wisdom when I speak with John Kwan tomorrow!"

CHAPTER 12

"Where Did You Get Your MBA?"

AT PRECISELY 8:15 THE FOLLOWING morning, Dan knocks on John Kwan's office door and enters the office.

"Mr. Burton," Kwan says in his cool voice. He is staring at his computer monitor and does not look at Dan. "You're here to discuss the day ahead?"

Dan has practiced the tone of voice he wants to use for this encounter—quiet but firm, polite and professional. "Yes. I have a meeting scheduled with Claudia Barnes, the Customer Service director, in fifteen minutes. All of our local Customer Service staff will assemble at 9 a.m. I'll be announcing the layoffs to that group. Sarah will be making phone calls to the managers at remote locations."

Kwan glances up from his computer monitor at Dan. "This was to be completed yesterday."

Dan nods. "Yes. I apologize. It will be made clear that the termination is effective immediately."

"Very well," Kwan says crisply. "I have nothing else to discuss."

Dan takes a breath. "There's something I'd like to say, Mr. Kwan."

Kwan's eyes are still on the monitor. "Yes?"

Dan can feel irritation rising at Kwan's rudeness. *"Better to control your temper than to conquer a city,"* he reminds himself. "Yes. I'd like your full attention, please." Dan's voice is still measured, polite.

Kwan's eyes shift from the monitor to Dan.

"I want to apologize for my behavior yesterday. I was unprofessional and unpleasant. There's no excuse for the way I spoke to you." Kwan's face is expressionless. "I have higher expectations for myself and for how I want to treat other human beings." Dan reminds himself not to drop his eyes, despite his discomfort. "I hope you may be able to forgive me."

Kwan shakes his head resignedly. "Mr. Burton, I am disappointed. Yesterday I saw flashes of the kind of management style that turn this organization around. You were forceful and commanding. Today you come in groveling and asking for forgiveness like a schoolchild." Kwan pitches his voice higher, mimicking a child. "'Please, Mr. Kwan, thank you, Mr. Kwan.'" He shakes his head.

"You have no courage, no sense of honor."

Yesterday, anger made Dan's voice grow loud; today, his voice softens as he feels a surge of bubbling rage at the sound of the world *groveling*. "Humility comes before honor," he says quietly, almost to himself.

"Humility comes before honor." Kwan's tone is mocking. "Where did you learn that? Did you get your MBA from the Mother Theresa School of Business?"

Dan looks steadily at Kwan. "I learned it from my mentor, Sifu Li. He says…"

"Sifu Li?" For the first time, Dan hears a note of genuine interest in Kwan's voice. "There is a Chinese man named Sifu Li who lives in the United States. He is one of the most renowned Kung Fu masters in the world."

Dan nods. "Sifu Li lives here in our city. He is my Kung Fu instructor, my mentor, and my friend." Dan hesitates, then pushes ahead. "It was Sifu who introduced me to the People First philosophy and continues to teach it to me today."

Kwan stares at Dan incredulously. "*Sifu Li* taught you these things?"

"Every word of it," Dan says sincerely. "I used to manage in the way you suggest, Mr. Kwan. I motivated through fear. I was high-command, high-control, and proud of it. One day I realized it wasn't working. It wasn't working at home, the company was struggling, and everyone around me was miserable. I went to Sifu and asked for advice. It changed my life."

Kwan shakes his head dismissively. "I have seen Sifu Li in the ring. Personally. He was a ferocious competitor. There is nothing soft about that man. We must be talking about two different people."

Dan decides to shift tracks. "You've been to Kung Fu tournaments?"

Dan imagines that he sees a trace of a genuine smile flicker across Kwan's face. "Almost every Chinese boy growing up in the 1970s wanted to *be* Sifu Li, just as Latin American children grew up wanting to be Pelé. He was the people's champion. Dominant in the ring, yet humble and unassuming…" Kwan stops suddenly and his eyes drift off. Dan wonders if the word "humble" has caused Kwan to stop and think. Kwan refocuses. "He moved to the United States in the 1980s and opened a string of Kung Fu schools."

Dan smiles. "I started attending the *kwoon* he operates in our city sixteen years ago. Sifu Li personally tied the black sash around my waist."

Kwan cocks his head at Dan. "You learned Walu Kung Fu from *Sifu Li*?"

Dan rarely talks about his personal accomplishments, but he feels this time is right. "I won the national championship for my weight class three years ago. Sifu was in my corner. His home is here. He is the senior instructor at the *kwoon* here in South Florida. You are welcome to visit any evening. You can walk up after class and say hello, but I'd be happy to introduce you to him."

The change in Kwan's demeanor is remarkable. He actually grins and stares off into the distance. "To shake hands with the Grandmaster. That *would* be extraordinary!" He looks up at Dan curiously. "You say this 'People First' idea was his?"

"People First is the philosophy he employs for teaching us, and he's had tremendous success with it. There are four men and two women from our *kwoon* who have won national titles in the last five years." Dan is about to mention the dramatic success at Prestigious Products after he introduced People First, but instinct tells him to wait.

Kwan is thoughtful, but his face has returned to its normal impassive expression. "I had no idea Sifu Li lived here. Perhaps I will accept your invitation one day." He glances back at the computer monitor on his desk, then back at Dan. "Is there anything else?"

The window of opportunity that had briefly cracked open is tightly shut again. But Dan is elated. He has finally found an opportunity to establish common ground with John Kwan. He is careful to keep his voice and expression neutral. "No, that's all. Again, I apologize for my poor behavior."

Kwan looks up at Dan with that curious light in his eyes. "You really believe that Sifu Li would want you to apologize?"

Dan's face is innocent. "He suggested it, Mr. Kwan. I've told you he is my mentor. He rebuked me for losing my temper."

"That is very interesting." Kwan looks back to his monitor. "Good day, Mr. Burton."

For the first time, Dan drops his eyes. "I'm afraid it won't be, Mr. Kwan." Dan's voice is very soft. "I'll be saying goodbye to a great many fine people today." He starts for the door.

Kwan's voice stops him. "And therein lies your problem, Mr. Burton. You have too many friends here. I myself form no friendships. I have no emotional attachment to anyone in this organization, which frees me to work at my best."

Dan turns to look at Kwan with genuine curiosity. "But what does that do for *them*, Mr. Kwan? What kind of freedom are you giving them?"

Kwan's eyes meet Dan's over the top of his computer monitor. "I don't care about their freedom. I just want them to work."

Dan looks at Kwan thoughtfully. He feels no anger whatsoever...only sadness. "Mr. Kwan, you spoke with great respect of Sifu Li. He once told me that the only true freedom you and I can hope to achieve will be found in discovering the desire to serve others without seeking anything from them in return." He does not wait for Kwan to respond; he turns and leaves the office.

After he has softly closed the door behind him, Kwan stares pensively at the door. "Serve...others..." he says slowly, as if testing the sound of the words. Then—"Ahh!"—he expels an impatient breath and returns to his work.

CHAPTER 13

"How Can You Do This?"

CLAUDIA BARNES HAS WORKED FOR Prestigious Products for thirty-five years, and has reported directly to Dan for the past fifteen years. She has always cheerfully put forth discretionary effort and encouraged everyone around her to do the same. Now her eyes are widening in alarm. Suddenly she bursts into tears and buries her face in her hands.

Dan Burton turns away and stares glumly out his office window for a moment. There is a steady drizzle falling, unusual weather for South Florida, and the world seems to be enveloped in gray gloom. Dan is hating every minute of this encounter—not that he holds any animosity toward Claudia, but he despises the bitter truth that he is the cause for her distress. Dan has just informed Claudia that she and the entire department she has directed for the past fifteen years—one hundred and thirty people—are being dismissed today.

Claudia struggles to bring her ragged breathing under control. She removes her glasses and wipes her eyes, smearing mascara across her cheeks. Dan wordlessly slides the box of tissues across the table to her. *I've been doing this a lot since Kwan got here,* he thinks sourly. Without looking up, Claudia grabs a tissue out of the box and dabs at her eyes.

Dan racks his brain for something comforting to say…something that might help soften the blow. But Claudia's situation is especially difficult, and Dan is at a loss for words.

Claudia's eyes are filled with pain and fear. "Dan, please explain *why* you're letting me go!"

Her makeup still stains her cheeks, but she makes no effort to wipe it away. "I thought since we became a People First company that this wouldn't happen—not to *all* of us! You said you cared about people more than profits; you said it over and over! How can you *do* this?"

Claudia's eyes begin to fill again, and she swipes roughly at them with the crumpled tissue. Dan shifts uncomfortably in his chair. "Claudia," he says softly, "I am so very sorry…"

"Then don't do it!" Her voice is harsh. "I know the economy is stagnant and we've lost market share, I know we've had an ownership change, but I've done *everything* you've asked! I've sat and told people who worked here all their *lives* that they're being laid off. I've worked late at the office, night after night, when my family needed me at home. I never gave up hope!"

Dan forces himself to meet Claudia's flinty gaze. *She's poured her life into this company,* he reminds himself. *The least I can do is let her speak her mind, however angry or unpleasant.*

"Claudia, the makeup of the new board…"

"The board!" Claudia practically snarls. "The board is John Kwan. Everybody knows that! And everybody knows he cares *nothing* about people—it's all about making money! We were praying you were going to be able to keep John Kwan at bay. *That* was certainly a false hope."

Dan takes a long breath to dispel a sudden rush of anger.

Claudia's voice is lower, but her intensity has in no way abated. "Dan, you *know* that when Paul came home from Iraq that this job meant *everything* to us. The disability payments are *so* meager, and there aren't many companies lining up to hire a man with one arm and no legs!" She pushes out a choked laugh. "Not much thanks for leaving most of his body overseas. And it seems like he left his heart overseas also. So *I'm* the breadwinner. *I'm* the one who might as well be a single mom while Paul's moping in front of the TV. *I'm* the only hope our kids have to finish college. What do I tell my family tonight? Tell me, Dan, *what?!*"

Dan drops his eyes for a minute. *I don't have the slightest idea what to say,* he thinks bitterly.

Dan raises his eyes, and his stomach starts to ache as he sees the hostility in Claudia's hot gaze. "Claudia, your severance package…"

"My severance?" she practically shrieks. "My *severance!* Do you think there are jobs out there for someone my age? Do you think in a few months, when the severance is gone, that it's going to be any different? Dan, what's happened to you? When you came in twelve years ago and said you'd changed, I *believed* you! I *saw* you change, and you led the way for change. These last few years we've been cutting and laying off, and I stood with you. I *defended* you! And this is *it?!* Thirty-five years, in good times and bad…I can't believe you're *doing* this!"

Dan speaks very softly: "Claudia, these are tough times, and tough times like this bring awful decisions like today. If left to my own devices, I would not have done this. I think you know that. I wanted to talk to you personally, rather than have Sarah do it—*certainly* rather than having John Kwan do it—precisely because you've been with us so long and you've been such a loyal Purpose Partner."

"Loyal!" Claudia's eyes are blazing, even as the tears begin to run down her cheeks again. "What a fine reward I get for being *loyal!*"

Dan pauses for a minute, hating the sound of his words. "Whatever I can do for you and your family during this transition, Claudia, you let me know. Whatever you need, you call me directly. I'm so very sorry."

Claudia stands abruptly and snatches her glasses off Dan's desk. "You're *sorry!*" Her voice is thick with disdain. "What do you think it's going to be like when I go home and tell Paul about this…*transition*?!" She practically spits the word. "What do I tell my kids? How 'sorry' do you think *they* will be, Dan?" She starts for the door, then turns. "Believe me, you don't have to worry about me calling. I don't ever want to talk to you again!"

After Claudia has stalked out, her back rigid with anger, Dan swings back to the window and resumes his inspection of the dreary landscape outside. After some time he drops his face into his hands and remains that way for some time, motionless. It may be that he is praying. Or perhaps it is simply Dan's turn to let the tears flow.

CHAPTER 14

New Beginnings

DAN IS DEEPLY DISPIRITED AS he returns home that evening. Immediately after the meeting with Claudia, Dan told seventy-five men and women that their positions had been eliminated—a grim chore that has become all too familiar in recent years. He watched the flicker of expressions across their faces: shock, fear, anger, grief. He stayed after the meeting to talk with anyone who wanted to talk. There were more tears, more anxious questions, and one man who, like Claudia, wanted to tell Dan exactly what he thought of him "for allowing this to happen."

And there were two women and one man who came up to Dan to thank him for bringing People First to Prestigious Products. The man had tears in his eyes as he said, "People First changed my marriage. It changed my life. Thank you, Dan, I'll never forget it." The words were undoubtedly meant to be a comfort to Dan, but they only served to deepen his sense of gloom.

A good portion of the afternoon was spent on the phone, notifying managers around the country about the layoffs and trying to explain the plan going forward. These calls are very difficult, because Dan lacks confidence in this new direction. Dan will not lie to his Purpose Partners or hold out false hope.

"Dan, is this the end of it?" is the question he hears over and over throughout this long day. "Are we finally done with these terrible layoffs?" Dan has no answers. It is difficult to be encouraging when he feels so discouraged.

His troubled expression lightens as he pulls into his driveway and sees an extra car parked there. He had forgotten that his son, David, was coming for dinner. As badly as he feels about the terrible turn that his daughter's life has taken, he feels great joy and satisfaction in David's choices. His twenty-six-year-old son graduated *summa cum laude* from the University of Miami, yet he clearly didn't spend all his time at "The U" studying. David began dating Lee Altman, a business major who also spent two years as a cheerleader for the Hurricanes, three years ago. The two have become inseparable, and Lee has virtually become a member of the Burton household.

Dan smiles as he parks his car. "Just what the doctor ordered!" he says aloud, and walks quickly toward the front door.

David Burton keeps his blond hair cut short and neat. At six-feet-two, he is an inch taller than his father; both Burton men are broad-shouldered and trim. David's bright blue eyes are filled with affection as Dan walks into the kitchen. He wraps his father in a bear hug. "Great to see you, Dad."

Dan holds his son close for a moment. "I never get tired of hugs from you," he says softly.

Lee is standing just behind David, waiting her turn to give Dan a hug and a kiss on the cheek. Her long, brunette hair and deep tan make her brilliant green eyes all the more striking. In a city which is home to supermodels and celebrities, Lee Altman turns heads wherever she goes.

Cheryl comes out of the kitchen to greet her husband. Without releasing Lee, Dan wraps an arm around Cheryl and gives her a kiss. Then he turns and grins happily at David. "I can now say with certainty that I have been kissed by the two most beautiful women in the world."

"And how you managed to pull that off is *totally* beyond me!" David says dryly. Everyone laughs.

Lee keeps her arm around Dan's waist and looks up at him, searching his eyes. "Cheryl said you had a tough day at work."

Dan's smile disappears. "Oh, brother!" He looks down at her and then at David. "I couldn't be happier to see you two." He grins at Lee. "I'll try not to be too much of a curmudgeon."

They all take their seats in the living room. "Mom said you had to let one hundred and thirty people go?" David asks, his eyes wide with concern.

Dan nods. "This is our third major layoff in five years. I don't know if Mom told you that we've got new ownership now and a new board. We're having some difficult days."

Cheryl returns from the kitchen with a tall glass of iced tea for Dan. He looks at her gratefully as she sits next to him on the couch. "How did it go with Claudia?" Cheryl asks.

Dan shakes his head. "Badly." He looks at the two young people. "Claudia Barnes had been with our company for thirty-five years. Great person, great leader, hard worker. She was in charge of the department that was eliminated today. Her husband, Paul, was career military, until he was nearly killed by one of those roadside bombs in Iraq four years ago. He lost both legs and most of his right arm."

Lee gasps at the description of Paul's wounds. "Do they have children?" she asks quietly.

"Four," Dan replies. "They're good kids, Lee, it's a good family, although Paul came home bitter and discouraged. Claudia said today that she might as well be a single mother, and she's better at it than anyone might expect. But if she can't find another job, this loss of income is devastating for them."

"How did she take the news?" David asks.

"Not well. She's frightened about the future. When we get frightened we get angry. When we get angry..." Dan purses his lips "... we say things we don't mean."

"She blamed you?" Cheryl Burton gently strokes her husband's back.

Dan nods. "I'm sure she already feels badly about it. She wasn't thinking." Dan looks down at the floor, and then up at Cheryl. "I want to help them. And she's just one of one hundred and thirty people who had their lives turned upside-down today. I want to do more for them than just tell them I'm sorry."

Cheryl gives her husband a reassuring smile. "We'll do whatever you think is best. But Dan, I'd like to change the subject for a minute."

"Of course!" Dan looks apologetically at David and Lee. "I'm sorry to come home in such a foul mood."

David waves a dismissive hand. "Dad, you've had a brutal day! We can talk about our stuff at a better time."

"Not on your life!" Cheryl's eyes are very bright. "This is the perfect time! You tell!"

Dan looks around the room with a faint grin. "There's something you all know that I don't."

Like Cheryl, David's eyes are shining with anticipation. "Yep."

Dan's smile broadens, and he looks at Lee. "And you're in on this too?"

"I am," she says shyly.

"You tell him, honey," David says, nodding encouragingly.

Lee looks straight at Dan with her fabulous green eyes. "I said 'yes.'"

Dan's brain is leaden from his long day, and he shakes his head, not yet understanding. "You said…'yes'?" Suddenly, his eyes widen and he looks quickly at David. "'Yes' as in…?"

David is nodding, grinning broadly. Lee touches the back of Dan's hand. "Would it be OK if I call you 'Dad' now?"

"Ho-ho!" Dan springs to his feet and throws his arms wide. "You bet!"

Lee quickly stands to embrace him, and David is there too. Dan grabs the two of them in a tight bear hug. "I'm so happy for you!" Dan turns to Cheryl, who looks radiantly happy. "I'm so happy for us!"

And for just a little while, there are no thoughts of layoffs or John Kwan; there is no anger or nagging guilt…just a deep, hilarious joy that his son has married so well.

One hour later, the two couples are seated around the dinner table. Meal time has been filled with stories—ranging from David's startling proposal in the middle of a coffee shop to the time a competitor actually threw Dan out of the ring—all of them punctuated with the full-throated laughter of people who thoroughly enjoy each other's company. Cheryl has brought a coffee pot and a plate of cookies, and everyone is leaning contentedly back from the table.

"Dad, I wanted to take you and Mom out to dinner tonight," David is saying sincerely, "but she wasn't sure you'd want to go out after your long day."

Dan chuckles deep in his stomach. "You didn't even take your fiancée out to dinner to propose! Why would I expect you to take us out?" There is gentle laughter around the table. Dan gazes happily at his son. And then, unbidden, a sharp stab of sadness. *Marcy should be here. That's the one thing that keeps tonight from being perfect…*He reaches out and takes his wife's hand under the table.

As if sensing a change in Dan, Lee is suddenly serious. "I can't stop thinking about that family whose husband was so badly wounded in Iraq. What will happen to them?"

"It's tough." Dan frowns. "Claudia is right around my age, mid-fifties. It's harder to find work as you get older, and she was earning a pretty nice salary that her family really depends on."

David nods soberly. "You might be surprised to know how many people we counsel at the center who got ground up in this economy. I saw an article that said that the poverty level in Dade County reached its highest level in fifty years in 2010. Things haven't improved much since then. A lot of folks are still unemployed or underemployed. They lose their homes, bill collectors are calling, their marriages are totally stressed, and then they start to drink or take drugs. It's a vicious circle. The worse they feel, the more they don't want to feel anything. And, of course, the worse the substance abuse, the more bills they can't pay, the marriage ends…it's pretty grim."

Dan glances at Cheryl and sighs. "David, I've got to ask you."

David raises an eyebrow. "Marcy?"

Dan nods. Cheryl stiffens slightly.

"No idea, Dad. We've looked, too. No sign of her. I don't know if she's even still in Miami."

"She's here." Cheryl's voice is almost a whisper. She looks at Dan apologetically. "I didn't tell you, Dan, because you were going through all this pain at work."

"She called?"

"Just over a week ago," Cheryl nods slowly.

"For money?"

Cheryl runs a hand through her hair and grimaces. "She said the most awful things. Hurtful things!"

"You didn't give her money, Mom?" David asks gently.

Dan gives his wife's hand a gentle squeeze. "We stopped doing that a long time ago," he explains.

"Oh, she always says it's for rent, or her car needs repairs, or something. We believe we'd be giving her money for drugs. I'm afraid we don't have trust any more, and we don't want to participate in her self-destruction."

Cheryl sounds as if she is talking to herself. "I told her I would come and pick her up right at that moment and take her to your treatment center, David, or any other one she would prefer." Her voice breaks. "I told her I love her with all my heart." She is silent for a moment and then says, "She said if I really loved her I'd meet her at *her* point of need, not at my point of need."

"But you did the right thing," David says firmly. "I know it hurts like crazy, but an addict will say anything to anyone in order to get what they want. I've had those same conversations with Marcy, Mom, and it *hurts* to hear my sister curse at me and tell me she hates me. But until she comes to her senses, to give her money is to be a party to her death."

"May I change the subject?" Lee asks hesitantly.

Cheryl smiles wearily at her future daughter-in-law. "Please do!"

Lee is frowning with concentration. "I know what David is saying is right, but what about the people who just need help putting their lives back together? Even our advertising firm hasn't been immune from this economy. We've had some layoffs. Every one of us knows somebody who went through a long stretch of unemployment or foreclosure or bankruptcy. How many lives got turned upside-down in the last six years?"

Lee is one of the most consistently cheerful people Dan knows, but now she is deadly serious.

"David and I were watching one of the *Christmas Carol* movies. When Scrooge was asked to give money for the poor, he basically said that he pays his taxes and those who are badly off should look to the government for help."

Lee shakes her head, and there is no mistaking the pain in her eyes. "I'm just like Scrooge! I hear about someone like your Claudia, Dan, and I think, 'Well, my taxes go to pay for unemployment and food stamps and welfare. People who are badly off should look to those programs.'" Her voice is angry, almost demanding. "What am I doing to help people in trouble? Nothing!"

Dan is looking at Lee thoughtfully. "What are you getting at, Lee?"

David gives his fiancée an affectionate grin. "She's gonna quit her job. It's just a matter of time.

She works for one of the most prestigious ad agencies in Miami, and she wants to come work with me. We go through this every couple of months."

Lee wrinkles her nose and gives David a playful shove. "It's hanging out with you Burtons that does it to me. David helps people every day at the counseling center and Cheryl, you do your volunteer work with Salvation Army. I feel like I'm a taker, not a giver."

David leans over and kisses Lee on the cheek. "You give to me every day. You pour love into me, honey, and you fill me up to do what I do."

"But it's not enough!" Dan's fist hits the table hard enough to make dishes jump, startling everyone. He has never stopped watching Lee's face. "It's not enough, is it Lee?" he asks again, more quietly.

Lee's eyes fill with tears, and she shakes her head silently.

Lee's pensive mood seems to have infected Dan. "I fought to get the best possible severance package for the people who were let go," he says, "but all that does is cushion the blow. It doesn't do *anything* to get them out of the pit I just threw them into. I'm like you, Lee. I want to do more!"

David is looking at his father curiously. There is only one other time he can remember seeing his father this excited. "Dad, you run a business that employs hundreds of people. Because of your efforts, at least in part, there are—what?— one thousand families who have homes and groceries and the like because they are gainfully employed. Isn't that enough?"

"We have eight hundred and twenty Purpose Partners left after today," Dan says softly. "I *know* that's important, David. I don't discount that. Since Sifu taught me the People First philosophy, I feel like I've contributed to the lives of others—both to their spiritual bank accounts *and* their actual bank accounts. And I'm learning more from Sifu and some other men about how building trust in our organization builds wealth in the lives of others."

"I'm a wealthier man from knowing you, Dad," David says warmly. "And you, Mom," he adds, looking over at Cheryl. He gently lifts Lee's hand to his lips and kisses the back of her hand. "And you."

Dan looks over at Cheryl. Where she had looked miserable a moment ago, her eyes are glowing now. "We are a wealthy family, aren't we?"

Cheryl smiles. "We certainly are." She takes her husband's hand. "Dan, I've had some thoughts about doing more to help people. I was hoping that this situation at work would ease before I brought it up with you."

Dan is instantly remorseful. "Were you afraid I was going to growl at you if you brought it up?"

"Oh, no, Dan, that's not it! I was just waiting for the right time."

"Tell me what you're thinking," Dan encourages.

"Well…" Cheryl gives a little giggle. "I'm afraid you'll all think I'm crazy!"

Cheryl shifts her chair to face Dan directly. She takes both of his hands in hers. "You've worked so hard for so long to provide for us. You set up the college fund for David and…" a shadow passes across her face "… and for Marcy, which we're keeping now for her 'rehab fund.'" Cheryl looks over at David and Lee. "We keep praying that we'll get a chance to spend that money."

Dan gives his son a soft smile. "And if Marcy doesn't use it, it'll become a college fund for *your* children." Lee's cheeks glow pink under her tan and she smiles shyly. *They look so happy together.*

Dan's smile widens. *How wonderful!*

Cheryl tugs at her husband's hands to get his attention. "About my idea." Dan smiles apologetically and nods for her to continue. "You've created a good retirement fund for us. I've been so grateful to know that's there." Cheryl hesitates, then takes a breath, and the words come in a rush: "I want to give it all away. Well, a bunch of it."

She hesitates as Dan's eyes widen in surprise. Cheryl looks at David and Lee and finds encouragement in their close attention. "I want to start a foundation with our retirement fund, Dan. A People First foundation. I want to help people who have lost a job or their home to get back on their feet." She searches her husband's eyes. Dan's look of surprise has faded into a gentle smile. "You think I've lost it, don't you?"

Dan shakes his head slowly. He reaches out and caresses his wife's cheek. And then, to Cheryl's surprise, Dan's eyes start to fill with tears. "Gosh, I love you!" He turns to look at David and Lee. "Just when I thought this night couldn't get any better!" He makes an odd sound, a laugh that catches in his throat as a sob. Suddenly, he slides off his chair and kneels in front of his wife.

"Cheryl Burton, I *love* you. Will you start a whole new life with me?"

Cheryl smiles tenderly at her husband. "I love you, too, Dan. But…what do you mean?"

"I mean," Dan throws back his head and this time pushes out a joyful laugh. "I mean, sweetheart, I was thinking about the very same thing on the way home tonight! That I want to set up a service to help people who are getting ground down in this weak economy. People like the Barnes family. But Cheryl…" Dan gently cups his wife's face in his hands. "That money is *your* nest egg future. There's no guarantee we'll be able to replace it once it's gone."

Now tears are starting to fill Cheryl's eyes, but they are tears of joy. "You really *like* my idea?" Dan nods, grinning. "Dan, I want us to *matter*. If we lose our money, we lose it. There are people who have already lost *everything*. Let's talk about what we can do to give them concrete help."

Still on his knees, Dan grabs his wife and pulls her into a long embrace. "I love you so much! I am so proud of you!"

He finally releases her, and Cheryl hastily brushes her eyes and looks over at David and Lee. "I'm sorry, you two. I should have brought this up another time."

Dan had forgotten that there was anyone else in the room! He turns hastily to look at his son. David is looking at him with love and wonder. Lee has one hand over her mouth, and her eyes are brimming. Dan gives Lee a crooked grin. "Are you sure you want to marry into this kooky family?"

"Oh my word!" she says in a small, choked voice.

David looks from his mother to his father. "You've both told me so many times that you're proud of me. It meant so much to me growing up. Have I ever told you how proud I am to be your son?"

Lee's eyes overflow, and the tears stream down her cheeks. "I'm so glad we came for dinner tonight!" She looks intently at Dan and Cheryl. "You're serious? You're going to do this?"

Dan and Cheryl look at each other, eyebrows raised in a mute question. Cheryl nods her head eagerly. She looks radiantly beautiful in her eager anticipation. Like Dan, she bursts into joyful laughter. "Yes! Yes, we are!"

David grins at his fiancée. "I'm thinking we ought to make this a family affair!"

Lee is still struggling to regain her composure. She nods her head vigorously.

Now it is Dan and Cheryl who are looking across the table in loving bemusement. "What do you mean?" Dan asks.

"You're going to need a director of counseling for this foundation, right?" David asks. "I'd work cheap."

Lee chimes in excitedly. "And I can use everything I've learned about public relations to help you attract donors. All of the senior account executives at my firm are encouraged to take on one major *pro bono* client, and I hadn't found one I liked yet. I *really* like this one!"

There is a moment of breathless silence at the table as everyone looks at each other in anticipation.

David breaks the silence: "So when do we start?"

Cheryl gives another giggle and looks at David. "Let's start tomorrow!" In that moment of elation, with every heartbeat seeming to pulse with love for his family, Dan is certain that his wife does not look a day older than the twenty-four-year-old Lee Altman. *And I don't think she ever looked so beautiful,* Dan thinks. *Even on our wedding day.*

Cheryl glances over at Dan. "Dan, the first call I'm going to make will be to Claudia Barnes, to ask her to consider being the Executive Director of the People First Foundation."

CHAPTER 15

"Confidence Doesn't Happen In a Losing Environment"

Ray Aschenbach of Iron Mountain

"WHEN YOU STOP SIGNING AUTOGRAPHS, that's an early sign that you're on the downhill slope." Ray Aschenbach, senior vice president of North American operations for Iron Mountain, is a big, broad-shouldered man who exudes a powerful, restless energy. He has been speaking rapidly, keeping his bright, dark eyes focused on Dan, checking to see if Dan has understood him… and he sees some doubt. "Maybe I should back up a bit."

Dan can't help but grin. *This is going to be fun,* he tells himself. He himself is a competitor through and through, and although he and Sifu have only been sitting with Ray Aschenbach for a few minutes, Dan recognizes that he is in the presence of another competitor, a man who will never be content with "second best." Dan feels his own energy level rising to meet Ray's. "Ray, I've been a CEO for years now; no one has ever asked me for my autograph!"

Ray chuckles. Even his laughter is abrupt, staccato. "I get energized when I have these moments to talk about the business and about people. My mind tends to jump from thought to thought."

Dan nods, still grinning. "That's OK. I'm enjoying it! I'll let you know if I don't make the leap with you."

"I went to college on a baseball scholarship," Ray resumes. "I actually had the opportunity to play for the United States with the World Port Team."

Dan whistles, impressed. "Did you pursue it through to the professional level?"

"I wanted to, right up to the day I was looking for the fastball down and away and the pitcher came up and in. The ball shattered my orbital bone and I went through five hours of surgery. That was the beginning of the end of baseball. I was one of those players who worked hard and knew the game well, but I was never an exceptional athletic talent."

"Do you miss it?" Dan asks curiously.

"No." Ray's smile is bright and his laugh is relaxed. "It all worked out for the best. But I do still like to go to games." His eyes narrow. "You see these professional athletes, and there are all these fans around, little kids, and Dad's taken them to see their first game. They come running up to a player and ask for an autograph and the player just blows right by them. You see that a lot. They've stopped signing autographs."

Ray frowns. "They've forgotten where they've came from! They've stopped appreciating the value in the individuals—the fans—who helped them get where they are. They've forgotten that at one time in their life *they* were the ones who were thrilled to spend just a few seconds with a pro ballplayer.

"You asked me when we first sat down, Dan, about the danger of a leader crossing the line that separates confidence from arrogance. The leader of an organization is like that professional athlete. I have twenty-five hundred employees in my division; most of them see me very rarely. When you walk into that room and they *do* get to see you, you've got to make time to *serve* your Purpose Partners. You sit with each one of them for as long as they want and sign autographs, so to speak."

Ray's bright eyes turn to Sifu. "You taught me those sayings, Sifu, that I keep remembering: 'You can't impart what you don't possess' and 'Whatever you want your external customers to feel, your internal customers must feel first.' When you forget that as leader—if you stop signing autographs—that's an early sign that you're on the downhill slope."

Sifu gives Ray a delighted smile. "Ray, you expressed that so very well! You have taken your background in athletics and applied it to People First. You are speaking about making deposits in the spiritual bank accounts of your Purpose Partners—you just have your own way of phrasing it. 'Signing autographs' is a marvelous concept!"

Ray grins at Sifu. "When you called me last week and told me you wanted to talk about trust and confidence, I started getting excited, especially since I had already planned this trip to Florida. The more I thought about it, the more I thought that confidence is the foundational characteristic of trust. Everything a leader does is built on confidence.

"No one wants to follow someone who is insecure or indecisive. That's the magic in instilling confidence in talented people: make them believe they are participating in something valuable and experiencing something extraordinary. When you've instilled that belief, you encourage them to commit to one another and to their customers. Then they'll make every effort to produce a successful outcome."

Dan reaches for his iPad and looks at Ray thoughtfully. "So you would say that an organization's level of confidence reflects its leaders' confidence?"

"Absolutely!" Ray nods a vigorous affirmative. "Leadership is the ability to lead people to success. There are certain things I do to project an attitude of confidence: smiling, enjoying my job, being proud of my family and the organization I serve.

"But there is something much more concrete that I do in addition to those things: I stress *winning*, both personally and professionally. Winning in and of itself builds confidence. Adjusting to circumstances in an effort to win is *much* better than conditioning yourself and your organization to surrender to challenges from the market, economic downturns, your competitors' actions, and so on. Our customers trust us to maintain a level of excellence in the protection of their information, regardless of any environmental or economic conditions the world may be facing."

Dan looks up from typing on his iPad. "Ray, I'm still a little hazy on what it is that Iron Mountain does."

Ray gives Dan a sheepish smile. "That's because I haven't explained it to you. I *told* you I get excited when I start talking about leadership!" He is serious again. "Iron Mountain helps organizations to better manage their information. To put it in a nutshell, Dan, we protect and store information. One of the main reasons for that protection is natural disasters, such as a hurricane or tornado or flood. It could be something even more dreadful than that; we had one hundred and thirteen customers who were in the World Trade Center during the 9/11 attacks. Or it could be the kind of disaster that doesn't make the evening news, like a computer crash or a hacker or even cyberterrorism.

"We store and protect the information that keeps that organization alive, because absent that information, the business is probably going to close down. I've seen reliable estimates that if a company is down for more than five days, the probability of them going out of business is north of 90 percent. Every hour of every day that a company is not operating, billions of dollars are lost. Our job at that critical time is to ensure that we get that information to a location where our clients can process it and get their business up and running again, even during the worst scenarios."

Dan has been listening with interest. "That must keep you *very* busy in today's information age."

"We have more than one hundred and twenty thousand customers in thirty-one countries," Ray answers simply. "Yeah, we're busy." The intensity in his voice builds again. "So a significant part of our job is to build confidence in our customers—confidence in what Iron Mountain does for them. So here comes your phrase again, Sifu: 'You can't impart what you don't possess.' Our customers won't have confidence in us if we aren't confident in what we do!"

"Ray," Sifu says in his soft voice, "I am curious to hear more of your thoughts about the importance of winning."

"Confidence doesn't happen in a losing environment," Ray says flatly. "Confidence comes through building a record of success over time, which creates a mind-set that winning is the expected outcome. To get there with any organization, you make a determination as a group that you're going to make it work and be successful—regardless of what's going on outside in the world today. If the economy goes bad, you pull yourself up by the bootstraps and figure it out. You'll have to make some tough decisions, but in the end you don't succumb to losing. You *don't* sit back and say, 'Oh well, it is what it is.' No, it *isn't* 'what it is'! You bring the group together, you put your collective minds together, and you figure out how to produce a successful outcome."

Ray raises his hand in a cautionary gesture. "Now, there's a fine line there; there's a balance on how that message is delivered, because you never want to cross the boundaries of ethics. Do I get up early and stay up late and work harder and smarter than my competitor? Yes! But do I do things to cheat my competitor or badmouth him or exaggerate my own services? No way! That's the line you don't cross."

Ray thumps a thick forefinger on the tabletop. "Here's the point: people who consistently stay at the top are those individuals who have *learned to win*. You can't establish a strong foundation of confidence unless you've actually experienced those successes over a period of time." Again, his forefinger *thunks* the table. "*That's* the winning component."

Dan is nodding enthusiastically as he types. Sifu smiles his encouragement at Ray and asks, "What about courage? Is courage part of the makeup of a great leader?"

"Absolutely!" Ray replies without hesitation. "It takes courage to examine both failure and success and learn from both. Great leaders take their organizations to places they have never been before…they experience things they never had before. It takes real courage to explore new ideas, new beginnings, new products, and new services in an environment where real uncertainty exists. In large measure, it's the leader's courage that fuels breakthrough performance, world-changing innovation, and individual legacy.

"If you aren't changing, you're losing ground. Business and technology are evolving at such a rapid pace, you cannot simply 'maintain' and hope to gain market share. You've *got* to constantly challenge yourself. You've got to explore and accept new ideas. When you do those things, there is going to be uncertainty—that sense of working without a net—but that's where innovation starts and that's how you get breakthrough performance."

Dan looks up from his iPad. "So you're watching your competitors and looking to stay one jump ahead of them in terms of innovation?" He is surprised to see Ray shake his head in disagreement.

"We keep our focus on ourselves and on our customers," Ray explains, "because we have control over ourselves. Our successes and failures are defined by our Purpose Partners, our shareholders, and our customers. I'm not going to invite the competition into that game. If we lose market share, it won't be because of something our competitors are doing, but rather because of something that we're *not* doing that's causing our customers to turn to somebody else."

Dan has stopped typing and is looking at Ray thoughtfully. "Say that again. If you were to lose market share…"

"I wouldn't see it as something our competitors have *started* doing, but rather something that we're *not* doing that's pushing those customers away from us. We honestly believe that we're the best organization to serve their needs, but we recognize that our customers have choices, and we don't *ever* want to reach the point where our customers think we're beginning to believe that we're larger than life, because that's just not the case."

Ray looks gratefully at Sifu. "You've reminded me of the proverb, Sifu, that 'pride goes before the fall.' When you stop doing the things that made you successful, that's the start of the fall. You've already tripped over the rock, but you don't know it. When you start getting comfortable and thinking that you're better than your competitors, you start getting lazy and you stop the disciplines that are necessary for continuous learning and ongoing improvement. Those are the early signs of an organization that's headed for a fall, and at Iron Mountain we are constantly working to guard against that happening."

Dan has been listening very closely. "So…you're always vigilant that confidence isn't turning into pride. But at the same time, you feel you must consistently communicate your confidence to both your internal *and* your external customers."

Ray nods decisively. "Yes, Dan, that's the balance. After good Purpose Partners, information is every company's most prized asset. You can't ask an organization to let you manage and protect their information unless you have their trust. Confidence is an essential component to establishing that trust. And as you just said, Dan, inspiring confidence in others starts from within. I know I keep saying it, but 'you can't impart what you don't possess.' All our Purpose Partners *must* buy in to our mission. They *must* possess the self-confidence that comes from success experienced over time.

"I've found that confidence brings a sense of conviction to a cause or purpose. And when you share that conviction, when you've communicated the 'what' and the 'why,' that leads to passion, and that passion creates an unyielding determination to do whatever must be done to make the organization great. That passion leads to extraordinary success, which in turn creates continued confidence, which establishes solid trust. It's a cycle of winning, Dan."

Dan shakes his head with an admiring smile. "Ray, I thought I could give a pretty good pep talk, but you have got me fired *up!* When you come back to Florida, I'd love to have you come and give a talk to our team." Suddenly, Dan's smile disappears and he looks off into space. "That is, if there's a team left for you to talk to." He looks back at Ray, and this time Dan's smile is almost shy. "I'm sorry, Ray. I don't want you to think that I wasn't listening to what you said about pressing on toward a successful outcome. It's just that my vision for success and my board of directors' vision seem to be at odds with each other right now."

Ray nods sympathetically. "If your organization is not unified around the same vision, it's going to be impossible to communicate the confidence that is so essential for trust and success."

"You can say that again!" Dan says feelingly. He looks back to the iPad. "Ray, assuming you have that unanimity of vision, how would you profile a leader who displays the right kind of confidence?"

Ray nods. "Sifu asked me about character clues, and I've identified six characteristics of the leader who displays the right kind of confidence." He starts to tick off the points on his thick fingers.

"First, you've got to be *authentic*. You have to be genuine and show that you have no hidden agendas. People respect a leader who is *real*; they reject a leader they find artificial."

Ray glances over at Sifu. "Grandmaster, I'm sure you've met leaders who are very guarded about what other people know about them. I take the opposite view. People who keep everything hidden are most likely trying to disguise some insecurity. I like to think that I'm a man of strong character, so I'm perfectly OK with people knowing who I am as a person. I'll open up and even create a sense of vulnerability, so that people will know that I don't see myself as some almighty being because of my job title. I'm a real person. That authenticity has proven to be of great value to me, because it helps me establish greater trust.

"The second point, which goes right along with authenticity, is *valuing your Purpose Partners and serving them*. Again, I meet managers who recoil at this idea. I believe it's because they think of a servant as someone in a menial position who waits on the more privileged and powerful."

Ray gives Sifu a grateful smile and he speaks slowly, emphatically. "It was *you* who taught me, Sifu, that every human being has exalted dignity, exalted worth, and exalted potential. You taught me that true power is the power that makes other people powerful. You told me to delight in my wife and my children and my Purpose Partners and help them develop their God-given talents. You told me to live in a model of discovery and celebration and to delight in their accomplishments *and* their efforts. And for me, Sifu, that has made all the difference."

Dan Burton, who once received the same challenge from Sifu, stops typing and looks at his mentor.

There is no disguising the love in Dan's eyes. Glancing over at Ray, Dan can see the same warm appreciation shining in Ray's eyes. "And for me too," Dan says softly.

"Ah." Sifu makes a gentle sound in his throat. He looks at Ray and Dan with pleasure and pride.

"My two good students!" For a moment, the three men remain silent. It is a comfortable, companionable silence, and Dan realizes that a bond has just been cemented among the three of them.

Sifu reaches across the table and grips Ray's muscular forearm. "I am so proud of you, my friend.

You have taken the People First philosophy and made it your own. I am a very proud teacher."

Ray's face lights in a wide smile. "You asked me if I miss baseball," he says to Dan. "Hearing something like that from the Grandmaster feels better than any home run I ever hit!"

Dan grins. "I know exactly what you mean. You just *did* hit a home run."

Ray nods, acknowledging the compliment. "Well, while I'm on a roll here, let me run through my last four points about how a leader displays the right kind of confidence. I've talked about authenticity and serving others. The third point is that a confident leader has *a track record of successfully setting and achieving goals.* How can you know you're successful if you have no goals? How can there be any confidence in that? A leader sets goals; a *confident* leader has a record of success in establishing and accomplishing those goals. That makes the leader confident, and it certainly makes the team confident also."

Dan is nodding and typing. "That's the history of successes you were talking about earlier."

"That's right," Ray agrees. "I've already touched on the next two characteristics of the confident leader. Point four is that confident leaders are *self-aware and organizationally aware.* These men and women maintain a discipline around continuous improvement, both as individuals and in their organizations. They've got a PhD in life, and they're confident that they're standing on the authority of the truth, a confidence that has been gained through the smelting furnace of experience.

"Such leaders are students, models of lifelong learning, and they've learned how to walk in truth.

At the same time, they are abundantly aware of the rich resources that exist all around them in the organization. They ask their Purpose Partners for feedback and celebrate their suggestions, because they know there is a treasure trove of knowledge and experience and ideation all around them. And they're good, intentional, active listeners.

"The fifth point goes right along with that; the confident leader is *ambitious*. He or she has developed a vision for organizational success, and that leader will work to stretch the Purpose Partners in the organization and to stretch the organization itself. He doesn't need the approval of others to lead according to the truth that he knows. He's not looking at a weather vane to get his direction; he *leads* with confidence and speaks with authority. The confident leader communicates passion and direction to everyone on the team."

Again, Ray counts off the points on his fingers. "So I've said that a leader who is modeling the right kind of confidence is authentic; the leader will value his or her Purpose Partners and serve them; the leader has a proven track record of setting and achieving goals; the confident leader will be self-aware and organizationally aware; the leader will be ambitious and passionate; and finally, the leader who projects the right kind of confidence *understands reality, yet sees it through an optimistic lens."*

Ray looks at Dan. "Sifu told me a little bit about the situation at your company. You're in a tough spot, Dan, one that a lot of leaders would probably have just walked away from. I believe you embody this last quality. You see the reality of your situation. You've made some tough decisions to address that reality. And yet the toughest decision you made was to hang in there and do everything you can to effect positive change. You're not looking at your boss and your board through rose-colored glasses, but you have remained optimistic that you can learn and grow and effect positive change. That's why you're here, right?"

Dan looks frankly at Ray. "That's right. But I have to admit that if you'd heard me whining to Sifu about my situation, you might not believe that I'm so optimistic!"

Ray waves a dismissive hand. "We all need a mentor we can vent to about the things that are causing us pain. That's not 'whining,' that's just making the intelligent choice to get a second opinion." Ray gives Dan a wry smile. "Obviously, Sifu hasn't told you about the times I've called him to vent...or you wouldn't be honoring me by taking notes of what I've been saying!"

All three men laugh. Ray is serious again. "Dan, I hope this will be helpful to you. I couldn't agree with Sifu more: confidence is a critical component when it comes to establishing and maintaining trust."

"Ray, I'm really glad to have met you. You've given me a real shot in the arm...a real shot of confidence!"

As Dan and Sifu drive away from their meeting with Ray, Dan turns in the passenger seat to give Sifu a happy smile. "Gosh, I enjoyed listening to that man talk! He seems to have struck just the right balance of confidence and humility."

Sifu nods and smiles. "I agree. Dan, you and I have talked about the importance of servant leadership. Ray just spoke of it, Tom Manenti spoke of it, and several outstanding business leaders have addressed that subject. And well they should! But as I was developing this concept of the seven keys of trust, I was struck by the fact that you don't hear very many men and women in business talking about the importance of *confidence* to establishing trust."

Sifu glances over at Dan. "You know who talks about confidence often? Men and women who serve in the military. They understand that people do not willingly follow insecure leaders; insecurity is not compelling! But people, whether they are on the battlefield or in the boardroom, *will* follow a leader who exhibits the trait of bold assurance that is based on unimpeachable truth."

Dan looks thoughtfully out the window. "It really is a fine line, isn't it? The line between confidence and arrogance?"

Sifu chuckles. "It certainly is! This is one of the things I love about the martial arts. I have learned more about humility from some of China's great champions than anywhere else!

Confidence is not a pedestal to exalt man's pride, but a platform that affords the freedom and boldness to speak with both humility and authority.

"And, Dan, the reason you can be an example of both humility *and* authority is because your foundation is not *you*; your truth does not have you as the source. When you are pointing away from yourself and pointing to truth, you are free to be humble and yet speak with authority at the same time. You feel no need to defend yourself, because you are not standing on the power of your personality or your accomplishments; you are standing on the truth."

Dan looks over at Sifu, his jaw set with determination. "Sifu, from now on, when I speak to John Kwan, I think I'll be able to keep from getting rattled like I did before. I'm standing on a solid foundation of character, competence, and confidence. I don't ever need to raise my voice or act as an intimidator, because I have something even more powerful: the truth."

Sifu smiles again. "Yes, Dan, that's very good. However, there are still some very important keys of trust that we haven't discussed yet. And we'll explore one of the most important ones tomorrow afternoon when we connect with Keith Guller. We've been fortunate to be able to meet our leaders face-to-face up until now. But I can assure you, Dan, even on a Skype connection, Keith Guller's caring will come through clearly."

A few moments later, Sifu swings the Lexus into the parking lot of Prestigious Products' corporate headquarters. Dan and Sifu shake hands and confirm the time Sifu will be coming to Dan's office tomorrow afternoon for the Skype call with Keith. "Sifu, I can't thank you enough for all the time you're spending with me," Dan says, gripping his mentor's hand. "Meeting these men is really making a difference in the way I think, and I know it's going to make a difference in the way I lead from here on out. I plan to work hard at building trust with John Kwan."

Dan walks slowly toward the building from the parking lot, pausing to look up at the brilliant, blue South Florida sky. Dan smiles up at the heavens. *What a beautiful night,* he thinks. *This is the most optimistic I've felt since I first heard of the Chang Tao takeover. We're going to get through this,* he tells himself firmly. *I'm going to find a way to build trust with John Kwan!*

Dan walks toward the front doors, whistling softly to himself. He smiles at the receptionist. "Hello, Molly," Dan says cheerfully.

"Dan!" Molly's eyes are strained. "Marcia Lundgren has called me twice in the last hour, asking if you were back. She told me that I should tell you to see her immediately before you do anything else."

Both the stress in Molly's eyes and the tone of Marcia's message are highly unusual. Dan feels a tightness in his chest. "Molly, what's wrong?"

Molly's eyes begin to fill with tears, which only adds to Dan's unease. "You'd better go see
Marcia right away, Dan," she says in a quavering voice. "It's bad news."

"Thank you, Molly." Dan turns without another word and heads for the stairs, not wanting to wait for the elevator. He springs up the stairs two at a time. *Something's wrong at home,* he thinks, his heart starting to pound. He breaks stride at the top of the stairs. *Marcy.* His breath catches in his throat. *She's turned up dead somewhere.* He strides rapidly down the hallway and turns the corner to Marcia's office.

Marcia is talking on the phone. She glances up as Dan enters. "He's here now, Sarah. Let me go."

Dan's stomach is churning with fear. "Marcia, what's going on?"

"Dan," Marcia says in a soft voice, "maybe you'd better sit down for a minute."

"Marcia, tell me!" Dan barks in a choked voice.

"Paul Barnes died this afternoon."

Dan exhales a deep sigh. *May God forgive me*, he thinks guiltily. *Not Marcy... that's actually a relief! Poor Claudia...what can I do to help her?*

"Dan," Marcia's voice interrupts his thoughts. "There's more."

Dan focuses.

"It was suicide, Dan." Marcia says quietly. "The kids were all off at school, and Claudia had gone to Miami for a job interview. Paul took a bottle of pain-killers. When Claudia got home, he was already gone. He left a note saying that he didn't want to be a burden anymore."

Dan lowers himself slowly into the chair across from Marcia's desk. His mind is swirling. "How...how did you get all this information so quickly?"

"Claudia called Sarah Woods. Sarah has been trying to help her find work, and they've been on the phone a lot recently. Sarah made the introduction to the company Claudia was interviewing with. Claudia worked here so long..." Marcia hesitates, her eyes flickering to Dan's face. "I guess the only friends she had to call are here. So she called Sarah."

"Is Sarah with Claudia now?" Marcia nods silently. "You're in touch with her?" Another affirmative nod.

Dan's eyes narrow and he looks across the desk at Marcia. "Claudia doesn't pay one penny for any of this—paramedics, funeral home, funeral service, any of it. Not one cent. You be sure to tell Sarah. As far as I'm concerned, we just upgraded Claudia's severance package. If I can't get that past John Kwan, I'll reimburse the company out of my own pocket. Whatever Claudia needs, Marcia."

Marcia begins to rapidly jot notes on a pad, grateful to do something natural and normal.

Dan is frowning in concentration. "Paul was a disabled combat veteran, which means he's eligible for burial in Arlington National Cemetery. If that's what Claudia wants to do, I'll pay for airfare and hotel for Claudia and the kids to go to Virginia. I don't..." Dan heaves a deep sigh. "... I don't think Claudia will accept it if she thinks I have anything to do with it, so Sarah should just tell her the company is paying for it."

Marcia is nodding and scribbling on her pad. "Marcia, are you going there yourself?"

"Yes," she replies promptly. "I would have gone sooner, but Molly said you were coming back here. I didn't want you to hear about it through scuttlebutt."

"Thank you," Dan says sincerely. His eyes meet Marcia's. "Whatever she needs, Marcia. Tell her she can direct any requests directly to you. If you have any question, let me know. I don't want her paying for flowers, food at the wake, none of it. Please keep it front-of-mind." Dan can feel a new emotion stirring—anger. He is thinking of John Kwan.

He looks at Marcia miserably. "I might as well have handed Paul that bottle of pills myself."

Marcia's eyes narrow with concern, and she looks straight at Dan. "Don't you go there," she says firmly. "You and I both know that Paul was never right after he was wounded in Iraq. He was so proud of his looks! He was an athlete and a weight lifter. When he lost his legs and his arm...he lost the most important thing in his world." Marcia shakes her head sadly. "Claudia told Sarah that she's been afraid that something like this would happen for the past two years. She said Paul was so miserable; he seemed to be waiting for something bad to happen to give him an excuse. Don't you blame yourself."

Dan's stomach is starting to ache. "I can think of somebody I *can* blame," he says in a low voice.

"Dan," Marcia says quietly, hoping to change the subject, "will you and Cheryl be going to see Claudia tonight?"

Dan's eyes soften as he considers the question. "Cheryl will want to go." He nods slowly. "And I should give Claudia the opportunity to tell me what she thinks of me. After all these years, I owe her that, at least."

"Pishposh," Marcia says briskly. "You don't owe her anything. But I know for a fact she would be grateful if you come. She feels very badly about the way she behaved her last day here."

Dan gives Marcia a crooked grin, but he does not feel like smiling. "I suspect she may not pick today to tell me that," he says drily. He heaves another long sigh and rises to his feet. "Thanks again, Marcia. Thank you for waiting for me."

"You're welcome," she says. "Dan?"

Dan is almost at the office door and he turns.

"Dan, it isn't going to do any good to tell John Kwan what you think of him."

Dan's eyes are ice cold. "Somebody's got to tell him."

CHAPTER 16

"What Are You Doing Here?"

JOHN KWAN ROLLS HIS EYES in that all-too-familiar gesture of impatience when Dan enters his office.

"Mr. Burton, our meetings are scheduled for the morning…"

"There has been a death in the family," Dan interrupts in a flat voice. "I assumed you would want to hear about *that*!"

Incredibly, Kwan does not even look up from his work. "A death in your family?"

The pulse that has been beating in Dan's temples begins to throb. "A death in the Prestigious Products family," Dan says through clenched teeth. "You may recall the name Claudia Barnes. She was the director of the Customer Service department that you eliminated three weeks ago. I wonder if you know anything about her personal circumstances?"

Kwan's eyes slide briefly from the computer monitor to Dan. "I don't have any interest in knowing about the personal life of a former employee." His eyes go back to the monitor.

Dan's peripheral vision is beginning to shut down. It is as if he is looking at Kwan through a long, hazy tube. He is consciously struggling to keep from shouting, but fury makes his voice throaty and unpleasant. He takes a step toward the desk. "If you have even one ounce of humanity in you, maybe you'll *start* to care! Claudia's husband committed suicide this afternoon. He was disabled in combat in Iraq four years ago, and he left a note saying he didn't want to be a further burden on his family. Claudia finds herself an unemployed widow with four school-age children."

Kwan sighs and looks up at Dan. "What are you doing here, Mr. Burton?"

Dan takes another step toward Kwan. "Does it not occur to you that you and I are responsible for driving that man to his death? That Claudia's loss of income was the final straw that broke that man's spirit?! Do you feel *nothing*?!"

Kwan is looking at Dan through narrowed eyes. "I feel that you are perilously close to talking yourself out of your job."

Reason and logic vanish. "*Take* your blasted job!" Dan bellows at Kwan. "I have to go to Claudia Barnes' home tonight and tell her and her kids that Daddy is dead because I was doing my *job*! You're going to go home tonight and sleep soundly while those kids cry themselves to sleep? What kind of man *are* you?!"

"A very successful professional one," Kwan says evenly. "I will ask you one last time, Mr. Burton: why are you here? What do you possibly hope to accomplish by coming in here and ranting like a child?"

Dan's eyes are bulging. "A *child*? It's childish to care about my fellow man?!"

"It is childish to come barging into my office, shouting about things which do not interest me. You want to help this family? Go help them! But know that the next time you raise your voice to me will be the last time you do it as an employee of this company." Kwan's voice is utterly cold.

Dan actually takes a breath…and then expels it. Kwan has turned back to his computer and does not see the effort that Dan must make to control his emotions. *What are you doing here, Dan? You just got done telling Sifu that you were going to build trust with this man…that you weren't going to get rattled. You just told Marcia that you were going to help Claudia and her family. You won't be much help if you get yourself fired!*

"I guess…" Dan says slowly, "I guess I am here because I was hoping you would feel as badly as I do."

Kwan looks up at Dan. Is that a glimmer of humor in Kwan's eyes? "No. You are here because you wanted to *make* me feel as badly as you do."

"I'm sure that's true," Dan says softly. *That is pretty childish when you get right down to it, Dan,* he thinks miserably.

"Then we have nothing else to discuss."

"Actually, Mr. Kwan, there is something else," Dan says, trying to sound reasonable. "I would like to add the cost of the burial to Claudia's severance package. As you know, something like that can run into thousands of dollars. Claudia has four children to care for and educate. I'd like to help her."

"*You* help her," Kwan says curtly. "Prestigious Products has already given her an absurdly generous severance package."

"The burial will likely be held at Arlington Cemetery," Dan continues as if Kwan had not spoken. "I will personally pay for the family to fly to Virginia. I think it would put a human face on our organization if we come alongside the family during this awful time."

"Mr. Burton," Kwan says heavily, "you must know by now that I care nothing about 'putting a human face' on anything. I care about the bottom line. Paying funeral expenses does nothing but harm our bottom line."

Dan's rage has dissipated as suddenly as it arose. The ache of sorrow returns to his stomach. "Our Purpose Partners' belief in us has been badly shaken in recent weeks. When this news hits the grapevine tomorrow, morale will hit rock bottom. I think it would be a relatively minor investment. We don't spend much more for our company picnic in the summertime."

"Good!" Kwan says brightly. "You've alerted me to something we can be sure to cut from next year's budget. Now this conversation has not been a complete waste of time. Thank you, Mr. Burton, and goodnight."

Dan feels utterly drained. He is too tired and heartsick to argue. *You lost your temper again*, he berates himself. *You're not building trust with John Kwan, Dan, you're destroying it!*

"Would you have any objection if I put out the word that the company is paying her expenses, as long as I pay them myself?"

Kwan looks up at Dan curiously. "Why on earth would you do a thing like that?"

"I feel responsible," Dan says frankly. "I want to do the right thing."

Kwan again rolls his eyes in disgust and looks back at his work. "Tell the employees whatever you wish," Kwan says brusquely. "But not one penny out of our budget. Understood?" He looks up at Dan. "And I meant what I said a moment ago. One more outburst and you are gone."

Dan sighs and looks back at Kwan. Then before he has even considered the words, he replies, "I don't stay here because I'm afraid of losing my job. I'm here because I want to earn your trust."

Kwan frowns. "If you want to earn my trust, start acting more like a businessman and less like a wet nurse."

CHAPTER 17

The Choice-Consequence Connection

AS OPTIMISTIC AS DAN was not even 24 hours ago, his emotional pendulum has swung in the opposite direction. He feels utterly defeated. He is sitting in his office with Sifu, waiting to connect with Keith Guller, CEO of Essex Industries, on a Skype call.

Dan tells Sifu about his outburst with John Kwan the night before, and then relates the details of his surprising visit to the Barnes home. As soon as Dan and Cheryl walked into the living room, which was crowded with family members and at least a dozen men and women from Prestigious Products, Claudia quickly moved across the room to embrace Cheryl first, then Dan.

"Dan!" Claudia exclaimed in a choked voice. "Can you ever forgive me for the way I behaved?"

Dan had literally rocked back on his heels in astonishment. "You're asking *me*...to forgive *you*?" he asked.

"I said such horrible things!" Claudia looked at Cheryl and squeezed her shoulder. "And you were so nice to call me. And offer me a job!"

"The offer still stands, Claudia," Cheryl said softly.

Claudia looked back at Dan. "Dan, I know you can't control what John Kwan does, and I know you're staying on at the company because you don't want to leave people behind whom you've invested so much in. I was upset, but that's no excuse for the way I acted. Please forgive me!"

"Pretty darn gracious, all things considered," Dan says to Sifu now. "I half-expected her to start screaming at me and instead she hugs me!" Dan heaves a deep sigh. "Unlike the way I behaved with John Kwan. He called me 'childish,' Sifu, and I think what made me most angry is that I knew he was right! I *was* acting childishly."

Sifu waves his hand dismissively. "Dan, you made a poor choice, just as Claudia Barnes did on the day you told her she was being released. We are choice-making creatures, after all!"

Sifu's eyes are very bright, and Dan almost unconsciously reaches for a notepad. The Grandmaster's focused expression tells Dan that Sifu is about to impart something important.

"There is no such thing as a human life that does not make choices, Dan," Sifu begins. "We are always moving in the direction of our thoughts, and our thoughts move us toward the logical outworking of our choices. Our lives are the direct result—the sum total—of all our choices. Like pearls on a necklace, all connected by a thin cord, our lives represent the cord of those non-refundable moments of time, punctuated by the pearls of our choices, and worn around our necks for everyone to see.

Sifu pauses for a moment, looking at Dan to see if he understands. Dan is jotting some notes, his eyes narrowed with concentration. He glances up at Sifu. "Keep going. I'm with you."

"Every choice we make creates an inevitable consequence." Sifu's voice is very gentle. "Until we become mindful that our choices have a direct conse-quence upon our present and future well-being, as well as the well-being of others, we will not assume full responsibility for those choices." Sifu stops again and looks at Dan quizzically.

"So…" Dan begins uncertainly, "each choice we make connects in a chain of choices which leads to an ultimate outcome. There's no such thing as a discon-nected choice."

"Precisely!" Sifu gives Dan an approving smile. "We make choices in our relationships. It is easy to point the finger at the other party. We tell ourselves, 'I am angry because he said this or because she did that.' We must stop playing the blame game and accept full responsibility for the problems that our choices have created in our relationships."

Dan nods thoughtfully. "So rather than blaming Kwan for being heartless, I must accept responsibility for choosing to react impulsively and emotionally."

Sifu smiles gently. "One way to become more mindful of the choice-consequence connection is to imagine that you have posted a sentry at the gateway of your mind for the purpose of discerning which choice will be allowed to pass through the gate and released into the outer world. Over the doors of that gate a question is inscribed: *'Helpful or Hurtful?'* The sentry is there to alert you to the fact that each choice you make will be helpful or hurtful to you…and ultimately to the world around you."

Dan's lips tighten in a grim smile. "I must have given my sentry the day off yesterday." He slaps his knee in frustration. "I had *just* finished telling you that I was going to do better with Kwan, and I turned right around and lost my temper again!"

"You have been forgetting your training, my friend," Sifu says in his kindly way. "We've encountered men like this in the ring, who will taunt you or intentionally foul in order to cause you to lose your temper and forget your plan. Kwan clearly desires to keep people off guard, and

I'm afraid he has enjoyed great success in that regard with you."

Dan shakes his head, still angry with himself.

"Dan, you had just been hit with some terribly upsetting news, and you wanted to hit back. Was it a poor choice? Yes, and I am pleased that you recognize it as such. The consequence of your choice is that your relationship with Kwan is more strained than ever. Did you go to his office for your morning meeting?"

Again, Dan shakes his head, shame-faced.

Sifu nods. "Certainly understandable," he says in an encouraging tone. Sifu looks at Dan, wanting to end this coaching session on a positive note. "Dan, are you a perfect person?"

"Heavens, no!"

Sifu nods, grinning at his friend's emphatic reply. "Nor am I. And that is why all trust involves risk, Dan. Placing our trust in imperfect people inherently carries some measure of risk. If all people were perfect, there would be no risk; all people would be totally trustworthy. That searching question, 'Should I trust this person?' would never enter our minds."

Dan is looking at Sifu closely. "Yes, that's true." His tone indicates that he is not yet tracking with Sifu's thoughts.

"Since you and I are imperfect, Dan, and therefore capable of creating mistrust, it is vitally important that we develop an assessment system in order to mitigate as much risk as possible. Do you agree?"

The light of comprehension is beginning to dawn in Dan's eyes. "Definitely."

"The seven keys of trust provide us with that system, Dan. We use them to make a conscious assessment of others, but even more importantly, as I've said, to assess ourselves! Are we building bridges of trust with others? Or are we—perhaps quite unconsciously—creating feelings of mistrust in others?"

Dan winces and looks down at the floor. "When I evaluate myself by the seven keys, I need look no further than to the one we discussed yesterday with Ray Aschenbach. Would John Kwan see me as a confident man? If I was confident, I wouldn't be in his office shouting. As long as I fail to show confidence, he will never find reason to trust me...or to listen to what I say."

"As long as he does not see that confidence," Sifu says softly.

Dan looks up at the Grandmaster, and there is a new certainty in his eyes. "I'm not giving up, Sifu," Dan says in a low voice. "I've made some dreadful mistakes, but I'm going to keep trying."

"That's what I hoped you would say!" Sifu exclaims. "Dan, Thoreau said that many people are mired in lives of quiet desperation. One reason why is because they have not learned to view everything that occurs as a life lesson. These lessons are often mysteriously disguised as painful ones, but these painful experiences are *gifts*, Dan, which teach us how to live our lives exceptionally well. If we can learn to accept heartache and suffering as rich lessons, they provide us with some of life's greatest growth opportunities."

"I must confess, Sifu, I've never pictured John Kwan as being like a present under the Christmas tree," Dan says drily.

Sifu chuckles. "All of life, that which we perceive to be good *and* what we might call 'bad,' offers a host of wonderful lessons from which we can learn to live exceptionally well. If we are to achieve the greatest moral good in our lives, we must be faithful to absorb these life lessons."

"I want to learn, Sifu," Dan says firmly. "I want to grow."

Sifu rewards Dan with his brightest smile. "That makes this an excellent day for you to meet Keith Guller. He is a fine man with a generous heart, and he will take us deeper into a very important key to trust: Caring."

CHAPTER 18

"Caring Is Contagious"

Keith Guller of Essex Industries

"FROM A LEADERSHIP STANDPOINT, CARING is integral to establishing trust." Keith Guller speaks slowly, as if considering each idea before he articulates it. "You must be truly sincere in what you say to people, and then you listen with an equal measure of caring to someone else's thoughts. That's how you serve people and that's how you establish trust."

Dan looks up from his iPad at the Skype camera mounted on his computer monitor. As often as he uses Skype, he still has to fight the impulse to look at the computer screen in an effort to make eye contact with the other person. "That's interesting, Keith. I ask you about the importance of caring and you go straight to listening."

Essex Industries is headquartered in St. Louis, Missouri. Dan and Sifu are seated close together so that Keith can see them both on the Skype camera. Even through a tiny camera mounted nearly 1,200 miles away, the cheerful good humor and genuine kindness that Dan will discover are so much a part of Keith's personality are clearly visible. Dan is already beginning to understand why Sifu selected this man to explain Caring.

Keith gives Dan a big, boyish grin. "Perhaps that's because proactive listening is a skill I still need to develop! And I want to improve at it because it really is such a significant attribute. Someone once told me, 'You're not the genius, Keith; the genius is in the room.' I try to remember that, and

I listen and learn on a daily basis. It's such a significant element to establishing trust! When you demonstrate to others by your active listening that you truly value their opinions and that you will consider their knowledge and experience and ideas, that's a strong indication that you really care."

"So you'd say that active listening is one of the best ways to demonstrate caring?" Dan asks.

Keith thinks for a moment, his right hand absently rubbing his beard. "I'd say that listening is more of an *outcome* of genuine caring. So much more is conveyed in a conversation when the other person can see and sense that you really do care about what they think and how they feel. That's when people will open up and be candid in their comments."

"Keith, may I push back at you for a moment?" Dan asks.

Keith grins. "Of course!"

"I've met people who will say things like, 'I'm not here to make friends; I'm here to do a job.' One executive told me that he doesn't build relationships with Purpose Partners because he may have to fire them some day! I think someone like that would ask, 'I demonstrate the integrity of solid character; I am competent and communicate confidence that I can perform in excellence; isn't that enough? Why does Caring matter if a leader has mastered these first three keys of trust?' How would you answer that?"

Keith nods. "When a leader demonstrates that he or she genuinely cares about the people in the organization, each Purpose Partner is motivated to excel and to make significant contributions. They reach for their highest and their best because they genuinely *want* to. I heard it said that people will work for a leader they fear; they'll work hard for a leader they respect; but they'll run through fire for a leader who loves them."

"That is *very* well said, Keith," Sifu murmurs.

"Thank you, Sifu. And the benefits don't stop there. As important as it is to get the most from your Purpose Partners, you're also getting leaders who are operating at their highest and best. You want a leader who is committed to process excellence, yes, but you also want that person to be committed to interpersonal excellence. Sifu, you introduced me to the concept of an organization that is high-tech *and* high-touch. That's what we're aiming for at Essex."

Keith's green eyes are warm and thoughtful. "I am convinced that when leaders demonstrate that they genuinely care and actively engage with others and reach out for their opinions, you have the best chance of developing operational excellence. Frankly, I don't believe there *is* such a thing as true operational excellence divorced from interpersonal excellence.

"Dan, you're in retail and I'm in manufacturing, but we would agree that if we're going to lead our markets, our companies must be marked by collaboration and innovation, with Purpose Partners actively collaborating to create products and processes that set us apart from our competitors. Right?"

"Absolutely right!" Dan agrees. His mood is brightening as he engages with Keith. "Years ago, Sifu promised to teach me how to make our company 'the purple tile on the gray wall.' It's the synergy you're talking about, Keith, which creates that breakthrough environment."

Keith nods vigorously. "And in that breakthrough environment you see two or three people having a conversation, and everyone is being respectful to each other as they state an opinion, everyone actively listens, and each person is allowed to speak without interruptions. Then you see a multiplicity of innovative ideas being generated.

"Covey used to say things like, 'When you can't see my point here, put my glasses on.' He was saying that others can and will interpret the same set of facts quite differently than I do…and their interpretation may very well expand my understanding—if I'll listen! We lose the benefits of the other individual if we don't demonstrate that we care by genuinely considering their perspective. We have to show that we *want* to put their glasses on!"

Dan is nodding and typing notes on the iPad. He looks up at the Skype camera again. "Keith, Sifu told me that talking with you was going to be one of the most important conversations I would have." He glances at his mentor and smiles. "As usual, he was right! So I'm sure you'd say that the caring of your leaders at Essex is important to your overall success?"

Sifu leans back in his chair, smiling delightedly. He has seen Dan warming to this subject and realizes that this conversation is a tremendous antidote for Dan's dreadful day yesterday.

"Important?" Keith asks rhetorically. "It is *imperative* that leaders model caring and encouragement if we want our Purpose Partners to believe they are significant contributors to our company. Every man, woman, and child needs to know that who they are and what they do has meaning and significance. As a leader, I *must* communicate that I care about you as a human being if I hope to inspire you to your highest and best.

"I am convinced that if you demonstrate to people that you truly care about them as individuals, not just about their output, they'll take pride in what they do and respect the importance of it. We work with the aerospace industry, Dan, and with the military, first responders, and hospital and medical technology. Our vision is to continue to manufacture products that enhance and protect lives."

Dan looks up at Keith on the monitor. "So getting your Purpose Partners to buy into the importance of what they do isn't too much of a challenge?"

Keith smiles. "We recently posted a video on our website of a firefighter who would have died in a burning building if not for our Last Chance Rescue Filter. And that's just one of hundreds of products we manufacture. We make seventy-seven different control grips for military and passenger jets and helicopters. Some of these grips have more than a dozen different functions for a pilot to operate from that one grip, so you can imagine how intricate the wiring is and how great the need for exacting quality control. We manufacture flame arrestors that are a standard safety feature on all Boeing commercial aircraft. Our Purpose Partners are engaged in engineering and manufacturing highly specialized products that *must* not fail, and I'm so proud of how they do that and how they embrace the responsibility for quality control.

"They *care* about what they do, and you see that our Purpose Partners also care for the next individual in the process; everything they do is done as carefully as if *they* had to take the next step in the process. If there's even one tiny error in a blueprint, or a mistake by an assembler or a machinist, somewhere down the line it impacts everyone and we have to go back to Step One and start all over."

Dan is impressed. "Keith, I didn't realize how involved your processes are!"

"That's why caring is so important, Dan. Those processes, as complicated as many of them are, can also be mind-numbingly repetitive. So that caring has *got* to exist within our Purpose Partners. Sifu says, 'You can't impart what you don't possess.' They have to know that they are important and valued, as people and as professionals, and that others are relying on them so they won't just let something pass on the line.

"Dan, if you get a chance to come to St. Louis and tour our facilities, you'll see that everyone expresses that caring. They take their work seriously. They can tell you where their part is going and how it fits into the overall manufacturing process. They'll tell you how their job supports our vision for creating engineered products that enhance and protect lives. We don't have people just showing up to pick up a paycheck; they feel that sense of significance and importance about what they do. But that only happens when they feel like their leaders care about them as *people*. Sifu, you've said it so well: business leaders need to see human beings, not merely human doings."

Sifu smiles his gentle smile. "My friend, you honor me by recalling so much of what we have discussed and putting it into practice."

"Sifu, I've put People First into practice because it's true and because it works! It brings out the best in people! And this component of caring is central to the People First philosophy. If our leaders will take ownership of caring for our Purpose Partners and let them know that who they are and what they do has meaning and significance, then those Purpose Partners will take ownership of the processes and products that they touch."

Sifu leans toward the camera again. "Keith, I would like to ask a question. Dan is currently working with a man who would probably say that this concept of caring is foolishness. 'I am here to run a business and turn a profit,' he might say. 'I am not here to hold hands and sing pretty songs.' How would you respond?"

Keith's face splits into a wide smile. "I'd probably sing, 'Come on people now, smile on your brother, everybody get together, try to love one another, right now.' I'd try to get him to lighten up! Seriously, I meet so many people who have this notion that creating a caring environment is fluffy, feel-good stuff that has nothing to do with operational excellence. It's a false dichotomy! It's just as easy to run a business that cares for people as it is to run a business that doesn't. In fact, it's much *easier* to run a caring company, because when your Purpose Partners know you care, they make an almost unconscious effort to excel."

Sifu nods his agreement. "I introduced this People First philosophy to a man who was working to create unity among four different locations in his organization. I spent a great deal of time with him explaining the principles and encouraging him to employ them at his company. After we'd had several meetings, our schedules kept us apart for a few months. Frankly, I wasn't sure if he would adopt People First or not."

"About three months later, he called and said, 'When you first explained People First, you could probably tell I was resistant. I knew that shaping a winning culture is important, but I thought we needed to improve our systems and processes first.' He said, 'I thought People First was like putting icing on a cake that hadn't been baked yet. But because of my respect for you, Sifu, I committed to giving People First an honest try for three months. And as I have practiced these principles, I've seen our Purpose Partners engage in the collaborative conversations that allow them to make those improvements to our systems and processes. Sifu, People First *is* the cake! We have a healthier, happier culture, and we have also begun to upgrade our systems and processes.'

"This man has used the People First philosophy to obtain that winning balance of operational and interpersonal excellence that you spoke of, Keith."

Keith's bright smile flashes again. "And there's the answer to someone who objects that People First is just touchy-feely fluff, Sifu. You can't just set numbers, throw them at people, and then crack the whip and shout, 'We've got to hit these numbers!' There must be mutual trust, respect, and understanding."

Keith leans closer to the camera. "There are two points in the manufacturing process where you're most likely to see errors: at the beginning of a job and then again at the end of it. If there is a lack of caring at the outset—if Purpose Partners are not engaged—they're more likely to make a mistake at the beginning. Mentally, they're strolling out of the starting blocks rather than sprinting. And then as they continue on through the process, particularly with a repetitive function, their attention may wander. They just want to finish the job, rather than staying focused, and that's the second point where errors occur.

"So we emphasize the importance of the individual—that each man and woman is critical to our success. And they are responding! They're engaged. If someone sees a piece lying on the floor, they pick it up. If someone spots a mistake or recognizes that a dimension is off, they care enough to step in and help put it right. And it all starts with building caring, trust-based relationships with our Purpose Partners and our customers. Caring energizes and focuses individuals."

"You're talking my language, Keith!" Dan says cheerfully; then he looks apologetically at Sifu. "I guess I should say we're both talking Sifu's language."

Sifu smiles at Dan. "It is not *my* language; you are both speaking the language of People First and you speak it very well!"

"Let me ask you this, Keith," Dan says curiously. "Is caring *caught* or *taught*? If a young manager came to you and said, 'I want to get better at caring,' what would you say?"

Once again that playful grin flashes on the screen as Keith replies, "I'd say go into a restaurant and ask for a chicken and an egg and see which comes first! Whether caring is caught or taught, it certainly is contagious, however you experience it. There *are* concrete things I do to build that sense of caring. I walk around our facilities and sit down during the breaks and ask people how things are going and what I can do to help make their work more productive or more joyful. I ask questions and listen.

"I talk to our leaders and managers about how we can demonstrate caring by asking our Purpose Partners, 'How can I help you in what you're doing?' It's all too easy to lapse into the old questions, like, 'Why didn't you do it *this* way?! What *took* you so long?!' Of course, there are times when we must speak the truth in love about opportunities for improvement, but we can be caring and respectful in those conversations and still directly address those issues.

"So, Dan, I can't say I'm *teaching* it, but I do try to make caring contagious in our organization. If I am transparent, it's a more subtle 'taught' than sitting down with someone and saying, 'Here's your caring lesson for today.' I'll tell people, 'I want to get better at caring about what you need,' and then listen to them speak about their perceived needs. Then I can encourage them to go out and listen to *their* Purpose Partners and communicate that they sincerely care about what *they* have to say."

Sifu leans toward the camera. "Keith, will you share some success stories about how the caring of leaders at Essex Industries has contributed to the success of your organization?"

Keith smiles and nods. "Not long after we began to implement People First at Essex, our Chief Operating Officer sent an email to one of our Purpose Partners, telling her that the work she does is very important, and why, and he finished the message by saying 'I am proud of you.' Well, this woman was absolutely energized. She called several of her Purpose Partners over to see the email.

'Look at this!' she'd say. 'Our COO took time to send this to *me*!' And then she told her supervisor, 'I'm going to start doing this too. I want to make other people feel as good as I feel today.'"

"My goodness, Keith," Sifu says warmly, "what a tremendous story! And it underscores the fact caring is contagious!"

"Yes," Keith agrees, "caring is contagious and I believe there's a snowball effect. There's a real sense of ownership growing here. I've seen customers who are touring the plant ask one of our Purpose Partners a question about their job.

That person will turn around and proudly explain to the customer what he or she is doing and then ask, 'Tell me a little bit about what *you* do and how this product is being used.' You see these things happen throughout our organization, in all of our locations. That's an expression of caring that exists here, and I like to think that's a reflection of caring leadership."

Keith grins at Sifu and Dan. "I'm so proud of the folks here at Essex, I could go on for hours!"

Sifu smiles back at Keith's image on the computer screen. "I would submit that the reason these examples of caring abound at Essex is because your Purpose Partners know that you care for them."

Thinking of John Kwan, Dan asks, "Keith, have you ever known a business leader whose effectiveness was diminished because he or she didn't care about people?"

Keith nods sadly. "Oh, sure! I wish I could tell you that we have a 100 percent success rate on hiring and promotions, but I'd be lying. I've seen men and women who had the operational excellence part down pat, but the interpersonal aspect was utterly lacking. People lose trust for an individual like that. The passion they would otherwise have for their jobs is subdued or disappears altogether."

Passion is subdued or disappears, Dan thinks. *Sounds like the atmosphere at Prestigious Products.*

He shakes his head, as if to clear the negative thought. "Keith, if you could only tell a business leader three things about how to build and maintain an atmosphere of caring within his or her organization, what would you suggest?"

Keith looks thoughtfully down at his desk for a moment and then looks back up at Dan. "Well, we already talked about this, but I'm convinced that you demonstrate caring by *asking questions and listening* to your Purpose Partners as they tell you what you can do to help them in their daily activities. I'd emphasize the phrase *listening with care*; it's not perfunctory listening, like you can't wait for the conversation to end. You really could lump the word *respect* right in with listening, because I know no better way to demonstrate respect for someone than to actively *listen* to what that person has to say. As you listen, you learn, you grow in your understanding, and you build bridges of trust and respect. And there you have it!" Keith grins.

Dan looks intently at Keith's image on the screen. "Keith, you've talked about asking people how you can help them several times. Is that how you would describe the phrase 'servant leadership'?"

Keith nods emphatically. All traces of humor have vanished from his green eyes. He speaks very slowly, clearly trying to communicate the heart behind his words. "Servant leadership is my own personal mission and vision. I believe I have the *honor* to be in the role of helping others, and the more that I can do of that, whether that's with my family, my Purpose Partners, or the community, the better! Giving to others and serving them is the most important thing I can do—helping them develop individually and developing the team here at Essex. I certainly hope I demonstrate that caring to my children and to my family. It's a blessing and a privilege, Dan, to be in the position where I can be of benefit to other people. I've put this down in writing, because I want to keep it front and center in my mind at all times."

Dan is no longer typing on his iPad. His whole concentration is directed at the man on the screen in front of him. "Serving others is more important than the business?" he asks softly. There is only a hint of a question in his voice. "More important than the bottom line. You believe that serving others is the most important thing you can do?"

Keith looks back at Dan, nodding slowly. "I believe that's why I'm on this earth."

CHAPTER 19

Family History

THE FOLLOWING DAY, DAN WALKS into John Kwan's office for their morning meeting. This will be their first interaction since Dan's explosion in John Kwan's office. And if that wasn't enough to cause Dan discomfort, the news he will deliver is.

As usual, John Kwan is seated at his computer. He glances up at Dan and looks back at his monitor.

"Mr. Burton, I have nothing to discuss with you today."

"Good morning, Mr. Kwan," Dan says, trying his best to sound professionally courteous. "I thought you might feel that way after my behavior two days ago. I feel very badly about that. But there is an issue I must to bring to your attention."

Kwan's eyes snap back to Dan. "An issue," he says flatly. "I sincerely hope this has nothing to do with Claudia Barnes or her family."

"No," Dan says, "this concerns the bottom line. We've gotten our first customer satisfaction scores since our recent layoffs. You'll want to see them."

Kwan looks back to the monitor. "Mrs. Lundgren sends me that information."

"You've seen the scores?" Dan asks.

"Yes."

"Store traffic is down," Dan says evenly, "gross sales are down, and our satisfaction scores are down significantly."

"When our inordinately long severance requirements are fulfilled," here Kwan gives Dan a cold look "we will see a profitable correction."

"Mr. Kwan," Dan begins earnestly, "I'm familiar with the equation. As you know, we had two rounds of store closings and layoffs before your group purchased us. And we did see a return to profitability. But unless we devise an entirely new marketing strategy, I see us going into a doom loop."

Kwan does not look up. "Mr. Burton, I told you before that I have no interest in what you think."

Dan can feel anger rising, but he keeps his voice calm and level. He is beginning to recognize Kwan's rudeness as a tactic designed to deflect conversation away from subjects he wishes to avoid. Dan has prepared for just this kind of response. "Yes, I recall you saying that. I also recall that our agreement about these meetings included you listening politely to what I have to say. Do you no longer intend to honor your end of that agreement?"

Kwan looks at Dan sharply. "When we entered into that agreement, you made no mention of the kind of infantile behavior you exhibited yesterday."

Dan bows his head for a moment, mostly so that Kwan will not see the sudden surge of anger in his eyes. Dan keeps his voice level. "You're right. I was completely out of line, and I can only hope you will forgive me." He looks back up at Kwan. "May I explain my thinking to you?"

"Quickly, please," Kwan says curtly.

"I'm sure you discovered in your preliminary investigation of our firm, Mr. Kwan, that we have never tried to attract the discount shopper. The name of the firm is *Prestigious* Products, as you know."

Kwan rolls his eyes. "This is pointless," he says heavily.

"I'm not finished." Dan takes a breath, wanting to keep himself in complete control. "After both rounds of layoffs prior to the buyout, we saw diminished market share and gross sales. Yes, those moves brought us back into the black, but at no time did market share return to prerecession levels. And as you dig into the numbers, our inventory turn has slipped and we've been forced to keep a close eye on our stock-to-sales ratios."

"Again, Mrs. Lundgren provides me with the same reports," Kwan says impatiently. "I have no desire to review them with you."

Unruffled, Dan continues, "Here's what's so disturbing: when you look at independent sources, you see that after the early shock of the recession wore off, the upscale buyers we're trying to attract resumed their prerecession buying behaviors. They may actually have increased their spending slightly. But they're no longer spending with Prestigious Products, Mr. Kwan. They're going elsewhere."

Kwan looks at Dan through narrowed eyes. *That got his attention,* Dan thinks grimly. His voice softens slightly. "We tested announcing sales and advertising lower prices a few years ago. And our numbers dipped again. Our customers perceived discount pricing as signaling a drop in quality."

"Get to the point," Kwan says, but there is a note of concern in his voice.

"I believe we have lost the trust of our customers. Our unique selling proposition has always been customer service and satisfaction. After our second round of layoffs, we communicated a recommitment to customer service. *That's* what moved our needle in a positive direction. Our customers don't come to Prestigious Products to save money, nor even to buy the highest quality merchandise, although quality is certainly part of it. They came here because no other retailer treated them with the care that we did. We made our margins on building relationships, Mr. Kwan, both our internal and external relationships. The layoffs and store closings have created doubt and mistrust with all of our constituents."

"I am here to get results, not build relationships," Kwan says inexorably.

"I understand. Your mandate from your employers is to create sustainable profitability. So if you see that a particular course of action is injurious to that outcome, you will want to make immediate adjustments. A mistake is only a mistake if one persists in it. I submit that we have reached the point of diminished returns. We simply don't have enough customer service personnel to provide the level of service our customers expect."

Kwan is staring at Dan with those cold, opaque eyes. Dan keeps his tone level and businesslike.

"Mr. Kwan, I've been doing some research on building trust. You mentioned your respect for the Grandmaster, Sifu Li. He's been helping me with that project."

Kwan's eyes flare. "You are not to be sharing sensitive information about our business with anyone, Mr. Burton, I'm sure you're aware of how serious such an action would be."

Dan waves an impatient hand. "I've shared nothing with Sifu that he hasn't read in the local newspaper. Sifu has been teaching me how individuals and organizations build trust. Sifu defines trust as an unwavering belief in the character, competence, confidence, caring, communication, consistency, and commitment of another person. He calls these the seven keys of trust. And we have violated every one of these keys in the eyes of both our internal and our external customers.

"Let's start with character. For years, we told our staff that Prestigious Products' most important asset was people; then we cut 30 percent of our staff. Now we've cut an additional 15 percent. We've left them confused, frightened, and resentful. Those moves, in their eyes, have made them question our competence and our confidence. As for our caring…"

"Pah!" Kwan exhales in frustration. "I suspected you were going to bring in this absurd People First thinking again! *That* is a mistake we will *not* persist in!"

"Mr. Kwan, I'm talking about unmet customer expectations being the direct cause of diminishing results that should concern you. If you'd let me explain the People First philosophy…"

"I need no explanation," Kwan interrupts sharply. "I've seen firsthand what a wretched notion this philosophy is!" He looks up at Dan, his eyes burning with contempt. "This one time, Mr. Burton,

I will share details of my personal life. And then we will speak no more of this People First foolishness!"

It is the first time Dan has seen John Kwan display any emotion, and he keeps his face carefully expressionless. "Let me tell you the history of my family name. In the first century there was a great hero named Guan Yu. He came to be known as General Kwan. He was wise and righteous and utterly fearless. Through the centuries the family of Kwan was known for bravery and possessing spiritual strength for the right and for justice. It was in this tradition that I was raised."

Kwan's eyes are burning. "I know a great deal more about this philosophy than you do, Mr. Burton. I watched it lived out from childhood."

Dan peers at Kwan, genuinely puzzled. "Then why…"

"Because the end result is poverty, not prosperity!" Kwan says sharply. "My father preached this drivel to our family every day, saying things like, 'Let no one seek his own but each one the other's well-being.' This is one of my earliest memories."

Dan's eyes widen with surprise. It is the very same phrase that Sifu used with him at their first meeting. "The Grandmaster…" he begins.

"I don't want to *hear* about the Grandmaster," Kwan interrupts harshly. "My father had a great name with our family and with our community, but this constant investment, as he called it, into other people only led us into poverty. *That* was the outcome of your philosophy, Mr. Burton.

"My father did everything he could to help me attend the university. He believed that an education would protect me from the poverty he experienced— the poverty he brought upon himself! I pursued dual majors in business and philosophy. My father kept working three jobs and urged me to pursue more learning, so I earned doctorates in both disciplines.

"After graduation, I taught philosophy at the university, making very little money, and things were deteriorating at home. The only difference between me and my father was that I was an *educated* poor man." The unpleasant sarcasm is thick in Kwan's voice.

"My father was ill, my younger brother needed higher education, and my mother had no marketable skills. I was recruited for the Chang Tao Group. They offered to teach me how to do business in a way that would give me a freedom I had never known. They promised a salary which would solve all my family's problems…"

Kwan's voice suddenly trails off and his eyes look past Dan into some distant memory. When he resumes speaking, his voice is quieter, but the smoldering anger has not subsided. "My father refused my offers of assistance. He spoke some piffle about a good name being more important than riches." Kwan swings back to Dan, his eyes blazing. "His body had utterly failed; he couldn't even get out of bed! And yet he was still prattling about his precious philosophy. He said the practices Chang Tao was teaching me stood against everything our family name represents."

Kwan's eyes turn inward. "The last time we spoke, we quarreled. I told my father that he needn't worry, that I would take care of my mother and brother.

"'I'm not pleased, son,' he said, 'you have abandoned everything I taught you.'"

"I said, 'Father, you are going to die, but I will look after your wife and son. There's no more poverty. I am a success, Father!' And he raised his head off the bed and whispered, 'Yes, but at what cost? You have fame, but you no longer have the family name.'"

"He died the next day." Kwan's voice is flat, dismissive. "I made sure that my mother and brother were well looked after, and moved to the United States. I have had no contact with them since that time."

Dan has been holding himself very still, watching Kwan's face. He almost recoils in surprise when Kwan looks back up at him, his eyes filled with hatred.

"Now, after all these years, I walk into your company and see these same failed principles plastered all over the walls!

"General Kwan was a conqueror. He was a winner. So am I! The Chang Tao Group introduced me to something real, which is how to make money. I learned that life is all about making a profit. I make money for my employers and they reward me handsomely. I make money for our shareholders and our stock continues to rise. This company, Prestigious Products, exists to make a profit—nothing more, nothing less. If our acquisitions are unprofitable, we sell them off. If Prestigious Products' metrics don't add up, we will sell it and acquire something that will earn us a handsome return. And right now, Mr. Burton, the metrics at your company don't add up."

Kwan's lips curl in a cruel sneer. "This philosophy you are contending for is a philosophy of weakness. It brought this organization to the brink of ruin, just as it did my father! He could not care for his family and he hated the fact that I could."

Dan is looking at Kwan closely, as if he is seeing him for the first time. "Mr. Kwan…"

"Enough!" Kwan makes a slashing gesture with his right hand. "I will not waste time speaking to you about philosophical theories or business practice. I had all those conversations when I was a young man, and it was a waste of time. I have just wasted time talking to you about my past. From this point forward, we will only discuss how you plan to earn money for this company. The clock is ticking, Mr. Burton. And know that any conversation you attempt to initiate about philosophy or People First will not be welcomed and will not be tolerated!"

Kwan spins back to his computer. "I will not be available to meet tomorrow. That is all."

Dan stands looking at Kwan for a long moment. *I suppose I should be angry,* Dan muses, *but really I can only feel sorry. No wonder Kwan is so unpleasant! He is harboring too much hurt to feel kindness or compassion.* Dan walks to the door of Kwan's office. He pauses at the threshold and turns to look at Kwan. "I'm sorry about your father," Dan says softly. "That must have been a very difficult time."

"I said *no more talk!*" Kwan's voice is shrill.

Dan nods sadly. "Good day, Mr. Kwan."

CHAPTER 20

If You Think You've Communicated, You Probably Haven't

Noel Fogarty, Former Vice President of Operations for Boston Scientific

"ONE OF THE THINGS I love about living in Miami, Dan, is that there are so many interesting people who live here."

Dan chuckles. Today is Dan's day to drive, and he is navigating the stifling congestion of rush hour traffic in the city's downtown area. "Sifu, one of the many things that I love about you is that you always find the ray of sunshine. I was just thinking how I *hate* the traffic here!" As if on cue, the traffic light ahead turns red, and Dan brings the car to a stop. He glares at Sifu. "It takes ten minutes to drive three blocks!"

Sifu smiles his gentle smile. "Dan, I am confident that after talking with Noel Fogarty, you will say it was worth every moment of discomfort."

Dan is glad to be diverted from their stop-and-go progress. "Would you refresh me, Sifu? Why did you select Noel as an exemplar of communication?"

Sifu nods. "Noel is a remarkable man and an outstanding leader. For years, he served as the vice president of Operations in Miami for Boston Scientific, which is an eight billion dollar-a-year international organization. He is working elsewhere now, but the work he did when he was there is truly exemplary."

The light changes, but the traffic does not move. Dan taps the steering wheel and frowns at Sifu.

"Is the traffic this bad in China?"

Sifu nods emphatically. "You would be most unhappy in Shanghai, my friend! It is the largest city in China. It holds twenty-two million people, more than live in the entire state of Florida!" Sifu looks at Dan gravely. "I shudder to think of going for a drive with you there."

Dan laughs aloud. "OK, OK. I'll try to relax." Sifu shakes his head in mock disbelief. When Dan has composed himself, he asks curiously, "So how does Noel build trust capital through communication?"

"I know of no one who is better at communication than Noel Fogarty. And that is intriguing, because Noel was not tapped for an executive leadership position primarily because his people skills, but because of his exceptional ability as an engineer. Of all the people I know with acumen for statistical process control and understanding Six Sigma and LEAN management principles, Noel stands out as superior. And that is why he is such a remarkable leader. He has tremendous balance in his knowledge and practice of the best business systems *and* the best human systems, perhaps the best I have ever seen. He honors and values people, and I expect he will tell us that he could get nothing done if it is not done through people."

The traffic has finally thinned, and Dan is guiding the car smoothly toward their destination. "He *does* sound like someone I'd like to meet." Dan glances over at Sifu. "The way my life is going, perhaps I should ask him if he needs a vice president."

Sifu grins playfully. "If you do, you would encounter this traffic every day!" He is serious again. "You would enjoy working with Noel, Dan, as he would enjoy working with you. You both understand that all Purpose Partners need to know that who they are and what they do has meaning and significance. The only way to create that sense of inclusion is to communicate. You exponentially increase your trust quotient by keeping people informed. Leaders who do not communicate increase tension and decrease trust."

"That's what John Kwan has done at our company," Dan says sadly. "There is *no* trust and a great deal of tension!"

"Yes, and what an insightful conversation you had yesterday, my friend! The father-son relationship is a significant aspect of Asian culture, particularly pride in the family name. For a father to tell his son that he has brought shame on the family name...for those to be the father's last words to his son...you can be certain that Kwan frequently replays those words in his mind. So his every action is driven by a need to be Kwan the Conqueror. He would guard against any show of kindness; he would see that as abdicating principle.

"When you think of it, Dan, Kwan is a highly principled man, but his principle is financial success at any price, and that principle creates enormous tension in an organization."

Dan shakes his head. "Just a few years ago, I was confident that the vast majority of our Purpose Partners were very positive and engaged. Today? People are frightened and confused and resentful."

Sifu nods. "And that is why communication is so important. It is one of the most effective means for overcoming disengagement and creating the People First Effect.

"I have been so proud of you, Dan, over the past ten years, as I've seen how intentional you have become in your use of language. Your words are intended to give others strength and courage and hope."

Dan swings the car into the parking lot of the office complex where Noel Fogarty works. Sifu looks at Dan thoughtfully. "If I was taking Noel to meet seven leadership exemplars, Dan, I would have selected you as the model for communication."

Dan recoils slightly and actually blushes. "Sifu, it's kind of you to say that, but I still have so much to learn."

"Yes, you are still under construction." Sifu says kindly. "As am I. And as is Noel. Come, my friend, I believe you will enjoy yourself!"

Dan's immediate impression of Noel Fogarty is that the concept of putting People First must have resonated with Noel the moment he first heard it. His bright eyes, wide smile, and enthusiastic tone clearly convey that he genuinely likes people. Dan recalls what Sifu said about Noel's exceptional ability as an engineer; if he had met Noel for the first time at a social function, Dan might have guessed from his engaging nature that Noel was a top sales rep.

Noel does not wait until they are seated in his office; he begins to engage with Dan from the moment he greets Dan and Sifu in the lobby. "Sifu told me that you wanted to talk with me about communication. I'm happy to help any way I can, but from what I've heard about you, Dan, I should be asking you for pointers."

"I'm afraid Sifu may have overstated my abilities," Dan says drily.

"It wasn't Sifu who first spoke about you, Dan. I worked with a former Purpose Partner of yours: George Blake."

"Oh?" Dan is pleasantly surprised. "George was one of those layoffs that makes you sick. Great guy, great head for marketing, tremendous copywriter. Losing him was a real loss for our company. We've…gone through some tough times in the last few years."

Noel nods solemnly and grips Dan's arm in a reassuring gesture. "As did many throughout the country, Dan," he says softly. Noel's tone brightens. "George and I were having lunch one day, and he was just raving about Dan Burton and what he'd done at Prestigious Products to introduce something called People First." Noel's blue eyes begin to twinkle. "As soon as I heard 'People First,' I realized you and I had a mutual friend." Noel looks over at Sifu.

Dan turns to Sifu with a broad grin. "You really *are* starting a movement!"

Sifu smiles happily at Noel and Dan. "With students like you two, I expect that creating the People First Effect will soon be just that: a worldwide movement."

The three men arrive at an unpretentious office. Noel gestures toward a small table at one end of his office, and the three men take their seats together. Dan recognizes that Noel made sure that his desk would not act as a barrier between them. Noel is studying Dan with bright, intelligent eyes.

"Tell me how I can help you," he invites.

"I'm curious about your accent," Dan says. "Are you from Ireland?"

"I am," Noel replies, with a nice note of pride. "I was based in Ireland for six years, running Boston Scientific's Galway plant, the largest manufacturing plant in their network, employing about 3,500 people. Galway was a fine plant when I arrived there, but they were going through significant changes. We had grown through a number of acquisitions, and we were very busy, but it had been made clear to senior leadership that from now on, our growth would not come from acquisitions, but through developing our own technology. That involved a significant shift in our operations. The change process required an operational plan, but also a strong communication strategy to create buy-in for the new program."

"Noel, we would love to hear more about that strategy," Sifu suggests.

Noel leans back and looks up at the ceiling, recalling the past. "There were a number of very talented people at Galway who weren't working to their fullest potential." He looks back at Dan. "The size of the plant presented its own challenges. We had four shifts running round the clock. Everyone knows *you*, but you don't know all thirty-five hundred people. In addition, we were ramping up to launch a new product. It was a huge commercial success, and communication was essential for creating that success."

Dan's professional curiosity is aroused. His interest, coupled with Noel's warm, easy manner, has caused him to completely forget that he just met this man five minutes ago. "Communication is *huge* when you're taking an organization through change. What did you do?"

Like Dan, Noel is energized by this subject. He leans closer to Dan. "You need to put in a planned structure of communication in an organization of that size, especially with the amount of change we were trying to drive at the time. And, of course, informal communication is a critical component also. Eventually, we had great success, and the system we put in place was eventually used as the pattern for all of Boston Scientific."

Dan gives a low whistle. "That must have been one heck of a system you put in place!"

Noel looks distinctly uncomfortable. Clearly, he does not wish to call attention to his own accomplishments. "I had a lot of help from a lot of Purpose Partners; my HR director was great, and we hired two communication specialists who were a tremendous help." Now that he has redirected the focus of the conversation from himself, Noel is relaxed and happy again. The two men have connected so completely that they seem to have completely forgotten Sifu, who is sitting quietly, watching his two prized students with pleasure.

Noel's eyes are narrowed in eager concentration. "Successful organizations are very clear about what they want to accomplish, what the outcomes will be, and how they're going to do it.

Communication is the glue that holds all that together. You get people to buy in by repeating the message and sharing the progress you're making along the way."

Both Dan and Sifu smile and nod in emphatic agreement.

"I'm talking about the internal stakeholders primarily," Noel continues. "With thirty-five hundred employees, you're like the mayor of a small town. Internal communication is essential. And then there's a whole different kind of communication with shareholders and the public."

"Tell us what you have learned about communicating to your Purpose Partners internally," Sifu suggests.

Noel begins to speak steadily. There is no hesitation in his speech; it is obvious that he has given this subject a great deal of thought. "Internal communication is tightly coupled to success in business; you need people who are engaged and willing to give more than just the hours they're paid for. Without that, you won't get far.

"Communication is a strong way to build that discretionary effort. Boston Scientific has a great, compelling vision. It was very easy for me and the other twenty-five thousand people employed by the company to engage with the overall mission, which is to help save lives and improve the quality of life for patients."

Noel gives Dan and Sifu a wide smile. "There aren't many industries where you have as valuable a proposition as we did. But you had to develop a broader strategy and actions around this idea of 'how are we going to make patients' lives better' every day?"

Dan is fascinated. "So even with a compelling vision like Boston Scientific's, you *still* worked to broaden the borders of the job with meaning?"

Noel gives a laugh filled with enjoyment. He turns to Sifu. "I think our friend Dan is the one who should be doing the talking and I should be listening! It's clear he's spent a great deal of time learning from you, my friend!"

Sifu gives Dan a look that pierces straight to Dan's heart—the look that he had always hoped for but never actually seen in his father's eyes. "Noel, I once introduced Dan as the Grandmaster of the People First philosophy. He has never done anything to change my opinion."

Now it is Dan's turn to gaze uncomfortably down at his hands. Noel cocks his head humorously at Dan and gives him a sympathetic grin. "It's always easier when the praise is being lavished on someone else, isn't it?"

Dan nods humbly. "Noel, I'd really like to hear more about what you did to establish good communication while you worked at Boston Scientific. My company is…struggling in that area."

"Perhaps I should tell you a little more about the company," Noel says in his cheerful brogue.

"Boston Scientific is an eight billion-dollar company with twenty-five thousand employees and locations all over the world, in the United States, Canada, Japan, Ireland, Puerto Rico, Costa Rica—fourteen manufacturing plants in all.

They have sales all over the world; more than half their revenue comes from outside the United States.

"With such a large and diverse group, we had to make a concentrated effort to help all our Purpose Partners make a heart connection with the mission. The vision is also hugely important, of course, and you must clearly communicate it. You can't just stick it up on a poster in the hallway.

"One thing I've learned, Dan, is that *if you think you've communicated, you probably haven't*. You need to multiply your effort by ten or twenty. The sad reality is that in a lot of organizations, people don't appreciate the importance of company-wide communication."

Dan shakes his head ruefully. "*I* was one of those people not so long ago."

"It's so easy to think, 'OK, we've developed a strategy, we've written it down, and we've told them about it.' But that's really only Level One." Noel raps his knuckles on the desk for emphasis. "You *must* continue to communicate what your Purpose Partners are expected to do, what the benefits are for all the different stakeholders, and what the impact will be for them. And you must *sell* them on those benefits if they're going to get behind what you're trying to accomplish."

Dan has activated his iPad and begun to type. He looks up at Noel with deep respect. "This is some of the best teaching on communication I've ever heard! I hope you don't mind me taking notes while you talk. Noel, you should write a book!"

Noel shakes his head, unconvinced. "The funny thing is, Dan, I feel like I'm still learning every day how to be a good communicator. I'm an engineer by trade and by training. I often feel very mechanical and methodical in my communication. It's not something that comes naturally to me at a personal level—to stand in front of a group of people and convince them to believe a certain concept and to behave a certain way. But I'm more convinced than ever that being a good leader and being a good communicator go hand in hand; they are synonymous with one another."

Dan nods thoughtfully. "For years, I had no understanding of the significance of what you're saying. I was just like you described a moment ago." Dan changes his voice to an angry whine, as might be used by a frustrated executive. "I told my direct reports, I sent a memo, and they still don't get it! What's *wrong* with these people?"

Noel grins sympathetically. "Didn't work out so well, did it?"

Dan rolls his eyes humorously to acknowledge the truth of Noel's state-ment. Then he is serious again. "Noel, I'm sure Sifu told you that we're linking this idea of communication to building trust. What are your thoughts about that connection?"

Noel is nodding vigorously before Dan has even finished his question. "The strength of all human relationships boils down to trust happening between two human beings. I don't think that trust happens unless you're sharing your feel-ings at a personal level—sharing more than your words, but also sharing your emotions. There has to be transparency. *That's* how trust is built."

Dan looks intently at Noel. "So it's not just *what* I say, but *how* I say it?"

"That's right," Noel agrees. "Trust doesn't happen just because I like every-thing you're saying all the time. We've all met people we wouldn't trust with a fifty-cent piece who told us all sorts of things we wanted to hear! For real trust to exist, you must believe that the person you're dealing with is genuine. They're not trying to put something over on you or gain some advantage for themselves."

Sifu clears his throat. "Dan and I have been using phrases like *building trust equity* and *creating trust capital.*"

Noel's eyes light with understanding. "That's exactly it, isn't it? Trust isn't a one-time event. You *build* it, just like an investment portfolio. Some leaders find it difficult to create that kind of trust on a one-to-one basis; they don't see it as efficient for dealing with large groups of people. I lean in the opposite direction; I believe that, as a leader—no matter what level you're on—there are a number of people whom you must deal with one-to-one if you're ever going to create that trust equity you speak of." Noel grins at Sifu. "I *like* that phrase!

"But the skill for the leader is to create that trust with a broader group of people," Noel continues.

"You may be great one-on-one, and that's certainly the place to start, but reaching several hundred or even thousands of people can be a tremendous chal-lenge. They don't know you personally and they usually see you in a forum that's a bit artificial. You're on a stage standing over them. It's hard to establish any kind of rapport. But over time, if you're consistent in what you're saying, and you're honest with the feedback you give people in assessing where you're at in the busi-ness, people will come to accept that you're genuine. That builds organizational trust, in precisely the same way trust is built up with an individual. Honesty is essential to communication. When people trust that you're coming from a good place, that you want their best, they respond with discretionary effort."

Sifu has been listening to Noel with just as much intensity as Dan. Now he asks, "Noel, I hear business leaders talk about the 'cascading communication' model. The senior leaders give information to their subordinates, who are tasked with disseminating the message throughout the organization. It seems like that should work reasonably well; after all, most people say that the grapevine is alive and well in their companies. So perhaps you are putting too much emphasis on the role of the leader. How much of a role does leadership actually play in establishing good communication, and how much of it just happens naturally?"

Noel smiles at his friend, knowing that Sifu is testing him. "You might reverse the question, Sifu, and ask, 'How does a leader separate himself or herself from good communication?' I don't think you can be a leader and *not* communicate. Communication is a critical component of building a solid organization—certainly not the *only* element, but critical nonetheless. Cascading communication is good, but you can't completely rely on that. It's like Chinese Whispers, or what some people call the telephone game; after the message is repeated a few times, it is certain to become garbled."

"Indeed." Sifu says approvingly. "Good communication in the executive conference room is not enough."

"Sifu, I believe it's important for the leader to be seen multiple layers down in the organization and in multiple forums. The leader must be out in front of the communication. You can't delegate it completely. Technology helps, and you can send out video clips to reach large groups, but I guess I'm a bit old-fashioned; I think there should be a strong personal component if you want to be most effective.

"At the same time, the sole responsibility can't rest on the leader, particularly in larger organizations like Boston Scientific, which has Purpose Partners located all over the world. You can't help but lose some of the personal aspects of communication under those circumstances. There's a delicate balance; you must make it a big part of your responsibility, but you have to rely on other people in your organization to deliver that message as well. But you mix in some skip-level communication, where you're making sure that you, personally, are talking to various stakeholders in your business."

Dan looks at Noel with undisguised admiration. "Noel, you've given this subject a great deal of thought, haven't you?"

Noel nods his head, acknowledging the compliment, and looks at Sifu. "It was something you said to me years ago, Sifu, that really crystallized it for me.

You told me that whatever I want my customers to feel, my Purpose Partners must feel first. I realized then that if I expect the men and women who work with me to treat our customers as if they are valuable and unique, I must effectively communicate that belief to my Purpose Partners about *themselves* if they are ever to convey that message to anyone else."

Noel's eyes swing back to Dan. "Communication is integral to helping your Purpose Partners engage with the business," he says matter-of-factly.

"And even in the manufacturing setting," Dan persists, "where you worked with a great many people who would never personally engage with a customer… you *still* feel like communication is that vital for sustainable success?"

Noel looks steadily at Dan, nodding his head. "Yes, absolutely. As leaders, we want to build a shared sense of values and culture. That's only going to happen through creating and maintaining solid lines of communication throughout the entire organization."

Dan glances over at Sifu with a jubilant smile. "*Man*, this is good stuff! Noel, can you tell me specifically about what you did to encourage and maintain good communication at Boston Scientific?"

"I'm more than happy to tell you!" Noel replies warmly. "At Galway, one important piece involved sharing what we called our strategic quality plan, which was our vision and strategy for the business. We established a mechanism so that, over a couple of days, I had talked to every Purpose Partner in the plant, all 3,500 employees. We did that four times a year. Now, these were very formal, one-way sessions, with just the leader talking and maybe a few members of the senior leadership team.

"We also assembled a communications team of twenty-five to thirty people who were selected from different levels in the organization, who performed different functions and worked on different shift schedules. These folks would share a lot more detail about change initiatives with their peers and get their feedback. Then they would come back to us and relate how people were responding to the message and share the practical discussions they'd engaged in about why the people they'd met with believed the initiative would or wouldn't work."

Dan is typing as rapidly as if he was listening to Sifu. "So Noel, you believe that if you want to effectively communicate change, you need to get out with the people on the front lines and find out how your stakeholders are buying into that change?"

Noel nods forcefully. "We gave our frontline managers a set of talking points on a weekly basis to share with their teams about what was going on with the company, as well as what was going well, or not going well, in their own departments. They'd talk about their challenges and priorities for the week ahead. And they would *listen*. The feedback is so vitally important!

"And then there's the informal mechanism, where you just walk the line and ask someone how they're doing and what they think is working well and what isn't. Sometimes we'd put ten to fifteen people together and sit them down with coffee and donuts and talk about what's working well in the business and what's not. You get a lot of honest, straight feedback that way, and you're able to discuss ideas for change and discover how well people are bought in.

"It's all about repetition and delivering a consistent message. We set up a communications hallway outside the cafeteria, with widescreen TVs, where we would share various stories. Some showed performance of various aspects of our business, others showed stories of patients who had been helped by our therapy or our treatments. We wrote a monthly newsletter and encouraged our Purpose Partners to contribute to that. One segment of the newsletter would focus on a particular Purpose Partner and what his or her function was. We wanted to reinforce our values and build a sense of interdependency."

"Noel," Sifu asks, "what clues do you look for in a leader that would indicate that he or she is an excellent communicator?"

Noel grins. "That's been on my mind a great deal lately. You only have one chance to make a first impression, right? It's all about credibility; do you believe the person you're listening to? I believe humility is important, and that's a quality you don't always see in leaders. There's a certain natural swagger that many leaders have that can be interpreted as arrogance. But I keep coming back to integrity. That's huge. You have to believe them! Men like Gandhi and Martin Luther King must have had *incredible* integrity.

"Bottom line: you must be true to yourself and be honest with people. You can't pretend to be someone you're not; it just doesn't work. I've seen very smart, capable leaders who destroyed their credibility in mere moments. You take hours and hours to talk with someone and build their trust, and then you can ruin all that good work very quickly if people sense that you're not acting with integrity. Then trust is gone and you may never get it back. So the first clue is that integrity. If you don't believe in what you're saying, say nothing.

"Repetition is important, and it's something I would reinforce with my leadership team, particularly younger mangers. Young managers tend to believe that if you've said it once that's enough. Wrong! It *never* hurts to repeat. If you have a compelling message, people don't get bored when you repeat it.

"Finally, Sifu, I look for people who genuinely like to communicate! A big part of a leader's role is being a good communicator and communicating often. If you see communication as insignificant or a chore, you're likely to keep putting it off, which is unacceptable. Your organization *must* communicate well, and there must be a consistency of message.

"That phrase you taught me, Sifu, 'Purpose Partners,' has tremendous significance. There must be a shared sense of purpose—an authentic partnership—among everyone in the organization. That will *only* be established through clear, honest, consistent, personal communication throughout the organization.

"You're communicating and you're asking for feedback. Do they understand what you're telling them? Do our values resonate with them? If they don't, we've got a problem! Are they proud to take part in accomplishing the mission? Are they excited about the vision? You have to *want* to communicate these things, you have to take pleasure in doing it over and over, and doing it with the utmost integrity. And you must encourage feedback and actively listen to it."

Noel stops speaking suddenly. "My goodness! I certainly got to talking there!"

Sifu leans closer to the table; his eyes are very bright. "Noel, you said so many very important things just now! Since Dan is taking notes, I'd like to draw out a few points, if I may."

"By all means!" Noel smiles apologetically. "I've been talking for quite some time!"

"And you just imparted more wisdom in one hour than many men speak in a lifetime." Sifu says warmly. "Noel, you said that your Number One clue is integrity. That is exactly right. There must be no disconnect between who the leader really is and what he or she displays to the world. There will never be trust if the leader does not display this kind of integrity.

"Second," Sifu continues, "your thoughts about the implications of the concept of Purpose Partners are splendid!" The Grandmaster looks at Noel, and his eyes are bright with respect. "I would simply add that a leader who is building trust through communication will regularly share information with Purpose Partners on the company's overall performance and how the partner's particular division is doing relative to strategic business objectives. This may be good news or bad news, but it must always be *accurate* information. As you said, Noel, a leader can work for years to build trust and destroy all those efforts in an instant!

"Finally, Noel, you spoke several times about the importance of asking for and receiving good feedback. It cannot be overstated that one of the most important qualities of a good communicator is practicing superior listening skills. One of the easiest ways to create a trust deficit is to interrupt and override others in the middle of a conversation. It demonstrates an utter lack of respect for the other person."

Dan and Noel glance at each other and chuckle uncomfortably. Both men are trying to recall the last time they interrupted someone. Was it as recently as this morning?

Sifu smiles at their discomfiture. "Every one of us should ask ourselves this question: Am I known as a great listener or a poor listener? We devalue and demotivate others when our poor listening skills communicate that we are not interested in what they have to say."

Noel is smiling and nodding enthusiastically. "You are so right, Sifu! Some of our very best communication is accomplished by saying nothing at all!"

Dan grins at Noel, and then impulsively reaches out and grabs his hand in both of his. "What an incredible delight to have met you, Noel! I know I'm going to be a better leader as a result of having listened to you for the past hour!"

Noel grips Dan's hand in a firm grip. "Dan, you and I are both better leaders for having listened to this man…" Noel looks warmly at Sifu "… when he introduced us to the People First philosophy!"

"And I am grateful to you both," Sifu says softly, "for being such wonderful models of that philosophy."

Noel grins at Dan. "Now *there* is some communication that ought to make you feel good!" He looks at Dan curiously. "From what Sifu told me about the seven keys of trust, you are down to the last two, correct? Where's your next stop?"

Dan smiles. "Actually, Noel, I'll be sitting down at my desk later today to talk to a friend of Sifu's about the importance of consistency."

CHAPTER 21

"Consistency Is Work!"

Richard Thorne of Kimberly-Clark Professional

"THE KIMBERLY-CLARK ORGANIZATION IS MORE than one hundred and forty years old. We have forty thousand employees in thirty-six countries, and we generated twenty billion dollars in sales last year." The voice booming out of Dan's computer speakers is cheerful, precise, and laced with a strong English accent.

Dan is seated in his office at Prestigious Products, talking to Richard Thorne, the leader of North American Business for Kimberly-Clark Professional, via Skype. Sifu was unable to attend this session, but he set up this call and spoke to Richard in advance to explain what Dan is hoping to learn from him. Dan began the call by asking Richard to tell him about his background with Kimberly-Clark.

"I've been with Kimberly-Clark for thirty-three years, Dan. I started in sales and spent a considerable amount of time working out of the UK. I came Stateside in 2006."

"And now you're in charge of all of Kimberly-Clark's business in the United States and Canada."

There was a time early in his career when Dan had believed that being the CEO of Prestigious Products made him a Very Important Person. If any traces of that hubris remained in him, meeting men like Tom Manenti, Noel Fogarty, and Richard Thorne has scrubbed it completely away. Their international scope of operations is so much larger than his! "Richard, I know it's difficult to point to any one thing, but what would you say is the reason you've enjoyed such success?"

Richard does not hesitate. "I believe it's because of my ability to work with people and collaborate with them. I am a firm believer that people make the difference—more accurately, *teams* of people make the difference. It's not about me as a leader; it's about the success of the team."

Richard's face breaks into a smile. "Sifu says wonderful things about your leadership, Dan. He said you teach *him* things about the People First philosophy. I'm honored that you would ask me for advice."

Dan hopes that the sudden flush in his face doesn't show up on the Skype transmission. "My goodness! Sifu is very kind to say that. I'm grateful to *you*, Richard, for making time for me. So you credit the People First philosophy for your success?"

Richard nods. "I've been fortunate to work with some very talented people and I've been *very* fortunate to work for a tremendous company that has given me wonderful opportunities. But I do like working with people. I'm outgoing and energetic, and I'm genuinely interested in people. People respond positively to that kind of leadership."

As always, Dan is taking notes on his iPad. "I couldn't agree more, Richard. I utterly lacked that interest in people before Sifu explained his philosophy. I was all about profits and not at *all* about people…even my own family!"

Dan looks up at the Skype camera. "And when I think about how consistently *wrong* I was for so many years, Richard, I have to tell you I've been looking forward to hearing what you have to say about the importance of consistency when it comes to building trust."

Richard smiles again. "I'll do my best to be helpful! Establishing trust in business relationships is all about being open and candid with everyone about what you expect from them. One of the key leadership behaviors that I encourage young managers to develop is building trust. In addition, I emphasize the value of listening to diverse perspectives and encouraging robust debate. Leaders build trust by maintaining that kind of consistent, two-way communication."

Dan's fingers are tapping rapidly on the iPad keyboard. "Richard, several of the men I've met have stressed the importance of leaders listening."

Richard nods. "It's essential!" he says emphatically. "You should get the broadest perspective from a diversity of background, experience, culture—whatever element of diversity you're talking about. You end up with a more aligned team, and that alignment allows you to lead to consistency. Alignment and consistency go together, in my opinion. Consistency is not merely a matter of production quality; it's a cultural thing."

"I'd like to hear more about that," Dan says quickly. "I get the consistency of production: you have sales all over the globe, so you want to make the very same quality of your products for Florida and for China, just like McDonald's wants their hamburgers to look and taste the same no matter where in the world you buy one. But if I'm hearing you correctly, consistency is *not* simply a process management issue. You're saying consistency is a function and an outcome of leadership, is that correct?"

"That's right," Richard agrees warmly. "Pushing that consistent message down through the organization is probably one of a leader's biggest challenges. You can't think about communicating just one level up in the organization or one level down and assume that will produce a consistent message. By the time what you *thought* was a consistent message has worked its way through the organization, it has morphed into something completely different, sometimes only two or three levels down from you! You must communicate to multiple levels.

"Consistency doesn't happen naturally, Dan. It's something you have to work very hard at. You must be consistent with your leadership team, and you then have to be very consistent in the way you talk to the team that works for them, and so on. As a leader, you model that behavior all the time, every day, if you're going to get a large organization to pull together in one general direction. In our case, Kimberly-Clark Professional is global, so we're trying to drive a consistent agenda across the world, not just in North America. As you might imagine, there are challenges in that."

"I thought I had a challenge maintaining consistency with my Purpose Partners in the United States," Dan says humbly. "That's just a tiny fraction of what you're tasked with!"

"But it's still an enormous challenge, isn't it? Just remember, Dan, if it's worth doing, it will require hard work. And this is where your leadership skills come in. If you maintain a People First approach, where you're recognizing and celebrating the team's success, that kind of leadership helps provide a foundation for driving that consistency. But you have to work at it!"

"Richard, tell me more about what that work actually looks like."

Richard nods. "You remember the old phrase, 'Managing by walking around.' That's what this is. You make sure you're out there leading by setting a consistent example. You're not just staying in your office, reading your emails, holding meetings, and doing all the things that you consider important—" here Richard's face lights in a wry grin "—and considering yourself a very important person.

"You have to get out! You can get caught up in sitting in the office; there's a very real danger of forgetting that you're not the one who makes the work happen. I'm not the one who gets it done; it's the fifty-seven thousand employees at Kimberly-Clark Corporation or the six thousand employees at Kimberly-Clark Professional who actually make it happen. Unless you empower your Purpose Partners to get the work done, it doesn't matter how many emails you send or how much you pontificate in your office." Again, Richard's face breaks into that playful grin. "'*Richard says*' just doesn't work in the modern world."

Dan throws back his head and laughs. "Oh my goodness!" he exclaims. "It wasn't all that long ago when I thought that '*Dan says*' carried all the authority of holy writ! Sifu made me see how wrong I was."

Richard chuckles and nods sympathetically. "Having a good mentor is so important!"

"Richard, I'm learning how much I still need that mentor today!" Dan is serious again. "You've been saying so many things that I really hadn't considered. No offense, but when Sifu first told me that we would be talking about consistency, part of me thought, 'This one is a no-brainer.' I mean, if I'm inconsistent in my behavior, how can anyone trust me? It's like the line in *Forrest Gump* about the box of chocolates: 'You never know what you're gonna get.' If a leader is like that, it kills trust."

"I never thought of *Forrest Gump* as a primer on business!" Richard grins. "But you're absolutely right. And Dan, I have to admit that when Sifu called and asked me to spend some time with you, I was happy to do it, but my reaction was much like yours. At first blush, the thought of being consistent doesn't sound very inspirational. But the more I thought about it, I started getting excited about what consistency really means.

"This key really resonates with me, Dan, because at the end of the day, it's all on you and me. It's the *people* who make the business and the processes work. And unless those people are getting a consistent message...I mean, you can hold two meetings that are identical to each other, but if two crews interpret the message two different ways, you'll get two completely different results."

Dan is frowning with concentration. "So consistency is not only a trust issue. Why would you say consistency is so central to the success of organizations?"

"A good leader will provide clear alignment to the team about what is most important, what's less important, and what's not important at all," Richard replies. "Consistency gives us the ability to prioritize."

Richard shifts closer to the Skype camera. "Look, in today's business environment, particularly in large organizations, unless everyone has a very clear, consistent understanding of what it is you're shooting for, you are in deep trouble. Whether it is a matter of understanding your company's corporate objectives or keeping your individual objectives aligned to those corporate imperatives, you won't be as successful as you could be if there is inconsistent understanding. People will interpret what they need to do and go galloping off in different directions. That's *never* going to deliver the best results!"

Dan is nodding thoughtfully as he types on his iPad. "Something my organization has worked hard to do is to create a consistency of customer experience in all of our outlets around the United States. Richard, would you say that consistency is even more of a behavioral concern than it is an operational one?"

"That's an interesting question, Dan. If you don't get the behavioral element of consistency right, it really doesn't matter what you do operationally! You'll never be consistent from a leadership perspective. Certainly, we all need to be aligned about where we're going operationally. But when you go back to your group and talk about how you're going to commercialize in the marketplace, if you don't have alignment at the behavioral level, you're going to get different levels of operational consistency.

"Of course, when you go into a mill and you're talking about machines and the way machines make things, there's a more functional element to consistency because of the engineering capability that the machinery brings into the process. But I would still insist that it comes back to people behaviorally; get that right *first*, then the people will perform more consistently, and *then* you get the consistent performance outcomes you're looking for."

Dan is delighted. "This is fascinating! Richard, I apologize to you and I will apologize to Sifu for thinking this was a 'no brainer.'"

"Dan, I'm delighted to talk with you. It's helped me crystallize my own thinking."

"Richard, what do you do personally to establish and encourage good consistency at Kimberly Clark?"

"I model the concept that we have an agenda and we know what our priorities are, and I work hard to make sure we stick to that agenda and remain true to our priorities. It's as simple as that, Dan, and it's one of the hardest things you can possibly do! There are things that come up in the day-to-day business environment that seem like they're sent to challenge you and knock you off track."

"Tell me about it!" Dan groans.

"It's at those points, Dan, if you believe your strategy is right, you go back to that strategy and stay true to it. People are looking to see if you're committed and serious about what you're trying to drive. If you give mixed messages, that consistency you've been working so hard to establish can quickly degrade into dysfunction and even paralysis in an organization."

"Disaster," Dan murmurs.

"Precisely," Richard agrees. "So you're out there with your Purpose Partners, modeling the behaviors and following the strategy. But you also make sure that you're telling stories about the successes in the organization that have come from those behaviors and from following that strategy. You *never* stop recognizing and celebrating the successes of people in the organization. Sifu speaks of the importance of demonstrating to people that you care about them as human beings, not merely as human doings. He's absolutely right. You must be *consistent* in valuing your Purpose Partners.

"And finally, Dan, there's the thing we've already talked about: building trust. We make sure that we are being honest with one another and that we are modeling adult behavior, which is a core tenet of People First."

Dan grimaces down at his desk when Richard uses the phrase "adult behavior." He is recalling his angry outburst in John Kwan's office just days before.

Richard is speaking rapidly, enthusiastically. "We engage in adult conversations—talking about the things people are doing well and the things people could be doing better—*in a two-way basis.*

One of the things we do here when we sit down as teams, we formally ask each other, 'What feedback do you have for me?'

"We *don't* say, 'Do you have any feedback for me?' That's a closed-ended question that allows for a yes or no answer. So we ask our Purpose Partners, 'What do you think I'm doing well? What do you think I could be doing better?' And that has to work *both* ways, in a two-way conversation! Unless you're

The People First Effect

having good, open, candid feedback, you're not really addressing the things that will affect a cultural shift. I can tell people to get out there and do the job, and that will probably make me 20 percent effective as a leader. But if I can help people really *believe* in what they're doing, that will make me 100 percent effective overnight."

Dan is silent as he finishes typing his notes. Then he looks straight into the camera. "I don't know how much Sifu has told you about the situation at my company. We've recently been acquired by overseas ownership. They are instituting a cultural shift that *nobody* believes in. You talked about 'dysfunction' and 'paralysis.' That would pretty accurately describe us at this time."

"Dan, I haven't experienced anything like that. I do know that culture is one of the most difficult things to shift in a business. Bricks and mortar are easy; people are much more complex. It takes a long time to shift a business culture. You have to be very clear about where you're coming from and where you're going—the steps you're going to take and the behaviors you're going to exemplify in order to accomplish that shift.

"You can take one step forward and slip two steps back very quickly, simply by saying the wrong thing or modeling the wrong behavior at the wrong time. Consistency is so *very* important, whether you're talking about interpersonal interaction or production process. Everybody is watching the leader very carefully to see, 'Is this really a transformation? Or can I just bide my time and wait for it to go away?'"

Dan is nodding as Richard speaks. "Shortly after I initiated People First at my company, one of my key reports came to me and said that it wasn't so much what I said that changed her mind as that she was sure I was committed to the philosophy."

"That woman was one of your classic early adopters, Dan, the people who get it and are excited. Then you have your fast followers; they are actually the critical group. In truth, it's not the person who starts, but it's the second person and the third person who join them, because now you've got a bit of a movement going.

"Then you have your 'wait-and-see' people; they're the ones you truly need to reach if you're going to effect change in the organization. If the wait-and-see group is active and excited, you're in great shape; if they aren't, they can slow any initiative. Obviously, you want them to come on the journey with you, but sometimes you reach the point where someone becomes so disruptive that you

162

have to have the tough conversation, perhaps even move that person—either to the side or moving them out—so that they don't become a cancer."

Dan nods, recalling a long-ago conversation. "Sifu once told me that a People First culture attracts and repels. Most people will be delighted to work in a People First organization and adopt the philosophy eagerly. But there will be those who are wedded to the old high-command, high-control style of management and they self-identify pretty quickly."

"That's right, Dan. There's one other group that must be reached and energized about change, and these are the key opinion leaders. They are typically two or three layers below you in the organization. These people engage in the corridor conversations and play a huge role in setting the belief in the organization. If they say, 'I think this is a great idea,' others will say the same thing. Or if they say, 'You don't need to do anything, it'll blow over,' people will follow their advice. So it's critical to reach those opinion leaders. It all comes back to consistency."

"Richard, may I ask you one more question?"

"Of course!"

"If you were mentoring a young manager, and you could only tell that person three things about how to build and maintain consistency in an organization, what would you say?"

"Well, a manager has to work at establishing trust. Without trust, it doesn't matter what you say or do, you will not be successful. And as important as celebrating success is to the People First culture, you don't build trust just by telling people how great they are. There must be an open, mature relationship.

"It's almost like an extension of your family. If you have that same open honesty with everybody, and if they know you sincerely value them as individuals, that you value their diversity and truly want to hear their opinions, that creates incredible trust. And when you have earned trust—not a blind trust, but earned trust—that's an incredibly powerful thing. People will go to the ends of the earth with you and with each other."

Dan's fingers are flying over the iPad keyboard. "Richard, this is fabulous! What else would you tell a young manager about building consistency?"

"The second thing I'd talk about is winning consistently. That's being accountable for asking your Purpose Partners, 'What can I do to help you be successful? How can I help you meet our short-term and long-term expectations?' And you have to be fully accountable for your own performance in terms of achieving the results. Don't wait for someone else to do it for you.

"Winning is very important! At the end of the day, if we don't win, that's extremely discouraging. Yes, there will be failures, and you want to help Purpose Partners learn from failure because that teaches us how to win! But winning consistently is very important to building confidence, consistency, and trust.

"And finally, Dan, I'd encourage a young manger to put consistent effort into building talent.

Building trust and developing talent go together. If I believe my leader is *for* me and is actively working to help me learn and develop, I'll trust that leader and make a consistent effort for that leader.

"So, for the leader, it comes down accountability again—not only for asking how you can create wins for others, but also asking, 'How can I recognize and celebrate the diversity of my team and take ownership of the development of everyone on that team?' You're consistently working to build your own talent and the talent of those around you."

Dan shakes his head admiringly. "Richard, all I can say is, any leader who has you for a mentor is going to develop in leaps and bounds. Thank you for what you've done today to develop me!"

CHAPTER 22

Running to Represent the Brand

SHORTLY AFTER FINISHING THE CALL with Richard Thorne, Dan dials Sifu's cell phone.

"My good friend!" Sifu answers warmly. "How did it go with Richard?"

"Sifu, I can't thank you enough for all the time you've spent with me and for these amazing leaders you've introduced me to. This has been so enormously helpful to my growth!"

"My friend, this process has been very instructive for me, as well," Sifu says warmly. Dan can clearly imagine Sifu's bright smile. "It is I who should be thanking you!"

"Sifu, you are always so gracious. You know, I can't believe I'm saying this, but perhaps I'm thanking the wrong man." He chuckles. "If it wasn't for John Kwan, we might never have had these conversations!"

There is no answering laugh from Sifu. "Perhaps that is the way to reopen this subject with him."

Sifu's voice is serious. "Thank him for sending you on this journey!"

"I suspect he might not be pleased to receive my gratitude," Dan says drily.

"You could sincerely thank him for presenting you with this opportunity for growth," Sifu says thoughtfully. "If he objects, 'What growth? Our customer base is shrinking!' you can reply that you were referring to your own personal and professional growth. And *that* would give you an opportunity to speak to him about the seven keys of trust."

There is a brief silence as Sifu gathers his thoughts. "You may remember hearing of Roger Bannister, the first man to run a mile in less than four minutes. He once said that every morning a gazelle wakes up in Africa knowing that it must run faster than the lion or it will not survive the day. And every morning a lion wakes up knowing that it must move faster than the gazelle or it will starve. Bannister concluded by saying that whether you are a lion or a gazelle, you had better start running when the sun comes up!

"Dan, you and I should *want* to wake up in the morning ready to run. We should *run to represent the brand*—the brand of putting people first, of building bridges of trust and treating people with the utmost dignity, respect, and honor! We run boldly, we run confidently, but we *run*, Dan, because there are many leaders just like John Kwan, who believe they can maximize profits by crushing the human spirit, rather than by setting it free. So you and I must put forth our best efforts to present the formula for true, sustainable growth."

A sudden thought causes Dan to heave a sigh. "Sifu, I've done a lot more falling than running lately."

"And that is precisely why we need to run, my friend!" Sifu says warmly. "We hit the ground running, because the lion is running also, and it seeks to overtake us and devour us! Every morning we run toward truth, wisdom, and excellence. When we stumble and fall—and I fall too, Dan—we spring right back up and start running again. Fall down seven times, get up eight!"

Dan leans back in his chair and grins up at the ceiling. "Sifu, if I spent every minute of the day talking to you, it still wouldn't be enough!"

Sifu chuckles. "I suspect it would make you very drowsy after a while! But tomorrow morning we will meet a man who will keep you wide awake. Keith Koenig is an outstanding professional and an even finer human being. He will teach us about Commitment, the seventh and final key to trust."

CHAPTER 23

"A Commitment to Integrity"

Keith Koenig of City Furniture

THE CONFERENCE ROOM ON THE second floor of the City Furniture offices is bright and airy. Dan, Sifu, and Keith Koenig, City Furniture's founder and president, are seated comfortably at one end of a large table, sipping coffee. Keith is a cheerful, friendly man with bright, intelligent eyes. Dan has met Keith several times at professional association meetings and trade shows. Keith Koenig enjoys an excellent reputation in the South Florida community, both for his business acumen and his desire to contribute to the community.

"I've heard so many great things about you, Keith," Dan says sincerely. "You know, I've shopped some of your stores; your displays and customer service are second to none. I've talked with our store managers on several occasions about emulating City Furniture."

"Thank you, Dan," Keith replies with a warm smile. "I've had some of those same conversations about Prestigious Products with our leadership, so that's quite a compliment! We like to think we're doing well, but we work hard to keep improving."

"Keith," Sifu says, "that is an excellent starting point for our conversation. I've told you about my seven keys for establishing and maintaining trust: character, competence, confidence, caring, communication, consistency, and commitment. Keith, I've always been impressed by your commitment to leadership excellence, so I'd like to ask you: Do you agree that commitment is essential to establishing trust?"

Keith is a deliberate man. He hesitates for a moment and replies, "Sifu, I'd like to back up just a bit and explain how I define 'commitment' and then answer your question. OK?"

Sifu nods, smiling.

Keith rests his elbows on the table and looks at Sifu thoughtfully. "I've been thinking about this ever since you called me. To me, commitment is a promise that one person makes to another, and it often goes two ways. Friendships, marriages, and business relationships all imply significant commitments. It's what I promise to do for you, whether it's written or implied, and what you promise to do for me."

Keith's steady blue eyes swing to Dan. "Trust is the foundation for every commitment. At the end of the day, even a contractual relationship without trust can be worthless. Warren Buffett said it very well: 'Without integrity, the price is never low enough.' If Buffett is considering buying a company, but he doesn't trust its integrity, the price—no matter how attractive—doesn't matter."

Dan nods thoughtfully as he types on his iPad. "Without trust, that low price may just add to the mistrust!"

Keith nods soberly. "I communicate commitments to my Purpose Partners in terms of our current business, what I see the future to be, how we're going to treat each other and our customers, and how we're going to act within the community. I've worked for nearly forty years to build this business and to develop that foundation of trust."

Keith swings his gaze back to Sifu. "That trust can be shattered in an *instant*." Keith snaps his fingers to punctuate the statement. "I've done business with people who made commitments that were worthless. Once I learned their integrity was not right, it was easier and smarter to avoid doing business with them. So a man's or woman's commitment to integrity is the very foundation of establishing trust."

"Keith," Dan says, "I'd love to introduce you to Sifu's friend, Tom Manenti. He has that same commitment to consistent integrity. Let me ask you this: if you were asked to rank the qualities of a great leader, how high would you rank commitment?"

Keith considers the question for a moment. "I think everything is interrelated," he replies. "We're talking about a commitment to integrity, which means doing the right thing, doing what you say you'll do, even when it hurts.

"Our leaders' follow-through on their commitments is crucial to building trust with their Purpose Partners. If a leader doesn't follow through on his or her commitments, it's very hard for the team to respect the leader, to want to follow that leader, or to want to fulfill the goals of the team or the organization.

"The bottom line, Dan, is that I see someone's *commitment* as being so integral to their underlying integrity that I don't know how you can pull it out and rank it by itself. Organizations with a commitment to integrity succeed; organizations that don't follow through on their commitments to their Purpose Partners, their customers, their suppliers, and the community are like a house with a weak foundation—sooner or later they come crashing down."

Sifu nods gravely. "The long-term profitability of such an organization will be severely compromised. Keith, how much of a role does your leadership play in establishing commitment at City Furniture, and how much of it just happens naturally?"

"I believe commitment is learned," Keith replies promptly. "Not everyone is born with it. People need a good example. We learn it from our families, our friends, and our Purpose Partners. I feel for those folks who get a bad example of commitment. How can they have trust? How can they learn to build trust?"

"Very true," Sifu says approvingly. "So if commitment is learned, how do you drive commitment through the culture here at City Furniture?"

"Our senior leaders must act with integrity," Keith answers decisively. "We have to follow through on our commitments and be trustworthy. I'm *very* aware how damaging it can be when I miss a commitment. I don't miss the major commitments that are important to someone or to our organization, but what if I tell someone I'm going to be there at 2:30 and I don't make it? That was a commitment! *Everything* matters.

"We won't always deliver the results that we expect or hope for. We certainly lived through that during the recession. We had different expectations for our business, but when the housing bust really set in, we were in uncharted waters. Our average daily deliveries dropped by nearly *half* during that time! We've always created an expectation that the future is bright because we believed it was…and then our sales cratered. We had to look at our commitments and make some difficult decisions.

"At that point we committed to deal with the issues as positively as we could. The people who had to be laid off were treated with the utmost respect and dignity in terms of severance and the way we delivered the bad news in face-to-face meetings."

Dan winces. "Those awful meetings!"

Keith nods sympathetically. "No fun for anybody. But truthfully, those results were surprisingly positive! I don't think we lost any trust with our associates. Everyone knew we were dealing with a change in the marketplace that was way beyond what we could forecast or manage.

"I learned something from that time: it's easy to keep your commitments when everything is going as you expect, but when the world turns in a completely different direction from what you'd forecast, you may have to change those commitments. The only way to do that is with honesty, transparency, and clear communication. And we held fast to our commitment to treating each person with respect and compassion. That's what maintained the trust of our team."

Dan nods. "Sometimes that commitment to integrity is all that's left," he says grimly. "The economy left us very little choice."

"And from what you've both told me, you maintained that commitment, even in the most difficult storm," Sifu says softly. "I am proud to call you both 'friend.'"

Dan and Keith both smile at Sifu. "Friend *and* student, Sifu," Keith says brightly. "I have been so grateful for your encouragement and wisdom."

"Keith," Dan asks, "how do the leaders at City Furniture demonstrate their commitment to the values of your organization? How do your Purpose Partners learn from your example?"

"We spend time discussing that in our meetings," Keith replies. "Leaders must be clear in communicating what's expected in terms of outcomes and fair in assigning accountability. They also must be transparent; we expect our leaders to take personal responsibility when things go poorly. When things go well, the leader celebrates the team that made it happen.

"We're working toward creating the concept of servant leadership at City Furniture. A servant leader doesn't take the machete and slash out the path; the best leaders organize the team, help them set goals, help them problem-solve, and encourage the team to work together to accomplish the goals. And they stay engaged, so they can keep any obstacles that confront the team from getting in the way of the goals."

"How about you?" Dan asks curiously. "What do you do, personally, to demonstrate commitment at City Furniture?"

"It's very important for me to personally touch and connect with as many of my Purpose Partners as I can," Keith says. "If I'm preoccupied and I walk by someone without saying hello, I've missed an important opportunity to impact them in a positive way.

"The higher up you get in the organization, the more important those interpersonal connections become. The general manager at one of our showrooms is a *very* important person. He or she must make sure all the facilities are run right and that their customers are served promptly, politely, and efficiently. The GM must be ready to address any problems so that the team can reach their goals with a high level of customer service.

"But if that same GM were to stop by and visit another one of our showrooms, no one at that location might even know who that man or woman is! They'd think it was another customer walking in off the street. But the higher up a senior leader is in an organization, the more important their interpersonal interactions become. Everybody knows who they are! The best leaders work to take advantage of every opportunity."

Dan looks at Sifu. "That's one of the things that stands out to me about People First: the commitment to be proactive about making people feel valued and important."

Keith nods assertively. "Exactly! Of course, it's important for me to cast a vision and help lead our team, but you're right, Dan, I also have a responsibility to impact lives in a positive way. You build a better sense of trust and strengthen commitment throughout the organization by building better relationships. It's critical for the leader to lay the foundation for peak engagement, rather than simply expecting Purpose Partners to give 100 percent.

"I hear some business leaders complain that their Purpose Partners have an 'entitlement mentality.' And all too often these individuals are the ones who make little or no effort to create engagement; they think the burden for engagement lies with the individual, not with the leader. I couldn't disagree more! It's critically important for leaders to create an environment where every Purpose Partner recognizes that we are an ethical company—" here Keith starts ticking the points off on his fingers "—that we've got good leadership and a good plan; we treat our customers the right way; we do the right things in the community;

and that this is a place where everybody cares about them as a human being, from their coworkers all the way to the top.

"If our Purpose Partners really believe these things, they will have trust, and there is a much greater likelihood they'll be effective and give 100 percent of their being to the organization. If they don't believe those things about us—" Keith spreads his hands in a hopeless gesture "—they have been effectively disempowered. There won't be trust and there won't be engagement."

"I've seen that disengagement firsthand," Dan agrees, glancing at Sifu with a wry smile. "It wasn't so long ago that I was the reason for it!"

Keith's eyes rest on Dan. "We've all made mistakes." He grins at Sifu. "We're all under construction. But when leadership is committed to creating trust—and that commitment has *got* to start with me—then our Purpose Partners have the best opportunity to be as fully successful and fully engaged in City Furniture as possible."

Sifu nods approvingly. "You are engaging the heart, not just the hands."

"Yes," Keith nods, and his eyes are very bright. "Work needs to be engaging and fulfilling, and I don't know how that can happen if we aren't committed to good interpersonal skills that let Purpose Partners know they're valued. When we do that, you see a strong commitment from our Purpose Partners to the organization, because they trust that the organization is fully committed to them. But unless that commitment is reinforced on a continual basis, trust will be eroded and engagement will decline. It's inevitable!"

Sifu is delighted. "You said that so *well*, Keith!" he says, gently slapping his palm on the table.

"There are economic laws that govern a business *and* there are the laws of human engagement. You have expressed that beautifully."

Keith nods and smiles. "Talk to Purpose Partners who are happy and engaged and ask them *why* they're engaged; they will almost always say up front that they like their coworkers. If we treat each other well, if we feel valued and important and cared for, we engage wholeheartedly. A commitment to interpersonal relationships is essential to organizational success.

"Sifu, this is where your phrase, 'You can't impart what you don't possess,' rings so *hugely* true.

"We're just one of many furniture companies. Customers can choose to buy their furniture from a great many organizations. We *must* forge superior relationships with our customers or we won't succeed. It's as simple as that. And if we want our Purpose Partners to genuinely *desire* to forge those relationships, then we who lead at City Furniture must commit to forging those relationships with our Purpose Partners first.

"I want to turn this emphasis on interpersonal excellence into one of our core competitive advantages. I am committed to creating an environment that is so engaged that a guest in any of our showrooms will have such a positive experience with every one of our associates that when they shop somewhere else, they won't feel as good. We want to turn those intangible interpersonal skills into a tangible competitive advantage.

"We work hard at constant, continual improvement operationally, so that we have the quickest delivery, the most efficient routing, the least amount of damages, and these are all *very* important to our customers. But if we also committed to adding a warm, genuine smile to that efficiency and expressing sincere respect and appreciation to our internal *and* external customers, we'll be that much more successful.

"How do you say it, Sifu? We want to have the best blend of hi-tech and hi-touch. We want to combine process excellence with the interpersonal excellence of the People First philosophy to the point where we become known for giving something 'extra' when you do business with us, just like a Southwest Airlines or a Chick-fil-A."

Sifu gives Keith a dazzling smile. "My friend, you have explained the balance of 'high-tech and high-touch' beautifully! There's one other area I'd like to cover with you. When you and I talked on the phone, I asked you to think about some clues which reveal the trustworthy commitment of a leader. Can you identify some clues?

Keith smiles. "I gave that a lot of thought. The first commitment clue I look for in a leader is *loyalty in both the personal and professional realms*. Of course, I want to see leaders who are loyal to the organization's values, mission, and vision; that's a given. Dan, you and I shop other retailers' locations to see what they do well. We're looking for ideas that will help make the shopping experience more pleasant for our own customers. I don't make these visits to find flaws in other stores, but you certainly do see them from time to time!"

Dan grins his agreement.

"One of the things I'll see, Dan, is an organization that pastes its values on big posters by the front door...except nobody who works there seems to know what those values are! Their behavior indicates that they value something quite different from what's on the poster! So my first clue is leaders who demonstrate that integrity between the organization's stated values and the way they actually behave toward their internal and external customers.

"But it's more than just professional loyalty. I believe commitment is demonstrated in the personal arena also: men and women who are faithful to their marriage vows, faithful to their promises. I've had it up to here with these politicians who are running around with someone other than their spouse and then say that it's a private matter. That's nonsense! It's a public office they hold, and these individuals have just given a clear indication that they have no loyalty to one of the most important commitments they'll ever make."

"You're right, Keith," Dan murmurs. "Even in the business world, that kind of personal infidelity is a *huge* red flag."

"Exactly," Keith nods firmly. "It builds trust for me whenever I see someone who is loyal to their personal and professional commitments. The second commitment clue is *engagement—a choice has been made to be 100 percent engaged.* I frequently tell our Purpose Partners that work is an experience that we create. We have to work together to create the environment we want to work in and build the organization we want City Furniture to be. It's not just me, not just the senior leadership team, we *all* must work together to create the kind of business that we're proud to be part of.

"Third, a committed leader is *responsible. Just like the best baseball managers, the leader takes the blame when the organization underperforms and celebrates others during times of prosperity.* The buck stops at the leader's desk. We believe in the concept of servant leadership at City Furniture, and we're committed to creating the right environment which will allow our Purpose Partners to flourish and grow.

"The best leaders, when there is a problem in their area, look for the root cause and take responsibility because it's in *their* area and it's on *their* watch. And when there's success, they celebrate the Purpose Partners who helped make it happen. Purpose Partners look at a leader like that and say, "He's a good guy—or gal. I like working with that person.'"

Keith grins slyly at Dan. "I know my fourth clue is one you've heard before somewhere. A committed leader will be *dedicated to truth in all things, wisdom in all things, and excellence in all things.*" Keith turns in his chair to include Sifu in his bright smile. "That was one of the first things you said to me, Sifu, and it stuck. We *must* be committed to truth in all things. Integrity is the foundation for everything every good leader does.

"Wisdom comes from learning and experience. I believe that the Bible is the best source of all information available. You have an entire book on living in truth, wisdom, and excellence, which essentially says that if you seek wisdom and if you ask for wisdom, it will be given to you. Solomon was given the opportunity to ask God for anything he wanted; he didn't ask for money or long life, he wanted to guide his people with a wise and kind heart. God prized that desire for wisdom above all other choices, and He granted it to Solomon, *plus* all the other things.

"My point is, you have to *want* to be wise and you have to *seek* it. We're very intentional about bringing this search for wisdom into our organization through all our training, the good books we read, the seminars we attend, as well as learning from other leaders—leaders like you, Sifu.

"Our vision for City Furniture is to be the ultimate furniture store, which is why we are committed to excellence in all things. We want each one of our locations to be the furniture store that our internal and external customer truly prefers. That means that the parking lot must be spotless; the greeting inside the showroom must be prompt and genuinely friendly; and the showrooms have to look great. The sales presentation and interactions and relationships must be positive and helpful. The product has to look fabulous and the values have to be great. When we make the sale, the delivery must be prompt and our Purpose Partners who handle the goods have got to treat every piece of furniture with care every step of the way. When our delivery teams come to our customers' homes, they've got to treat them with respect and care.

"All those things are hard to do consistently! But we're working and training and seeking excellence in all those areas. That's the way to success—not just in the business world but in all of life. We should be committed to striving for excellence in all things. When I see a person who is committed to living that way, it builds tremendous trust in me."

Sifu chuckles in sheer delight. "Keith, you are sharing such *wonderful* truths!"

"I learned a great many of these truths from *you*, Sifu," Keith says earnestly. "You are very kind! I have one final commitment clue, and that is *a committed leader is dedicated to the development of others.* We're looking to put even more management focus into the development of our Purpose Partners, and we're investing in people every way we can. We've always had some of the most effective training in our industry, but we're redoubling our efforts to help our Purpose Partners be the very best that they can be, personally and professionally."

Keith sits back in his chair with an air of finality. "Here's my commitment: I want our customers to experience a tangible difference when they visit one of our showrooms. I have great respect for our competitors, but we want to create a noticeable gap between us and them and then continue to broaden that gap. And I'm committed to making our Purpose Partners happier—to strive to continue to create the ultimate environment for everyone who enters it. That's the kind of business I want to be a part of."

CHAPTER 24

Bitter Change

JUST A FEW HOURS AFTER Dan and Sifu have left City Furniture, twenty-six-year-old Johnny Kwan gulps a shot of cognac. "Aaah!" Johnny lets out a deep breath and reaches for his glass of beer, draining it in one long swallow. The noise level in the crowded South Beach nightclub forces him to shout at the bartender. "Hey! Hit me again!" he bellows, waving his hand at the empty glasses. "And I'll take the tab."

The bartender looks at Johnny closely. "How about I call a cab? You've been hitting it pretty hard."

"No need," Johnny lies easily. "I've got a friend coming to pick me up." He points again at the empty glasses. "One more time." The bartender refills his shot glass, and without hesitation,

Johnny throws down another cognac. He *thunks* the empty shot glass down on the bar. *Yeah*, he thinks bitterly, *I'd have a friend coming to get me...if I had any friends.* He takes a long swig of beer. *Maybe I should call dear old Dad.* The thought causes him to push out a bitter chuckle, which turns into a loud belch.

The bar is crowed with young people, but in the din from the dance band in the next room, no one sees or hears Johnny; he might as well be sitting in a glass bubble. He slides an American Express Platinum card across the bar. "Put fifty dollars on there for yourself."

If the bartender is pleased by the large tip, it does not show in his eyes. Perhaps it is because the tip is barely ten percent of the bill. "Thanks," he says shortly.

Johnny Kwan pushes his thick, shaggy hair out of his eyes and quickly scrawls a signature on the credit card slip. *I wonder if Dad even looks at these receipts. Probably just has his secretary write the check to AmEx every month. Just like the check that comes to me.* He gets slowly to his feet and steadies himself against the bar. *I sure got a good buzz on,* he thinks. *Shame it doesn't make me feel any better.* He takes one more long swallow of beer and turns for the exit.

The night had started out much like any other. Already mildly intoxicated after an afternoon of drinking beers at a bar on the beach, Johnny had returned to his Miami Beach townhouse, expecting to find Dianne, the tattooed young woman who had so troubled his mother, waiting to go out for a night on the town.

Johnny was under no illusions about what Dianne wanted from their relationship. She laughed at his jokes and acted as if she found him interesting, but what really interested her was Johnny's shiny new Porsche Carrera and the bank balance the one hundred thousand-dollar car represents. That was fine with Johnny; he cared nothing about what Dianne thought or felt; he simply liked her looks and the fact that she wore very revealing clothing. He had planned to enjoy her for as long as his talk of marriage would hold her; when he grew tired of her he would discard her, as he had several young women before her.

Johnny knew that Dianne was shopping for a man with money when they met, but it never occurred to him that she might keep right on shopping after she moved into Johnny's townhouse. And he completely missed the calculating look that came into her eyes when he confessed after one long night of drinking and drugs that his father might one day pull the plug on Johnny's wildly extravagant lifestyle. So he was dumbfounded when he arrived home this day and found a two-word note: "We're done."

Johnny did what he has always done when confronted with some difficulty; he went to an upscale dance club and began to drink. People there know him; they know if they hung around, they would enjoy several free drinks. Johnny did not disappoint them. After all, it wasn't his money he was spending.

Johnny began to brood, wondering why he was in such a foul mood. He asked himself if he had some feelings for Dianne, but that wasn't it. He realized that he was only angry because the breakup was *her* idea, not his. Johnny began to throw down shots of cognac, and his disposition became increasingly sullen. Before long, all the people who surrounded him had drifted away and Johnny sat alone drinking…thinking.

Who needs that bunch of moochers? Johnny thought sourly. He paid the bill with his father's credit card and weaved his way to the door. No one speaks to him as he leaves. He has no idea where he will go next. *I sure don't feel like going home. I never thought I'd miss Dianne, but now I don't want to go home. It's empty…like my life is empty.*

Why does it bother you so much? Johnny asks himself as he waits, swaying slightly, for the valet attendant to bring the Porsche. *You've been alone all your life. Why are you feeling so crummy?*

You know why. That sneering inner voice, the one Johnny tries to silence every day with alcohol and drugs, begins whispering cruelly. *Where's it all gonna end, champ? Do you want to be like Dad? He's got all that money, and he's all alone. Mom can't stand him. He acts like he hates everybody. He doesn't even know you're alive!* Depression hits Johnny like a punch in the gut. He actually puts his hand to his stomach as his loneliness flares like physical pain.

Johnny is momentarily distracted by the arrival of his car. He slides behind the wheel and steers the Porsche out onto the main road. He turns up the volume on the 12-speaker CD player, but that hateful voice is not silenced. *What now, ace? Gonna go out and rent yourself a new bimbo tomorrow? What a wasted life. Remember what Dad said? "You're a waste of life, Johnny!"*

He never once *said he cared about me…just about what I do. That's all I ever hear from him: "What are you doing, Johnny?" So what* are *you going to do, ace? What kind of a "change" are you gonna make? Huh? You think it'll make a change if I stuff this shiny new piece of junk into the biggest palm tree I can find?*

Johnny Kwan flips the volume up to an ear-splitting level and savagely stomps on the accelerator. The Porsche surges forward, pushing Johnny back into the driver's seat. *Huh, Dad? Is that the kind of change that will make you happy?*

Five miles away, David Burton is straightening up the meeting room at the counseling center. The center hosts a Narcotics Anonymous meeting on Thursday nights, and David is always there to offer encouragement to the attendees. *And let's face it,* David admits to himself, *every week you're hoping and praying that Marcy will come walking in.* David takes one last look around the room and shuts off the lights. *I guess she made it clear that I shouldn't hold my breath on that one.*

David sets the building alarm and walks out into the parking lot. He pauses for a moment, enjoying the breeze coming off the Atlantic Ocean. David smiles up at the night sky. *What a great meeting tonight! Lives are changing. Thursday is a long day, but I always feel so good on the way home. I can't wait to tell Lee!*

A warning bell on a nearby drawbridge starts to clang, signaling that the bridge spanning a canal is about to open. The sound is so familiar that David scarcely notices. *It feels great to make a difference. And when we get Mom's and Dad's foundation up and running, it's really going to fill a need in the community.* He closes his eyes. *I hope it isn't wrong to be so happy when other people aren't. I don't think I've ever felt so great!*

David's happy reverie is interrupted by the scream of a high-performance motor. *Some idiot is really on the gas! You suppose he's trying to beat the drawbridge opening?* A glance at the bridge tells him the two panels of the bridge have already started to lift. Almost unconsciously, David has started to walk toward the bridge, which is only a few hundred feet away. The turbocharged whine of the motor grows louder. "Stop your car!" The voice is loud, mechanical. The bridge operator is shouting into a loudspeaker. "The bridge is open!"

Seconds later David hears a loud *crack* and sees headlights approaching the edge of one leaf of the bridge. *He drove right through the gate and now he's gonna try to jump the bridge!* David thinks incredulously. Time seems to have slowed to a crawl. A bright red car hurtles over the edge of the bridge. It actually clears the gap between the two leaves of the bridge and lands on the other side with an ugly, metallic *crunch*, sending up a swirl of sparks. The car swerves hard right and crashes through guardrails, plunging down toward the dark water of the canal, landing on its roof with a loud splash. Immediately, the car begins to sink.

It has been said that heroes act without thinking while others are still wondering what to do. David Burton's mind is consumed with one thought: *There are people inside!* He sprints toward the edge of the canal. Horns are blowing, the bridge warning bells are clanging, the voice is blaring on the loudspeaker, but David hears none of it. *Deep breath, David, deep breath!* Without pausing to remove his shoes, he sucks in a lungful of air and leaps into the water...

CHAPTER 25

Midnight Call

AT 11:30 THAT NIGHT, JOHN Kwan is jolted awake by the ringing of the bedside phone. He glances over at Peijing, who is lying on the far side of the king bed, then peers at the clock. *Who could be calling at this time?* He stares at the phone, tempted to let it go to voice mail.

Peijing shifts in the bed beside him. "Johnny," she mumbles. "Johnny could be in trouble."

Kwan glances at his wife, frowning. *Who else could be calling?*

"John." Peijing is insistent. "*Please* answer it!"

Kwan reaches for the phone. "Hello?"

The man's voice at the other end of the phone is crisp, impersonal. "Is this the residence of John Kwan?"

Something turns over in Kwan's stomach. "This is John Kwan."

"This is Sergeant Kendrick of the Miami Beach Police Department. I'm sorry to disturb you at this hour."

Kwan's voice sounds strained to his own ears. "What is it?" Peijing sits up straight in the bed.

"Mr. Kwan, are you the registered owner of a red 2014 Porsche Carrera S?"

Kwan's heart begins to thump in his chest. "I bought that car for my son."

Peijing snaps on a light. "What is it?" she whispers. Kwan waves a peremptory command to be silent.

"Is your son named John Liu Kwan Jr.?"

"Yes." Kwan's heart is pounding now. *Johnny's been arrested,* he tells himself. *They're calling to tell me Johnny is in jail.* He glances at Peijing. "It's the police," he says curtly.

Peijing's eyes widen in horror. "Oh no! Please no!" Kwan swings away from her.

"Your son has been involved in a serious accident. He apparently tried to jump the Porsche over an open drawbridge. His car went into the canal."

Kwan looks at Peijing. "Johnny's been in an accident." She gasps, but Kwan has already refocused on the voice on the phone. "How badly is he hurt?"

Peijing starts to sob. For the first time in years, Kwan reaches out and takes his wife's hand. "Your son is alive," Officer Kendrick is saying. "He was taken to Jackson Memorial. You'll have to call the hospital for more information."

"Alive," Kwan breathes. He gives Peijing's hand an encouraging squeeze. "Thank you for calling. We'll get to the hospital." His wife gasps, but Kwan feels anger beginning to simmer. *This time I'm going to apply some discipline,* he tells himself. *Stupid kid.*

Officer Kendrick's voice interrupts his thoughts. "Mr. Kwan, there *was* a fatality. Witnesses say a man dove into the water shortly after your son's car went into the water. Your son came to the surface a moment later…but no one else. We've already notified that man's family."

Kwan sits motionless. "You're saying that someone died trying to rescue my son."

"It looks that way, Mr. Kwan."

"I—I don't know what to say."

"The man's family lives here in South Florida. He was engaged to be married. I certainly wouldn't do it tonight, but you may want to reach out to the family in a few days and express your gratitude."

"Of course." Kwan reaches for the pad of paper he keeps by the bed. "What was his name?"

"His name was Burton. David Burton."

Kwan writes the name on the pad. Blinks. Stares at the name. "Burton," he murmurs. His stomach is starting to churn again. "And the family's name?"

John Kwan will never forget this moment…the sound of his wife sobbing behind him…the ache in his stomach…seeing the name *Burton* in the dim light from the bedside lamp. Officer Kendrick's voice seems to echo into the phone. "His parents are named Dan and Cheryl Burton."

"Dan Burton." Kwan says softly. "There's no chance you could be mistaken about the man being dead?"

"I'm afraid not. Divers found Burton's body. It looks like Burton was able to free your son, but somehow he got caught under the wreck and drowned. Good night, Mr. Kwan."

The line clicks and Kwan sits motionless, the dial tone humming dully in his ear.

CHAPTER 26

Life After Death

IF ONE HAS NOT EXPERIENCED the horror of the late-night phone call, there is no way to empathize with the Burtons' experience. Lee Altman called the Burton home within minutes of the call from the Miami Beach police. Her voice, choked by sobs, is barely recognizable. Dan has no clear memory of either conversation. He was once kicked squarely between the eyes early in a Kung Fu competition. Although Dan went on to win the match, he remembers very little of that round or the round after that. Badly hurt and thoroughly dazed, Dan's years of training took over. Sifu later told Dan that he had scored several clean points shortly after absorbing the kick, but to this day Dan has no memory of it.

This night is much like that. Dan functions as if he were in the middle of a horrible dream; every moment seems slow-motion and surreal. He remembers holding Cheryl close while she weeps but has no idea what he said to her. He remembers Lee Altman appearing at their front door, her eyes wide and hurt, her face streaked with tears. He hopes he was of some comfort to her. He remembers the terrible trip to the morgue to identify David's body. Driving in silence with his weeping wife beside him and Lee in the back seat. Dan desperately wishes he could push the thoughts away: *How long does it take to drown? How terrified was he? What was he thinking when he finally took a breath and nothing was there but water?* Dan will not voice these questions, hoping that Cheryl or Lee haven't gone there in their own dark thoughts…but he is quite sure they have.

Dan enters the morgue alone, insisting that Cheryl and Lee wait in the outer room. He has been dreading seeing his son's face, but David's eyes are closed and there is no expression of terror. Other than the deathly pallor, David might have been sleeping. Looking down on his son's body, Dan's mind spins through a kaleidoscope of memories…holding David immediately after his birth…the look in his two-year-old son's eyes on Christmas morning…watching David wobble down the sidewalk on his bicycle after removing the training wheels. But perhaps the memory that has stayed in the forefront of Dan's mind during these awful hours is that lovely dinner in the Burton home just a few nights ago—the laughter and the tears. He hears David's voice in his mind, over and over: *Have I ever told you how proud I am to be your son?*

It is not until the next morning that the Burtons learn that it was John Kwan's son whom David died to save. For Dan, this feels like being kicked in the stomach when he is already down and gasping for breath.

The following day, the local newspaper runs a feature detailing the different paths that David Burton and Johnny Kwan Jr., both twenty-six years old, had taken. Johnny Kwan—expelled from three prestigious private schools, drunken driving arrests, a drug overdose, failing grades at the university…and yet his wealthy parents continued to keep him in expensive cars, clothes, condos…even a speedboat!

South Beach playboy Johnny Kwan has already been discharged from the hospital, presumably to resume his irresponsible life, free from any consequence other than a possible trial for driving under the influence. David Burton—graduated with highest honors from the University of Miami, who could have written his own ticket in the business world but chose to devote his life to helping others, engaged to a beautiful professional woman—is dead…killed in the act of trying to help someone who apparently wanted no help.

Young Kwan, whose blood alcohol level was three times the legal limit when his car plunged into the canal, told police that his memory of the incident is hazy. Officer Kendrick told Dan privately that Johnny had frankly admitted that he didn't care if he died. He'd had the wind knocked out of him by the crash and the impact with the deploying airbag, but he was fully conscious when his Porsche flipped into the water and began to sink.

"I thought, 'This is it,'" Johnny told Kendrick. "The car was filling with water and I just sat there and figured it would all be over soon. Suddenly the door opened, and there were hands on me, fumbling with the seatbelt, pulling me out of the car. I didn't help, I didn't fight…I didn't do anything. I didn't know if I was dreaming or maybe an angel had come to rescue me. Then I was out of the car, and those hands gave me a push…and I was on the surface. I kept looking around for the angel or whoever it was to come up next to me…but he never did. I don't know what happened to him."

I know what happened, Dan thinks savagely. *It was my angel, you worthless punk! And you didn't even think to go back down to look for him?!* Dan forces himself to stop. David had invested all of his passion into helping unhappy people who were mired in hopelessness and despair. And at the end, he gave his life for a deeply troubled young man who didn't even know what was happening. *He died doing what he loved to do, that's the bottom line,* Dan tells himself. *He died the way he lived. I wonder what John Kwan is feeling right now…if he feels anything at all.*

Dan does not know what he himself is feeling. Dan has not wept for his son…not yet; he is afraid that if he starts, he may not be able to stop. He has tried to sleep, but he keeps jolting awake from hideous, half-remembered dreams of drowning. *I keep thinking that if I shake my head hard enough, it'll be like when I was a kid having a nightmare; I'll wake up and David and Lee will be sitting here, telling me about their plans, their dreams, and David will tell me again, "Have I ever told you how proud I am to be your son?" But it won't go away. Dear God, I don't think this one will ever go away!*

A sob works its way up Dan's throat, but he grimly pushes it back, making an odd, choking sound. *You've got to be there for Cheryl. And Lee. Tomorrow is the memorial service, and the funeral is the day after. Plenty of time to go to pieces after that. Stay strong now! What was it Sifu said the other day? "If we can learn to accept heartache and suffering as a rich lesson, these things will provide us with some of the greatest growth opportunities in life." Grandmaster, I'm not feeling too rich right now…*

Cheryl is upstairs trying to sleep. Dan has not dared to ask her what her dreams are like. He is sitting alone on the living room couch. Dan knows he should be doing something—anything—but he feels no initiative, no desire to move. His mind is swirling and his stomach aches with grief.

The doorbell rings.

Dan sighs and heaves himself up from the couch. *Somebody else from the church,* Dan thinks wearily. There have been dozens of phone calls and several visitors bringing dinners and sympathy. Dan saved one precious text message from Sifu Li: "I am here for you any time of the day or night. You are always welcome to call or come."

That was nice, Dan thinks. *Now you be nice, Dan. These folks just want to show us their love.* A trace of a grin flickers across his face. *When this is over, I could write a book: "One Hundred Recipes for Chicken Casserole."*

Dan swings the door open, trying to muster a welcoming expression. A thin young woman is standing on the front step. Dan's brain locks for an instant; he stands frozen.

"Daddy?" the woman says hesitantly.

"Marcy!" Dan has not seen his daughter in two years. Her pale blue eyes, once so bright and vivacious, seem milky and lifeless. The dark circles under her eyes accentuate the unhealthy pallor of her skin. Marcy's long blond hair is stringy and unkempt. Dan's eyes run down over her body. She is rail thin; her wrinkled dress seems to hang off her. Marcy Burton is just twenty-five years old, but she could easily pass for forty.

She takes a cautious step forward. "Daddy, I'm sorry." Dan's eyes snap back to Marcy's face.

Her eyes are brimming, and a single tear runs down her cheek. "Oh Daddy, I'm so sorry!"

Dan does not think; his little girl is crying, and he sweeps her into his arms. "I'm so glad to see you!" His daughter smells of stale cigarette smoke, she is little more than skin and bones in his arms, and Dan doesn't care. He holds her even tighter. "I'm so glad you came!" Marcy buries her face in her father's neck. Suddenly she begins to sob—deep, soul-tearing sobs. Dan says nothing; he simply holds her and strokes her coarse hair. "I love you, sweetheart," he whispers. "I love you so much."

Dan hears a sharp intake of breath behind him. Cheryl is approaching softly, looking at the weeping woman in Dan's arms. Wide-eyed, she silently mouths a question: "Marcy?"

Dan nods his head and raises his eyes toward the sky. *Can it possibly be? In the week that we lose our son, our girl has finally come home?*

Marcy's sobs are shaking her bony frame. "He was so good…and I'm so bad. I'm so awful!"

Dan can feel the tears on his own cheeks now. "Shhh," he whispers. "You aren't 'awful.'" His voice is husky. "Don't talk like that."

Marcy's voice is so soft, he has to press in to hear…and he hears the words he has prayed for: "Daddy? Can I come home? Please?"

Cheryl joins them in the doorway, gently rubbing her hand on Marcy's arm. Marcy lifts her tear-stained face. "Mom!" Dan releases Marcy so that she and Cheryl can embrace.

Dan has learned from counseling and bitter personal experience that an addict will tell any lie in order to get money for drugs. But he is certain that is not why Marcy is here. *I have no reason to trust her…but perhaps this tragedy has brought her to the end.* Dan shakes his head in wonder and again raises his eyes to the heavens. *Did David give his life for more than one?* A sob wells up in Dan's throat, and this time he makes no effort to hold it back. He wraps his arms around his wife and daughter…

"There's something I have to tell you." Marcy is seated on the living room couch, holding a steaming cup of coffee in both hands as if she needs the warmth. Dan and Cheryl are seated on either side of her, pressed in close, their arms around her.

"Honey, you don't have to tell us anything," Cheryl says warmly. "We're so happy you're here."

Marcy shakes her head decisively. "No. I *have* to tell you this. I can't hold it in." She glances up at Dan, her eyes brimming with tears again.

Dan, still tortured by images of David flailing desperately beneath a sunken car, steels himself.

He doesn't want to hear about Marcy's life on the mean streets of Miami… not now. He needs no new ugly mental pictures at this time. But gives his daughter what he hopes is an encouraging smile. What Marcy says next catches him off guard.

"I saw David four days ago." Marcy's voice is very soft. She frowns down at her coffee as if it contains answers for the shattered shards of her life.

"How did he find you?" Cheryl asks curiously.

"I've been sharing an apartment with some people in Overtown," Marcy begins. Dan's lips tighten. Torn by riots in 1989, the Overtown area of Miami is notorious for violence, drugs, and prostitution.

"David showed up at the front door," Marcy continues. "Somebody at his rehab center must have told him that I was there." She takes a deep breath. "There were a bunch of us there." Marcy seems to hunch even lower over her coffee "We'd been…partying all day."

Dan understands the word "partying" to mean drug use. He says nothing, but gently rubs Marcy's back, encouraging her to tell her story her way.

Marcy's voice is almost a whisper. "I've been thinking about…making a change in my life for the past few weeks." Her eyes are locked on her coffee. "A good friend of mine died of an overdose a few weeks ago and I…I didn't want it to be me next."

Dan and Cheryl exchange glances over the top of Marcy's bowed head. *It could have been Marcy who overdosed,* Dan thinks dully. *We could have lost both our children in the space of a month.*

Marcy takes a sip of coffee. "I hadn't seen David in months. I actually thought this might be a sign that it really was time for me to get straightened out. And David is—" Marcy sucks in a breath "—*was* so warm and low-key." Marcy glances up at Cheryl. "I've known people who were enrolled at David's center. Every one of them trusted him and loved him."

Dan rubs Marcy's back again. "And he loved you, sweetheart."

Marcy winces and peers at her coffee again. She is silent for a moment, and then suddenly her shoulders start to shake with more sobs. "It doesn't make any sense, but it had to be *my* idea to get well." A tinge of bitterness enters her voice. "As soon as David asked me if it was time to make a change, I got all defensive and nasty.

"I knew what was best for my life," Marcy says bitterly. She looks up at Dan, her eyes stricken.

"I told him to leave me alone. I cursed at him, Daddy. The last thing I said to him—the last thing he heard from me on this earth was me screaming at him to get out of my place." She pushes out a choked sob. "And he went! Now I'll never see him again!"

Marcy begins to weep. Dan and Cheryl both lean closer to her and hold her tightly.

Cheryl waits until the sobs subside a bit. Her voice is low and urgent. "Marcy, I want you to listen to me. David *knew* you loved him. Your father and I know you love us. You've been caught in a trap for some time now, honey, but that doesn't change who you are at your core.

You are our daughter. We love you. David loved you like crazy, Marcy! Nothing can change that…no unhappy words, no tragedy, no stupid, lost kid hot-rodding on a bridge. *Nothing* will change that."

Dan is vaguely aware that both he and Marcy are staring at Cheryl. There is a fierce strength burning in her eyes that Dan has never seen there before.

Cheryl gently touches her daughter's cheek, but her intensity has in no way abated. "It's important that you hear this, Marcy. There is *no* looking back, only pushing forward. You haven't met Lee, David's fiancée. I told her right after this happened that, as much as David loved her, she was always going to have to share him. She would never have had him all to herself—never. He had such a huge heart! He loved with all of his being!"

Cheryl's eyes are filling with tears, but her voice is strong. "David gave and gave and gave his love to everyone he met! When people responded, he kept on giving. When they pushed him away, he gave that much more. And he finally gave himself completely away to a young man he'd never seen before!

"He…" Cheryl's voice breaks and the tears stream down her cheeks, but she presses on. She grabs Marcy's hands and holds them tightly. "He *never* stopped loving you, Marcy. And you never stopped loving him. You just lost your way for a time."

"Mom…" Marcy stares at her mother nakedly and her voice is shaking. "I *am* lost. I'm *so* lost!"

Cheryl Burton pulls Marcy into a tight embrace. "Of course you are! We're *all* lost! And all we can do is admit it to each other and get up out of the mud and keep walking!" She glances at Dan. "What has your father been telling us for years? 'Fall down seven times, get up eight!'"

Dan is afraid to speak; he does not want to interrupt. *I thought I had to stay strong for Cheryl?* he muses, astonished. *We've been married for thirty-two years; when did my wife turn into such a rock of strength? Or was it always there and somehow I missed it? Talk about character and caring! Talk about commitment!* Love for his wife fills Dan's heart. For just a moment he has completely forgotten the crushing weight of grief. *I wish Sifu was here to see this! He'd be talking about Cheryl having the heart of a champion.*

Cheryl is holding Marcy by her shoulders and looking into her eyes. "Marcy, take the first step, honey. Make that life-change! We'll back you every step of the way."

"I will, Mom." Marcy turns on the couch and looks into Dan's eyes. "Daddy, I know I've told you every lie under the sun these last few years. You have no reason to believe in me. But I want to change. It's *time* to change."

Dan's face is filled with love and wonder and hope. "It's *your* time, sweetheart. Like Mom says, we'll do everything we can to help you. Whatever you need. We believe in you with all our hearts."

CHAPTER 27

An Unexpected Visitor

TWO DAYS AFTER DAVID'S FUNERAL, Dan and Cheryl are sitting in their kitchen, drinking coffee and talking quietly.

"So…you still want to go ahead with the foundation?" Dan asks with a small smile.

"Oh yes, Dan, more than ever!" Like Dan, Cheryl is utterly exhausted. But there is no mistaking the determination in her eyes. Cheryl Burton has been knocked down, but, like her husband, she is not out of the fight. "Of course, I intend to keep my promise to Marcy. If she asks me to come to meetings or visit or whatever, I'll be there for her."

"Me too," Dan says quietly.

Marcy checked into a detoxification facility the day after David's funeral. As soon as that step is complete, she will enter a sixty-day residential program. Marcy insisted on the center where David worked. "David poured his life into that place," she told her parents. "I want to be a part of that."

Marcy cannot receive visitors during her first two weeks of treatment, but Dan and Cheryl have already planned a visit on the very first day she can invite them. And Cheryl has been on the phone with Marcy, offering encouragement.

"I know this is only her second day in detox, Dan, but I'm so hopeful! She sounds so determined."

Dan gives his wife a gentle smile. "We've been praying all these years. And then we're surprised when our prayers are answered."

"We need to pray that much harder now, Dan."

"Yes," Dan agrees.

"What about you, Dan? What's next for you?"

"I honestly don't know," he says quietly. "I can't picture myself in the same room with John Kwan."

Cheryl nods sympathetically. "I can imagine."

"We haven't talked about it, but I was relieved that he didn't come to the funeral." Dan manages a wry grin. "I guess I had put him in a no-win situation in my mind. If he comes, I hate him for intruding on our grief. If he doesn't come, I hate him for not acknowledging David's sacrifice."

"He did send the flowers, Dan. And it was a very nice card."

"Yes it was," Dan agrees thoughtfully. "Do you suppose his wife wrote it?" The handwritten card, printed in elegant, flowing script, read, *"Words cannot describe how deeply grateful we are that our son is alive...and how truly sorry we are that we cannot thank your son in person."*

"It *was* nice, Dan. Like you say, whatever they decided about coming to the funeral would have been the wrong decision."

"I know," Dan nods. "But I just don't think I have it in me to go back to work. Not *that* work."

Dan looks at his wife curiously. "Do you think you could stand working with me all day?"

Cheryl's eyes widen. "Seriously? You'd like to be a part of building the foundation?"

Dan's heart is warmed by his wife's reaction. He smiles. "If you'll have me."

Cheryl reaches across the table and squeezes his hand. "Any day, every day!"

The doorbell rings.

Dan looks plaintively at Cheryl. "I know people mean well, but I'm so tired..."

Cheryl pats his hand and gives him a mischievous smile. "Maybe somebody is bringing lasagna instead of chicken. I'll get it."

Dan sips his coffee while Cheryl walks to the front of the house. He wants to talk to Sifu before tendering his resignation, but he feels certain that this is the course he should take. *Seems funny that I'm thinking about following in my son's footsteps…Isn't it supposed to be the other way around? But I want to help people. I…*

"Dan?" Cheryl's voice interrupts his thoughts. Her voice sounds strained. "There's a man at the door who says he wants to talk to us. His name is John Kwan."

CHAPTER 28

"I Am Empty"

DAN'S MIND IS RACING FURIOUSLY as he follows Cheryl to the front door. *What is Kwan doing, coming to my home?! I have* no *desire to speak to him…Dan, get a grip! There is absolutely nothing to be gained by speaking your mind. He's probably come to say thank you. Keep your mouth shut! Listen.*

John Kwan is standing by the front door. Dan actually breaks stride when he sees him. Kwan is dressed as always—neat gray suit, brightly shined shoes, conservative tie perfectly knotted—and yet there is something strikingly different about him. His imperious manner has vanished. He looks exhausted; his shoulders seem slumped, and his eyes are lifeless. *He looks like he's aged five years!* Dan thinks. *You'd think it was his son who died!*

Cheryl speaks into the stillness. "Won't you sit down, Mr. Kwan?"

Kwan's eyes dart to Cheryl's face, then to Dan's, then back to the floor. "Thank you, Mrs. Burton." His eyes flicker up to Dan. "If it's not too inconvenient?"

Dan's gestures to an armchair. "Please." His voice sounds cold, and he tries again, working to inject a note of courtesy. "You're not interrupting anything."

Kwan sits on the edge of the chair. His eyes are still lowered and he brings his hands together, clenching and unclenching them. He does not speak.

Dan and Cheryl sit close together on the couch opposite Kwan. Dan peers at Kwan curiously.

What happened to him? He looks for all the world like a schoolchild who's been called before the principal for a scolding. You wouldn't even know it was John Kwan.

"Mr. Kwan, we were very grateful to receive the flowers and card from your family," Cheryl says, trying to prompt conversation.

"My wife was furious," Kwan says softly, almost to himself. He raises his eyes and looks at Cheryl, then at Dan. "She said if Johnny and I were men at all, we would have come to your son's funeral and got on our knees and begged for your forgiveness." He looks back down at his feet, his hands still working.

Were those tears in his eyes? Dan asks himself incredulously. Still struggling with his ugly feelings for Kwan, Dan concentrates on keeping his voice neutral. "You were in a tough spot…whether to come or not. It was a difficult decision."

"My wife is moving back to China." It may be that Kwan didn't hear Dan. "She says I have destroyed three lives: hers, our son's…and the life of your son." He raises his face to Dan and Cheryl and there *are* tears on his cheeks. Dan is so startled that he actually rocks back on the couch.

"She says I am a killer." Kwan's eyes are locked on Dan's eyes now. Dan's mind is reeling.

Kwan looks wounded, defenseless, hopeless…Dan feels that he is looking at the tear-stained face of a complete stranger.

"She says I have killed our marriage." Kwan's eyes swing to include Cheryl. "She says the only reason I haven't killed our son is because your son gave his life to save him. She says I have made a fortune killing businesses—businesses like yours, Mr. Burton."

"Maybe you'd like to try calling me Dan." The words are out of Dan's mouth before he considers them. *I can't believe I just said that! I don't like this man. I don't trust him. My son is dead because of his son. But he looks so hurt…he looks like Marcy did the night she came home…like there is nowhere else to go.*

"And I'm Cheryl." Cheryl gives Dan a loving look that goes straight to his heart. She might as well have spoken aloud: *I'm proud of you, Dan.*

"I…my first name is John." Kwan shakes his head and looks at Dan with a wondering expression. "Would you believe I have never invited anyone to call me by my first name?"

That's because you're always busy trying to intimidate, Dan thinks, and then mentally checks himself. *Knock it off, Dan! This man is sitting in your living room crying. He's asking for help. You've got to find a way to forgive. He will never trust you if you don't genuinely care.* "John,"

Dan says softly. And then, almost unbidden, he musters a genuine smile. "I'm glad you came."

Kwan does not return the smile, but there is no mistaking the gratitude in his eyes. "You are both very gracious to welcome me into your home." His eyes swing to Cheryl. "Mrs... ah, Cheryl, my son wanted to come to the funeral." Kwan shakes his head and his eyes turn inward. "I just felt that the sight of either one of us—" he shoots a quick glance at Dan "—might be more than you could bear."

Dan opens his mouth to reply, but Kwan keeps speaking, the words tumbling out in fits and starts. "Johnny doesn't understand. How did things go so terribly wrong? I...have funded a very self-destructive lifestyle." Kwan's eyes are clouded with pain. "I read the article in the newspaper about our sons. It was all correct. Your son was so good! He gave his life so that Johnny could live. He gave his life freely; no one asked him for help...Johnny says he didn't deserve to be saved. He told me he wanted to die because it would hurt me! He said it would have made us even for all the hurt I dealt him over the years." Kwan looks back and forth between Dan and Cheryl with anguished eyes. "*I* should have gotten the phone call that my son was dead. And instead it was you!"

Kwan's eyes drop to the floor, and all the energy drains out of his voice. "I don't know where he is. I don't know where my wife is. I woke up this morning and the house was empty...and I realized...that I am empty."

Dan and Cheryl are both frozen into stillness. Kwan wipes his eyes and looks straight into Dan's eyes. "All my life I have been focused on achieving financial success. Whatever it took—however many hours I worked, however many people I trampled—I would be a success. And 'success' meant becoming a millionaire. Well, I have reached my goal. And I sit here in the home of two people who have every reason to hate me because I have *nothing*. I could buy five homes like this and not even ask the price...and I am bankrupt."

Kwan sucks in a breath with a choking sound. "My father was right. He was so right! Everything

I worked for, everything I crushed people's lives to acquire...it is worthless." Kwan's head drops. "I don't expect you to understand."

Dan realizes that he has been motionless for several minutes. *He's just like that man Sifu told me about. What was the phrase he used? He said the man had "an impoverished view of wealth."*

Dan glances at Cheryl; her eyes are narrowed in sympathy. She turns to Dan, and there is no mistaking the smile at the corners of her mouth. She raises her eyebrows and nods pointedly toward John Kwan. The gesture is unmistak-able. *Go ahead,* she is saying. *Tell him!*

Dan shakes his head and cannot suppress a wry smile. Kwan, head down, does not see it. But there is no mistaking the warmth in Dan's voice. "John, I must admit that I never imagined that I would hear myself saying this, but you and I have a lot in common...a *lot* in common!"

Kwan looks up at Dan blankly, not comprehending. "You...and I?"

Dan smiles again, a smile of genuine friendship. "Let me tell you about the first time I had breakfast with Sifu Li."

CHAPTER 29

"I Want to Change"

HOURS PASS WHILE DAN EXPLAINS the People First philosophy to John Kwan. Cheryl stays close, bringing a pot of coffee, some snacks, and later some sandwiches. She watches John slowly relax and become absorbed as Dan explains the People First philosophy. John loosens his tie and sets his suit jacket aside. He asks questions, listens attentively, objects occasionally, but his focused attention never wavers. Both men shed some tears, and both make heartfelt confessions of failure.

And through it all, as morning turns into afternoon, Cheryl's love for her husband burns brightly.

With every reason to dislike and distrust John Kwan, Dan chooses to take the high road. He is warm and engaging, gracious and forgiving. At one point she hears Dan say with genuine emotion, "John, I'm no better than you; I'm just at a different stage of my journey. I was so incredibly fortunate that Sifu Li was there for me when I needed help. But I haven't 'arrived' at some point of mastery of this philosophy. None of us ever will.

"John, that newspaper article highlighted my son's virtues and your son's flaws. But it didn't mention that Cheryl and I have a son *and* a daughter. And right now our daughter is in a treatment facility, trying to beat her drug addiction. Before anyone holds me up as some kind of exemplary father, we have to talk about my abject failure with Marcy."

Cheryl's eyes begin to fill. She recalls how diligently Dan worked to reconnect with both David and Marcy after adopting the People First philosophy. David responded immediately, but Marcy maintained a certain distance from both of her parents. Dan kept trying, taking his daughter out for special "date nights" and seeking opportunities to interact with her personally. Marcy was clearly being pulled in another direction by friends at school. Shortly after graduating from high school, Marcy announced that she was moving into an apartment with two friends. From that point, her descent into addiction and degradation had been rapid and heartbreaking.

In the living room, John is looking at Dan as if he is seeing him for the first time. "So…you're not just sympathizing with my troubles with Johnny? You can *empathize?*"

Dan nods. "I watched Marcy's life spin out of control and I felt like there wasn't a thing I could do about it. I don't know if there's anything that's more devastating emotionally."

Dan looks away as John's eyes fill with tears. *I disliked this man so much, and he's just like me! Or just like I was… He's feeling so much pain…*

John's voice interrupts his thoughts. "You are a good man, Dan," John says quietly. "I don't know why I couldn't see that before."

"But that's just it, John," Dan says excitedly. "I was just thinking that you I and were exactly alike not so long ago! When my mind-set was 'profits first,' I only saw people as a means to maximizing those profits. I didn't see human beings; all I saw was human doings. All I cared about was what people could *do* to help me reach my financial goals.

"I was a high-command, high-control leader all the way. I was perfectly willing to sacrifice long-term relationships on the altar of short-term gain. It's like printing counterfeit money, John. The counterfeit bills *do* work. If you go into the store, you can buy one hundred dollars' worth of goods with your bad bill. The counterfeiter says, 'What's the big deal? The bills work; I'm getting results; I'm making money.'

"For years, Prestigious Products was making money and I was making a ton of money. But I was using a counterfeit currency! It wasn't a trust currency; it was a currency of fear. It worked for a time…but the counterfeit currency inevitably proves to be false. I was demeaning the human spirit of people in my personal and professional life, and the cost was becoming painfully apparent. My marriage was falling apart, I was a stranger to my kids, and our Purpose

Partners at Prestigious Products were increasingly disengaged. All my encounters were transactional, not transformational.

"John, you said that you are bankrupt and empty. So was I! For a long time, the only person who occupied the totality of my mind was *me*; there was no room for other people! And that self-absorbed mind-set inevitably leads to an impoverished existence. I was riding the same elevator to the basement that you feel like you're on today. I was just fortunate that Sifu helped me get off maybe one floor sooner than you. That's the only difference between you and me.

"Sifu taught me to see people as Prestigious Products' most important asset and to pour my energy into *people* first, not profits first. When I did, I discovered that, with a committed team of people who really care, you can be the most competitive company in the world. And *that* was when I began to see the dramatic change in the bottom line I'd been wanting all along."

John winces and looks at Dan frankly. "And that change *was* dramatic. I read the financials, Dan. I didn't say anything to you…but the company was showing tremendous improvement until the crash in 2008. And you worked very hard to get things turned around after that."

Dan shifts uncomfortably in his seat, feeling a hot surge of anger. *It would have been nice if you had said that before,* Dan thinks acidly. Then he chides himself. *Dan, how difficult do you think it was for John to admit that? You should be grateful, not angry!* "I had hoped to continue to increase our dividends and work toward reopening some of our locations," Dan says softly.

John nods. "And then the Chang Tao Group and I turned all that upside down." He is silent for a moment and then looks at Dan searchingly. "Dan, you have been very gracious not to talk about the counterfeit currency that *I* have been using and the terrible cost my family is paying. And yours too!" John pauses for a moment, his eyes narrowed in concentration. "Your son was a product of this People First philosophy?"

Dan looks at John, nodding wordlessly.

John shakes his head in wonder. "Imagine a company filled with people like your son! No organization would be more productive or more sustainable!" There is a new light of hope burning in John's eyes. "I want to lead a company like that! I want to change.

"Let me ask you a question, Dan: if I adopt this People First philosophy—let me rephrase that, *when* I adopt this philosophy—do you think that will be enough to regain the positive momentum you had generated at Prestigious Products?"

Dan hesitates. He is elated that he has enjoyed so much success in helping John see the importance of embracing People First...but the first key to trust is *Character*, and Dan knows that he must now speak the truth in love.

Dan speaks slowly, carefully. "John, I'd love to say, 'Yes, that's all it will take.' But that would not be good counsel. It's *part* of the solution, not all of it." Dan looks straight at John. "It's time for a little truth-telling of my own. After you held your first meeting with our company, I had another breakfast with Sifu Li the next morning. I was pretty discouraged," Dan admits. "I was thinking about resigning."

"I seem to recall pushing a lot of buttons that might have prompted you to do just that," John says matter-of-factly.

Dan grins. "Well, maybe one or two," he says drily. And then, to Dan's surprise, John Kwan grins back at him. Dan has discovered during these last several hours that John Kwan is not the one-dimensional, dispassionate autocrat that Dan had imagined him to be. John has a dry sense of humor, and the twin tragedies of David's death and his family's collapse have made him humble and teachable. Dan sincerely wants to help this man, just as Sifu has helped him.

"John, Sifu talked to me about the work we must do to build trust capital at Prestigious Products. The People First philosophy will act as a catapult which will propel us toward establishing the trust our Purpose Partners must have in us if they are to give their highest and best. Sifu gave me a definition of trust that I've memorized: *Trust is an unwavering belief in the character, competence, confidence, caring, communication, consistency, and commitment of another person.*

"John, we are suffering from a trust deficit at Prestigious Products. It had formed before your arrival, John, because of all the layoffs and store closings. Our Purpose Partners were questioning whether our leadership—whether I— truly possessed these seven keys of trust. They wondered if I truly cared about our Purpose Partners when I was laying off so many workers. Was I really committed to People First when my focus seemed to be so firmly locked onto restoring a profitable bottom line? We were running a trust deficit at Prestigious Products. You inherited that deficit, John."

Dan hesitates, but continues gently, "Unfortunately, John, you followed a course that caused that deficit to grow." Dan fully expects John to object, but John says nothing. He looks at Dan intently and nods thoughtfully. Dan continues, "Our Purpose Partners feel like they're getting close encounters of the impersonal, non-trusting kind. So do our customers. We have a broken culture, John."

John looks at Dan steadily. "Tell me what we must do to rebuild that culture."

Dan smiles and reaches for his iPad. "OK, let me show you the seven keys of trust."

CHAPTER 30

Turning the Corner

"SIFU, I'M HAVING A HARD time believing it! Just a few months ago our CFO asked me, 'Do you *really* believe John Kwan can change?' And I said I wasn't hopeful. Oh, boy, was I wrong!"

Sifu looks at Dan with his bright, curious eyes. "Tell me more," he encourages. The two men are sitting in the same restaurant where Dan first told Sifu about John Kwan's arrival. Today, Dan's mood is noticeably lighter.

Dan chuckles. "People probably said the same things about me twelve years ago. But it's like coming to work with a different person, Sifu. For two months, I met with that man every morning in his office. There was no place to sit down! He kept no chairs in his office. So he would sit behind his desk and I would just stand there. When I came back to work, he not only had two chairs—comfortable chairs—on the other side of his desk, but he's also set up a table and chairs in one corner of his office. We hold our morning meetings at that table, and he has his assistant bring us in fresh coffee for the meeting. We spend an hour a day talking about People First and mastering high trust."

Dan shakes his head, as if he is struggling to believe his own words. "He asks great questions and takes copious notes. He's so eager to get it right, Sifu! My first day back on the job, he called a meeting of our executive team. It was very much like the meeting I had with them the day you first told me about People First. He *apologized*, Sifu. He told them he had done everything wrong and destroyed trust among our team and within our organization. He didn't hold anything back. He talked about David dying to save his son…" Dan's voice is suddenly husky and he looks down at the table for a moment, struggling to regain his composure. When he looks back up at Sifu, Dan's eyes are anguished. "I'm sorry, Grandmaster. It's going to be a while before I can talk about David."

"Of course," Sifu says warmly. "You have nothing to apologize for, my friend." He looks at Dan with frank curiosity. "I thought that after the tragedy you might choose to walk away from the company."

"Sifu, that's one of the remarkable things about this! The day John Kwan came to my house, I had just told Cheryl I was going to resign and come work at her new foundation. But after John sat in my living room and bared his soul, it would have been wrong to leave. My wife was in complete agreement. The three of us sat in my living room and talked about it. John said he would understand completely if I resigned, but that he would be forever grateful if I didn't. He said that he needed me." Dan looks at Sifu wide-eyed, shaking his head in wonder. "Can you believe that, Sifu? John Kwan said, 'I need you, Dan.' He said those very words!"

Sifu reaches across the table and grips Dan's forearm. His eyes are very bright. "My friend, I have been so proud of you all these years I've known you. But I don't know that I have ever been so proud of you as I am today. You walked through a furnace that few could withstand. And you have come out the other side, not talking about yourself, but talking about the goodness of others. You are *living* People First, Dan; I am so very impressed!"

"Thank you, Sifu." Dan grips his teacher's hand. "That means a *lot* to me! Anyway, John brought the leadership team together, and he laid his whole story out. He talked about getting the phone call in the night about his son and about David's death. He told everyone about how angry his wife was, and he admitted that he still has not been able to speak to her or his son. He told them that he'd been climbing the ladder of success all these years and he's just now discovered that it was leaning against the wrong wall—that the wall had just collapsed on him. It was remarkable! And he gave our team two immediate assignments: the first was to let everyone in the organization know that we are reinstating the People First philosophy, effective immediately; the second was to develop an action plan for rebuilding our customer service department. It was an incredibly positive meeting."

Sifu nods and smiles. "Indeed it was! How did your team respond?"

"Cautiously," Dan admits. "John was tremendous. He was human; he was transparent. But these folks have been pretty beaten down, particularly our CFO and VP of Sales. So the response wasn't quite as enthusiastic as the one they gave me on the day I introduced People First.

"I stayed back with John after the meeting and talked with him about what you told me about building bridges of integrity. I told him that a bridge isn't built in a day. It takes steady work. But I told him he had put in a *great* first day's work. He was grateful for the encouragement. And he said he wants me to assume a much more proactive role in steering the organization, as I had before Chang Tao bought us."

Dan grins at his mentor. "When I got back to my office there were members of the team practically lined up to ask me if this is for real." Dan chuckles. "I'd be talking to one person and someone else would walk by the door, looking to see if I was alone. I felt like air traffic control at Miami International!"

Sifu smiles, but he is watching Dan closely. "And in the two weeks since the meeting?"

Dan's grin widens. "People First works! John and I have been talking a lot about the philosophy and how the seven keys of trust are so integral to its success. We've spent a lot of time on caring and communication, and he's taken it to heart. He's met with every member of the executive team one-on-one. He went to their offices, rather than summoning them to come meet with him. The feedback I've gotten on those meetings has been extremely positive. The ice is melting."

"That's wonderful, Dan!" Sifu says warmly.

"But that isn't all; John seized on Noel Fogarty's idea of skip-level communication. He's been meeting with people at various levels of the organization. He even asked me to take him on an all-day tour of some of our locations. He sat and talked with store managers and sales reps. He even spent 15 minutes chatting with one of the facilities managers. It turns out he's very good at asking questions and proactive listening. It's been *very* impressive, Sifu. He genuinely wanted to change, and he's doing it! I asked him the other day if it was OK to tell him that I'm proud of him, and his face lit up like a little kid. It's really been an amazing couple of weeks."

Dan turns away and looks out the window, wincing in sudden pain. When Dan looks back at

Sifu, his eyes are suddenly full of tears. "Tomorrow will be one month since David's death. And it still hits me like a hot iron in my guts."

Dan takes a deep, quavering breath and gives Sifu a look of utter incomprehension. "I can't explain it, Grandmaster. So many truly wonderful things have happened since David died! It's not just work, although that's been amazing. Marcy is doing great in her rehabilitation. Cheryl talks to her every night, and I've been on the phone with her..."

The emotion is too much. Dan puts his hand over his mouth to stifle a sob and the tears spill down his cheeks. "I've got no reason to trust her, Sifu, but she sounds like my little girl again! She sounds so happy and so *hopeful!* And Cheryl!" Dan roughly wipes his eyes and smiles. "Sifu, my wife is such a rock of strength! The first few days I thought I needed to be strong for *her.* Oh my word, Sifu, that woman is a tiger! She's been pouring into Marcy, pouring into me, and she was so gracious and kind with John Kwan. And *now* she's working to launch our new foundation. What a woman!" Dan's joy is returning. "I wouldn't want to get in the ring with her, Sifu. She'd have me tapping out in two minutes!"

Sifu is smiling gently at Dan, but there is a question in his eyes. "You say you don't understand...?" he prompts.

"Here's what I don't get, Sifu: How is it that so many wonderful things can be happening in the midst of the most awful thing that's ever happened in our lives? I don't think I've ever been so much in love with my wife as I have been these last few weeks. It's been years since I enjoyed going to work so much. I'm part of the *solution*, and I'm helping to teach another man how to be too. And then, in the middle of it all, something reminds me of David and that awful pain comes. I'm almost guilty, Sifu, because I'm having so much fun! How do you explain that?"

Sifu's eyes turn inward as he collects his thoughts. Then he looks at his friend with deep compassion. "Dan, you and your family have been in my thoughts and prayers every day. I've given a great deal of thought to your son. I know this wound is very raw and real. Please stop me if this becomes too painful."

Dan looks into the Grandmaster's eyes with complete trust. "Grandmaster, you have never uttered one word to me that was not intended to make me stronger and better. Please tell me your thoughts."

Sifu speaks slowly, carefully. "Dan, there is a proverb that teaches us that unless a kernel of wheat is planted in the soil and dies, it remains unprofitable. But if it dies it will produce a plentiful, profitable harvest of changed lives."

Sifu hesitates, looking at Dan to gauge his reaction. Dan nods earnestly, indicating his desire for Sifu to continue. "David may very well be that kernel of wheat, Dan. You've told me that your David was laying down his life for others. He could have made a handsome living in the business world; he died to that because he wanted to invest in people. He was looking to reap that harvest of changed lives. He died to himself and allowed his heart to be planted in the rich soil of service and sacrifice.

"Dan, some of the greatest movements in human history were born out of such sacrifice. This country, Dan, and the freedoms we take for granted today, were born out of the sacrifice of a group of men who pledged to each other their lives, their fortunes, and their sacred honor in the pursuit of creating a new kind of freedom that had never been seen in history. Many of those men paid the full measure of that pledge. And what a harvest grew from that sacrifice!

"Dan, my personal choice is to live life with the idea that everything happens according to a plan and purpose. David's death was not a random event; it was not meaningless or insignificant. Is John Kwan more or less motivated to change his life as a result of your son's gift of life to his son? Is Cheryl more or less committed to establishing the new foundation? It has changed from being a nice idea to a life's mission! Could David's death have been the catalyst for greater growth for your foundation? Is Marcy more or less motivated to change course because of David's example? In just one month, Dan, we are already seeing those first green shoots of new life springing up through the soil."

Dan's eyes are widening with comprehension and new hope. "Marcy told us that she dreams of picking up where David left off," Dan says softly. "She wants to reach out to other young women and show them the power of a changed life."

"You see?" Sifu's eyes are filled with the light of intensity. His voice rises with excitement. "Dan, you and Cheryl have an opportunity to allow David's life *and* his death to impact a great many lives. And I would encourage you to let your vision expand. Could it be that David is telling us in his sacrificial death that we should *all* be willing to lay down our lives for one another? Could David's death be the impetus that we have all been looking for to understand the true effect of People First? Dan, a single idea can spark a worldwide movement. There is no better way to give meaning to David's death than to let it be the seed that produces a rich harvest of changed lives!"

Sifu leans back from the table and relaxes, taking a breath and letting it out with a sigh. "That is how I understand something so awful that none of us can really understand it, my friend. It is not a perfect answer, Dan, but it is the only one I have for you."

Sifu does not need to ask Dan if his words have been helpful. Dan's eyes are shining with purpose and strength. "But it makes so much sense, Sifu! I told you I feel guilty because I've been having 'fun.' The proper word is *joy*. I've been feeling a sense of joy at the new light of hope I see in John Kwan and in our Purpose Partners. I'm joyful about this strong, dynamic woman I'm married to, Sifu. And I'm overjoyed that my prayers for Marcy..." here Dan's voice grows husky "...prayers often offered through tears, are being answered. You're right, Sifu, I'm seeing new life everywhere! I heard a song years ago that went something like, 'Though sorrow may last for a night, there's joy found in the morning.' I know this sorrow over David's death is going to last a lot longer than a night, but the joy is there too. Isn't that incredible?"

Sifu nods vigorously. "It is an incredible path of strength and hope and faith. It is the strength that I've always seen in you, Dan, the strength that reached out twelve years ago and admitted that it did not have all the answers. There is *strength* in admitting one's weakness, Dan! It is the hope that believed a new way of thinking and behaving could accomplish great change. And it is the faith that trusts that, even in the midst of the worst kind of storm, you *will* see the rainbow...that there is the promise of new life."

Now it is Sifu's turn to look at Dan with wonder in his eyes. He shakes his head. "Dan, you have been very gracious over the years to introduce me to others as your teacher and your mentor. My friend, those days have ended."

Dan looks at Sifu quizzically. "I don't understand."

Sifu's face is suddenly solemn. "Dan, there is more I can teach you about Walu Kung Fu. There is even more that I can teach you about People First and mastering high trust. But I am no longer your mentor. You are my friend, if you will have me. You strengthen me. You are teaching me. I see it as iron sharpening iron. I sharpen your blade and you are most definitely sharpening mine.

From this day forward, Dan, I would have you introduce me to others as your friend."

Dan is looking at Sifu incredulously. "Sifu," he says huskily, "to say that I am honored is to wildly understate it. I hope you will never stop teaching me, Grandmaster!"

"And that is just how I feel about you...Grandmaster," Sifu replies warmly.

CHAPTER 31

Not Again!

THE NEXT MORNING, DAN IS eager to sit down with John Kwan for their morning coffee—John has insisted that they no longer call it a "meeting"—because he wants to share the last thing Sifu Li had said to him the previous day: "Tell John Kwan I'd very much like to meet him and congratulate him on embarking on the way of People First. If he'd enjoy it, perhaps you and Cheryl would accompany him for a dinner at my home."

Dan strides cheerfully down the hall toward John's office. He realizes he is actually whistling softly to himself. He hears himself speaking to Sifu yesterday: "I almost feel guilty that I'm having so much fun!" Dan actually grins. *Feeling so much* joy. *Joy at the new life David died to produce.*

He enters John's office, still grinning. "Good morning, John," he booms cheerfully...and freezes.

It is as if the John Kwan Dan has come to know and genuinely like in these recent weeks has disappeared. The man sitting behind the desk looks up at Dan coldly, without a trace of the warm smile that has appeared with increasing frequency. "John?" Dan asks. "What's wrong?"

John looks at Dan and his eyes flash with anger. "I received a phone call last night from my employers in China. They expressed their great displeasure with the new direction we have implemented here. They directed me to resume all cost-cutting operations immediately."

Dan stiffens. John's face is so utterly cold that he is unsure what to say. He nods once, waiting.

"And?"

The angry flame burns even brighter in John's eyes. "I told them that I am a man of integrity and that I would do no such thing!" he snaps. His shoulders slump and the anger in his eyes turns to sadness. "I met with our executive team and our Purpose Partners. I looked them in the eye and told them I am as committed to People First as you have been." His eyes flare again. "Am I now to tell them that it was all a ruse? That I am the most monstrous kind of liar?"

Dan actually relaxes and gives John a crooked grin. "John, you looked so angry...I thought you had an issue with me!"

"I do have issues!" John snaps, still unsmiling. "All sorts of issues!" He looks down at his desk.

"I have come to understand that the life I lived for so many years was utterly unprofitable. The cost to me, to my family, and to *your* family, Dan, has been horrific. I go home to my empty penthouse every night and think about how many lives I destroyed in my pursuit of wealth—the homes that are empty now, just as my home is, because I was driven to own a penthouse. How many marriages disintegrated because one partner could no longer pay all the bills after I had killed their spouse's business?"

John looks up at Dan, his face taut with pain. "How many men and women are living empty, aimless lives because I took away their livelihood and sense of purpose in order to maximize profits? How many people turned to drugs and alcohol, like my son has? How many suicides?"

"John," Dan says softly. "You can't let your thoughts go there. There's no profit in that either, my friend."

John is looking back down at his desk. "There was another thing I worked for all these years," he says in a flat voice. "Respect. The respect of my employers and the respect of my family. If I was respected, I cared nothing about the lives I crushed."

He glances up at Dan, and his eyes filled with bitterness. "Lives like yours, Dan."

"John..."

"My wife decided early on that being married to a corporate raider gave her no pleasure. It enraged me that she would not honor me for my great skill." His voice softens. "It was like experiencing my father's disapproval all over again."

John leans forward and puts his head in his hands. "I did not deal with that well at all. Instead of listening to my wife, I pushed her away."

Dan slips into one of the chairs across from John's desk. "John," he says softly, "men like you and I can't change the past. We can only work to craft a new future."

"The future!" The words are pushed out in a bitter laugh. John raises his eyes to Dan's. "Through that unhappiness, Dan, I was always able to count on the respect and support of my employers in China. They told me time and again that I was their top operative. 'Kwan the Conqueror,' they called me. When I visited the home office, younger men turned in their seats to look at me when I walked by." John's voice takes on a sardonic tone. "Ah, that was worth it all...all the shattered dreams and a wayward son and an unhappy, alcoholic wife."

John heaves a deep sigh. "Last night I told my superiors that I had discovered a new business model. I told them the existing leadership at Prestigious Products was unlike any we had ever encountered. I pleaded with them to give me one quarter to prove the worth of this philosophy."

John looks at Dan, his eyes wide. "I actually said, 'I beg you!' I said I was supremely confident that we would provide an ROI unlike anything they had ever seen."

"I gather they weren't interested," Dan says drily.

"They are selling Prestigious Products, Dan." The words seem to hang in icy stillness. Dan feels himself go dead inside.

"They are selling the company," John continues, "and I am unemployed. We can only hope that the new owners will be willing to listen to what you have to tell them. But I must tell you that the Chang Tao Group has no interest in the business philosophy of the buyer; they simply want to maximize the profit."

Dan's mind is racing. "But John, why are you unemployed? Simply because you deviated from standard procedure for three weeks?"

"No." For the first time, Dan sees a glint of humor in John's eyes. "I am no longer employed because after I tendered my resignation, I told my superiors precisely what I think of their philosophy. I remembered something you had told me and I gave it back to them as best I could. I said they had money without meaning, cash without contentment, finances without fulfillment, prosperity without purpose, success without significance, and shadow without substance." John looks quizzically at Dan. "Did I say it correctly?"

212

The ache Dan feels in his guts dissolves in a burst of hearty laughter. "You said it beautifully!"

John nods in apparent satisfaction. "I said they had acquired many *things*, but that I had learned through the price of great pain that people are more important. That was when they hung up."

Dan looks at John with undisguised astonishment. "John, I don't know what to say!"

John tries to look stern, but now there is no missing that dry humor that Dan has come to enjoy so much. "Oh, you've said quite enough already, Mr. Burton. All this talk about integrity and caring has turned my life upside down!"

Dan laughs again and raises his hands in mock surrender. "My apologies!" Still grinning, he gestures to the table John has set up in his office. "John, let's have our coffee and talk this through."

John nods and gets to his feet. "One thing we will *not* be discussing," he says as he walks around the table, "is my resignation. That is final. I may not have honored my father when he was alive, but I can certainly honor him now. I may be unemployed, and I may go home to an empty house, but I *will* stand on my integrity. I know now that one can have an enormous bank account and be poor beyond measure."

Dan grins. "You may not be unemployed for as long as you think. I've heard there is a new foundation in town that needs a Chief Operating Officer. The pay won't be too great right away, but the people are pretty nice to work for."

John stops in his tracks, his eyes searching Dan's face. "You and Cheryl would consider hiring me?" His voice is almost a whisper. "After all I have done to your family?"

"John," Dan says warmly, "if I didn't make the offer, I might be unemployed at home! My wife is a big fan of yours!" They move to the table and take their seats. "There's someone else who wants to meet you. Sifu Li has invited you to join him for dinner."

John's eyebrows shoot up. "The Grandmaster invited me for dinner?"

Dan nods. "I hope you don't mind if Cheryl and I join you." Dan grins. "You can tell Sifu about your new career path."

John shakes his head, clearly astonished. "Dinner with Sifu Li! I'll be delighted to accept!"

Dan looks at John curiously. "I know you haven't had much time to think, but how are you feeling?"

John looks at Dan frankly. "The whole life that I knew, that I was quite comfortable with just one month ago, has completely unraveled. The last few weeks have been like riding up and down on an express elevator. And yet there is a part of me that feels more free than I have felt since I was a child." He chuckles. "I guess I would have to say that I am very confused."

"I don't think you're confused at all, John," Dan says confidently. "You were confronted with a decision, an ethical dilemma, and you reacted instinctively! I'm so proud of you, John! You *are* a man of integrity. In just a few weeks, you have taught me to trust you, John. My wife trusts you, and she doesn't give her trust lightly. And there are others here in this company who have come to believe in you in a remarkably short time! You are *not* confused, John. You are walking in integrity."

For the first time since they have met, John Kwan reaches across the table and gives Dan's forearm a quick squeeze. It is quick and tentative, but Dan can't help but recall Sifu Li's gesture of respect and affection the previous day. "I have never had a friend like you," John says simply.

Dan is touched. "In spite of all the unhappiness that has gone with it, John, it has been my privilege to get to know you. I am honored to be your friend." *More new life growing,* Dan thinks happily. And then suddenly there is that awful, unexpected ache in his stomach. *Oh, but I miss you, David! I'd trade it all to have you back!* Dan quickly looks down at the table so that John will not see the grief in his eyes.

John turns away from Dan and looks out the window at the bright sunshine outside for a moment. "Dan, I need to ask for two kindnesses."

"Of course!" Dan is only too happy to have his thoughts interrupted.

"First, I am technically a trespasser here. I am quite sure that my resignation was accepted in China. I'd like your permission to remain here in this office for one week."

"Certainly!"

"Thank you. The second kindness may be more difficult. You have been teaching me about the importance of clear, consistent communication. I'm sure you will want to share the information about this pending sale with everyone in this organization immediately. I have no authority to stop you from doing that. But I ask you to keep this between you and me for one week. In the meantime, I want you and the executive team to continue what you have been doing: getting customer service up and running and catching people doing things right. "

He looks earnestly at Dan. "Not a word to anyone other than your wife. At the end of one week, we'll schedule an all-company meeting like the one we had when I first arrived here. I will make the appropriate announcement at that time. If anyone must tell our Purpose Partners that I have failed to keep my pledge to revive People First at Prestigious Products, it will be me."

Dan looks at John doubtfully. "Tell me...why," he says slowly.

John Kwan looks straight into Dan's eyes. "Dan, you have very little reason to trust me. You honor me greatly when you tell me that you do. Now I am asking you to let me trade on that trust. Do you trust me, Dan?"

Dan looks at John for a long moment. "Yes, John," he says sincerely. "Yes I do."

John looks out the window again. A slight smile is tugging at the corner of his mouth, but his face is inscrutable. "One week, Dan. Perhaps I may yet live up to my family name."

CHAPTER 32

People First

DAN AND CHERYL ARE SEATED in the back of the large meeting room. *I was uncertain the last time I came to one of these meetings,* Dan thinks; *today I am utterly clueless!* It will all end, apparently, where it began a few short months ago. Once again, the entire corporate staff and all senior managers of Prestigious Products are assembled for a meeting with John Kwan. Once again, Dan feels anxious eyes scanning his face, and he works to keep his face impassive. *If I was wrong to trust John, I'm going to have to apologize to a great many people.*

The week since John first told Dan about the pending sale of Prestigious Products has been slightly surreal. Having promised to keep silent about the pending sale of the company, Dan has felt extremely uncomfortable about interacting with the members of his team. He has kept to himself much more than usual, relying on telephone and email to communicate, a practice he had worked hard to change ever since he introduced People First to Prestigious Products.

Two days ago, John Kwan told Dan privately that there had been an agreement in principle to buy the company. True to his word, he asked Dan to schedule the all-staff meeting. The strain showed on Dan's face as John was speaking, and John actually broke into a smile. "I asked you to trust me for one week, my friend. I promise you that this meeting will not be as unpleasant as the first one I held with the company."

Dan had looked at John in confusion. "John, people will be asking me questions. Can you give me some information?"

John had actually given Dan an impish smile. "Tell anyone who asks you that you expect this to be a positive meeting. And there's one other thing, Dan. I'd be very grateful if Cheryl would attend."

Dan was nonplussed. "*My* Cheryl?"

John's smile widened. "Yes. I plan to talk about the People First legacy that you created for Prestigious Products, and I'd very much like for Cheryl to be there to hear it. Please tell her that I would take it as a personal kindness if she would attend. You'll ask her?"

Dan had nodded his head, but his doubts and confusion had been clear in his voice. "John, I can only hope you're not building a plank of trust for me to walk off."

John actually laughed aloud. "No planks, my friend; a bridge to the future. That's all I can tell you now. If anyone asks you what this meeting is about, you can honestly tell them that I have kept you in the dark."

"That certainly won't be an exaggeration!" Dan had said with some feeling.

"Dan, in two days and I will explain everything to you and the entire organization."

There have been other things that seemed slightly "off" to Dan's internal radar—*highly sensitized internal radar*, Dan admits to himself now. Dan is aware that John has held several meetings with Marcia Lundgren. It has been another cause for joy for Dan to see how hard John has worked to reset the relationship with his CFO, and how gracious Marcia has been to forgive and move forward. Marcia had visited Dan's office several times to share her delight over John

Kwan adopting People First...until this week. Dan assumes that Marcia is assisting John with the details of the pending sale, but it has almost seemed that Marcia has been avoiding him in recent days. *Could it be, Dan, that she's wondering if you've been avoiding her?* Dan nods to himself with a wry grin. It *has* been an unusual week.

Because Dan has been spending so much time with Sifu in the past few months, he has felt more comfortable picking up the phone to call his friend and sort through his thoughts. He has been trying to reach Sifu all week long, and has been disappointed not to get a return call. Sifu has sent two apologetic text messages, explaining that he is "very busy with a new business venture" and promising to call Dan in a few days.

Well, I have no earthly idea what John has planned, but I'm sure I'll have a lot to discuss with Sifu after today. At that moment, the conversation in the room begins to hush as John Kwan enters the room. And he is not alone. Just as Dan's eyes start to narrow in disbelief, Cheryl leans close and whispers, "Dan, isn't that Sifu Li with John?"

Dan is so startled that he does not immediately reply. There are actually two familiar figures flanking John: the first is Bill Newell, the former chairman of the Prestigious Products board of directors; the second is Sifu. All three men are smiling broadly. John gestures to two chairs in the front row; Bill and Sifu are seated and John climbs the stairs to the stage.

Dan's mind is whirling. True to his word, Bill Newell had submitted his resignation shortly after the announcement of the Chang Tao takeover. Cheryl's voice interrupts Dan's thoughts. "What in the world is *Sifu* doing here?" she whispers. "I didn't know he and John had met."

Dan looks at his wife and shakes his head wordlessly. He inclines his head toward the stage. "I guess we're about to find out," he murmurs.

The dramatic change in John Kwan is apparent even before he begins to speak. The stark black business suit he wore to the last meeting has been replaced by a tan summer suit and bright, cheery tie. But the biggest change is that John's cold, imperious stare has been replaced by a warm, genuine smile. Their eyes meet, and John's smile widens. His eyes widen with pleasure when he sees Cheryl and he nods a silent "Thank you" to Cheryl.

"Good morning, ladies and gentlemen," John begins. "Thank you for coming. Since our first meeting together, I have had the pleasure of meeting some of you personally and speaking to you about a change that has taken place in my life and in my thinking in recent weeks. But for many of you, your only interaction with me was seeing me stand on this stage to tell you that 'tough times demand tough leadership' and that I was planning 'austerity measures.' Perhaps most discouraging to many of you was my announcement that the People First philosophy which Dan Burton initiated here twelve years ago was being discarded. I told you I was here to maximize profits, and I'm sure you realized that the recognition and celebration of the human spirit played no part in reaping those profits, as far as I was concerned."

John takes a deep breath and lets it out slowly, looking around the room. Just as on the first day when he addressed this room, there is complete silence.

John smiles again. "Today is a day of many firsts for me. Until just recently, I do not remember a time in my life when I told a single human being that I was wrong; today I stand here before you all to say that I was deeply, disastrously wrong that day. And it got worse! Just days later I ordered layoffs which impacted the lives and families of 130 Purpose Partners, which crushed their hopes and dreams and further dispirited all of you. I did these things because I cared about profits first and people last. I did not care about people at all. Not you, not even…" John suddenly hesitates, and Dan realizes John is struggling to control his emotions. When he speaks again, his voice is soft. "Not even those who were most important in my life."

John's voice strengthens. "I'm sure you are all aware that my indifference has had catastrophic consequences for two families. My son, John Jr., decided that he had no desire to live in a home with a father who cared nothing for him as a human being. He decided—" John's voice is rough with emotion, but he pushes ahead "that he had no desire to live. He drove his car into a canal in Miami. A heroic young man dove into the water to save Johnny. That young man saved my son's life, but died during the rescue. His name was David Burton, Dan Burton's son."

Dan reaches over to Cheryl and takes her hand. *My goodness,* Dan thinks. *I thought I was courageous to get up in front of the senior executive team to tell them about my failures as a leader. How hard is this for John?* Cheryl tightly grips Dan's hand. There is no sound in the room, not even a chair squeaks.

John looks around the room slowly. "The next day, my wife, Peijing, packed her bags and left our home. All the years of frustration of living with a man who cared only about profits and nothing about people poured out of her. And as she stood there, weeping, saying things that she hoped would hurt me as much as I had hurt her and my son, I realized that all the profits I had earned for my employer and the money amassed in my bank account are virtually worthless.

Another man's son gave his life to save my son, and my son did not care if he lived or died. When my wife walked out the door, I realized that no amount of money could repair the damage I had done."

Dan glances over at Cheryl. She is looking intently at John, but sensing Dan's eyes on her, she glances at her husband and silently mouths the word "Wow!" Dan nods.

"I had no idea what to do," John says. "For the first time in my life, I was forced to recognize that I had no friends…that I had never *had* a friend—only business associates. And so, in utter desperation, in anguish of soul, I went to see two people whom I half-expected would order me out of their home. They certainly would have had every right to do so. I went to see Dan and Cheryl Burton."

A low murmur wafts through the room like a breeze. A few people turn in their seats to look at the Burtons. Cheryl shifts uncomfortably in her chair. Near the front of the room, Marcia Lundgren turns to look at Dan, and inexplicably her face lights in a big grin. *What in the world is she smiling about?* Dan wonders.

"And that brings me to another first," John says. His face lights in a wide, warm smile. "I realized this morning that, although I have made dozens of introductions at business meetings throughout my career, I have never introduced anyone as my friend. Well, ladies and gentlemen, I would like to introduce you to two of the kindest, most caring people I have ever known, my two remarkable friends, Dan and Cheryl Burton. May I ask you both to come up here, please?"

Cheryl glances at Dan, a question in her eyes. *Oh, well,* Dan thinks bemusedly. *This whole morning has been an exercise in trust anyway…* He smiles wryly at his wife and inclines his head toward the stage. *Shall we?* the gesture says. Aware that hundreds of eyes are on them, the Burtons rise and self-consciously make their way to the front of the room, still holding hands tightly.

Someone begins to applaud. Dan sees that it is Marcia, who is on her feet and pounding her palms together, her eyes shining. The applause quickly spreads throughout the room, and more and more people rise. Soon Dan and Cheryl are walking down a narrow corridor of applauding men and women. He looks up at the stage, and John is beaming down at them, applauding as vigorously as anyone.

They mount the stairs to the stage, and greet John. The noise level in the room only increases, and now there are cheers and whistles from the crowd. Dan glances down at Sifu and is amazed to see something he has never seen before—the Grandmaster's cheeks are wet with tears! Yet Sifu's smile is wide and bright, and he is applauding loudly. Dan is afraid that his own eyes are beginning to fill; he looks around the room and waves his thanks. Then he steps back slightly and gestures to Cheryl in a *Please say hello to my wife* gesture. The applause swells again, and Cheryl blushes. Dan can't help but grin, and he joins in applauding Cheryl.

Finally, the raucous greeting begins to die down, and Dan, still grinning, motions to his Purpose Partners to be seated. He looks back at Sifu and Bill Newell, who are both smiling and taking their seats. Dan shrugs his shoulders slightly, palms up, shaking his head in a *What's going on?* gesture. Sifu nods and smiles, gesturing confidently toward John. Dan moves back toward Cheryl, taking her hand and looking at John quizzically. "John," Dan begins, "I am… clueless."

John actually chuckles. "I know you are, Dan." He turns to look out at the people assembled in the room. "Ladies and gentlemen, I have said that I went to the Burton's home just days after the death of their son, fully expecting them to tell me they had no desire to talk to me or even look at me. Instead…" John turns and looks at Dan and Cheryl with a warm smile. His eyes are very bright. When he resumes speaking, his voice is rough with emotion. "Instead, they welcomed me…I poured out my heart to them. I…" John hesitates, and then his voice strengthens. "I told them that I had failed in every way imaginable. I had failed as a husband, as a father, and I had failed all of you as a leader."

Once again, a hush falls over the room. John looks around for a moment, letting his words reach every person in the room. Instinctively, the Burtons move closer to John on the stage, as if unwilling to leave him standing alone while making this incredibly difficult admission. John understands the gesture and smiles at them gratefully. John takes a deep breath. "This man and this woman," he continues, "who had every reason to see me and my family as directly responsible for the death of their only son, sat with me for hours. They spoke of a dramatic change that had taken place in their own lives as a result of a philosophy they had learned from a man named Sifu Li, the philosophy you have come to know as People First.

"Dan went further; he explained to me very kindly, very humbly, that events of the last few years had conspired to rob many of you of the trust you once had in Prestigious Products. But as gracious as Dan was, it became clear to me very quickly that I was the one who was most responsible for this loss of trust." John turns his head. "May I have the PowerPoint please?"

The large screen behind them is lit with a very fine graphic representation of Sifu's seven keys of trust. Dan looks at the slide with fascination; the graphics are beautifully done. Dan glances at Sifu with a smile, and Sifu nods his head vigorously, indicating his approval. Bill Newell is also grinning broadly.

"I want to present you with the seven keys of trust, which were developed by a man whom I'll introduce in a moment. I've had the opportunity to sit with this man over the last few days and get his thoughts on these concepts, concepts which you'll be hearing a great deal more about in the months ahead."

Dan is aware that people are watching him, and he struggles not to let his confusion show on his face. *John has been meeting with Sifu? Why wouldn't Sifu have told me about that? And what in the world is Bill Newell doing here looking so cheerful?*

"Have you ever met someone for the first time," John is saying, "and walked away from that encounter thinking, 'I cannot be specific, but I do not trust that person'? It may be a vague feeling of mistrust, more intuition than something concrete, but you are on guard. I suspect that many of you walked out of this meeting room the last time we were all here feeling that way about me! The reason for this feeling of unease is that the person you have just met has failed to demonstrate one or more of these seven keys of trust. Whether we are conscious of it or not, we evaluate everyone we meet by these seven keys of trust: character, competence, confidence, caring, communication, consistency, and commitment.

"Take a look at the screen. Did you find that the person you have just met is a man or woman of *character*? Do they have integrity? Will they keep their word? Are they *competent*? Have they demonstrated the ability to complete the action they have said they will perform? Are they *confident* in their ability? Or do they seem worried and unsure—which, of course, would cause *you* to worry! Perhaps they have very strong character, and they are competent and confident, but are they *caring*? I was recently reminded of a phrase that was frequently used by one of the world's great sales trainers, who said, 'People don't care how much you know until they know how much you care.'

"What about the person's *communication* ability? Does he or she clearly communicate principles, purpose, and plans? How is the person's *consistency*? Do you know what to expect from this individual? Or do attitudes and actions seem to frequently change? And finally, does this individual demonstrate a *commitment* to building and maintaining trust?"

John raises a cautionary hand. "Please understand that I do not introduce these seven keys of trust to you so that we can all begin roaming the halls of Prestigious Products, examining our Purpose Partners to see if they measure to all seven keys. To the contrary, I present them to you so that you and I can evaluate *our own* behavior and determine if we ourselves are building bridges of trust with family, friends, and Purpose Partners.

"When Dan Burton presented this concept to me, I was forced to evaluate myself—to see myself through your eyes. I have always thought of myself as a man of *character*. I am very committed to my principles and live them consistently.

Unfortunately, those principles were entirely rooted in an all-consuming desire to maximize profits. I did it legally, but I did it ruthlessly and relentlessly. I was highly *competent* in my role as a venture capitalist and supremely *confident* in my ability. But then we come to the fourth key of trust: *caring*."

John looks around the room again. All eyes are on him, and the room is very still. "When I stood up on this stage a few months ago, did I communicate caring? Or something quite different? Just days later, I ordered the dismissal of one hundred and thirty of your Purpose Partners, eliminating an entire department, and made no effort whatsoever to communicate the reason for that drastic move. I left you to wonder and whisper among yourselves. Did I build bridges of trust? No; my callous indifference to the lives of people and my noncommunication utterly destroyed any rickety bridges of trust that might have remained.

"I may have been very consistent in my behavior and fully committed to earning profits, but I consistently demonstrated that I was not committed to *you*...only to the bottom line. So I clearly failed in at least two of the seven points—caring and communication—and gave you good reason to doubt me in two more of those points: character and commitment."

John looks around the room. Dan has been watching faces in the audience. Men and women are staring at John with rapt attention. Even with the culture of transparency that Dan had worked so hard to build at Prestigious Products, Dan is sure that no one in this room has ever seen a leader speak with such complete vulnerability.

"And so," John continues in a softer voice, "because you were rightly questioning the character and competence of a man who would eliminate the entire customer service department, a man who had communicated nothing but that he did *not* care about what you thought or what you were feeling, a man who had clearly demonstrated that his only commitment was to the bottom line—and probably because you were overwhelmed with being understaffed in the first place—your sales and customer service fell off. Our customers responded to our new 'People Last' culture by shopping elsewhere."

Another pause. *There were a number of people in this room who could have told John all that before the layoffs,* Dan thinks matter-of-factly. He does not realize that he is nodding his head.

But it wouldn't have registered. It took this awful tragedy to open his eyes and make him see. What did Sifu say? David's death was the seed that produces a rich harvest of changed lives, and it's happening right in front of my eyes!

"During the course of the past few weeks I have been meeting regularly with Dan Burton," John is saying, "and he has given me a crash course in People First. I've come to understand that whatever I want our external customers to feel—that they are wanted, that they are the life's blood of our business—I must make you feel that first. Dan made me see that I could not just stand up here on a stage and tell you that I need you and that I believe in you, but that my words must be SSIP—sincere, specific, immediate, and personal. I've been meeting with many of you and visiting many of your locations, trying to communicate that sincerity as best I can."

Now Dan sees smiles and heads nodding around the room. John is hitting themes that the leaders of Prestigious Products have come to embrace as their own. Cheryl gives Dan's hand a squeeze. She, too, can see and feel the people in the room coming on board with what John is saying.

"I asked the Burtons to come up here because they have been in a very difficult situation for the past seven days, and, as always, they handled it with the utmost character. You see, eight days ago I learned that my former employer, the Chang Tao Group, which had purchased Prestigious Products just a few months ago, is selling the company immediately in order to maximize their profits."

A sound, something like a collective "Ahhh" sweeps through the large meeting room. *Ouch,* Dan thinks. *John was just starting to win them, and now all the air just went out of the balloon.*

"I was as disappointed as you are," John says, raising his voice slightly to quiet the murmurs.

"For the first time in my life, I had found something I believed in, a cause other than myself, and I was being told that I could no longer pursue it. Which is why I refer to the Chang Tao Group as my 'former employer.' I offered my resignation and it was accepted."

Again, another jumble of subdued conversation sweeps through the room. John waits, letting his listeners absorb the information. "I will not be a part of a 'profits first, people last' philosophy any longer. But where does that leave you— my Purpose Partners? I felt that I had got you into this unhappy situation; would I now abandon you? It was fresh in my mind how my son had felt abandoned, and that cost another man's son his life."

Cheryl's hand tightens again on Dan's. Dan scarcely notices. It is starting to dawn on him why Sifu and Bill Newell might be in the audience, and his heart begins to thump in his chest.

"David Burton did not turn away when he saw my son's car plunge into the water," John says steadily. "He did not tell himself that it was not his problem. And he did not have the slightest idea who was in the car. But he did not hesitate. He knew he had to do what was right."

John pauses, but there is no need. The room is utterly still again. Dan glances at Marcia and looks hastily away. Her cheeks are stained with tears, and she is looking at Cheryl with a love and compassion that makes Dan's heart ache. "In the face of such great love, the example of a man who gave his life for someone he did not know, I had no choice but to do what was right," John says quietly. "And unlike David Burton, *I* was the reason that this business is underwater! I could not turn away. And that meant that I would have to reach out and ask for help…once again, to two people who had no reason to accept me or listen to me.

"I'd like to introduce you to two men, one of whom you know and one of whom most of you have never met. You all know Mr. Bill Newell, or know of him. He was the chairman of the board of Prestigious Products for a great many years. He resigned recently in protest of the leadership style that the Chang Tao group was bringing to your company. Bill, would you come up please?"

The room fills with warm applause as Bill takes the stage. He embraces Cheryl and gives her a kiss on the cheek. He moves to Dan and grabs his hand in a firm shake. Then he pulls Dan close;

"Hold on to your hat, buddy," Bill says softly. Before Dan can reply, Bill has moved past him to shake hands with John.

"The second man is a living legend in my home country of China and to practitioners of martial arts the world over. For twenty years he was the undefeated people's champion of China and the undisputed Grandmaster of Walu Kung Fu everywhere in the world. Today he is a very successful businessman and a very wise one. Perhaps of greatest interest to all of you, he is the man who introduced Dan Burton to the People First philosophy twelve years ago, and it is he who devised the seven keys of trust that I presented to you a moment ago. Ladies and gentlemen, if you have appreciated working in a People First company, would you please give your warm welcome to Mr. Sifu Li?"

Sifu bounds lightly up the stairs to the stage, smiling broadly. The group welcomes Sifu with hearty applause. Dan can think of no better way to greet his mentor than to bow and offer the two-handed salute that all the students at Sifu's school use to acknowledge the Grandmaster. Sifu bows and solemnly returns the salute, but then he grabs Dan's hand in a firm grip. He looks up at Dan, and his eyes are very bright. "I hope you enjoy this day, my friend," Sifu says warmly. "You are the reason I am here." Sifu turns to Cheryl and they embrace.

John Kwan looks at Dan, and his smile is every bit as wide as Sifu's. "Dan, you must be wondering what on earth is going on!" He looks back out at the room. "All Dan knew was that I was coming here to announce the sale of Prestigious Products. He has no idea who the buyer is."

John pauses again, his eyes dancing from Dan to Cheryl. Dan suddenly realizes that he is holding his breath and he makes a conscious effort to relax. *Hoping against hope,* he thinks.

"Ladies and gentlemen," John says formally, "Prestigious Products has been sold to a group of investors who call themselves the People First Leadership Group. The three primary investors are on this stage. They are Sifu Li, Bill Newell, and myself. We intend to show the world how the People First Effect, as Sifu calls it, will make Prestigious Products the model for creating trust and organizational excellence."

It takes a moment for the words to sink in. Now it is Dan's turn to break out in a huge smile. He looks at Marcia, understanding now why she had given him such a big grin before. Marcia grins back at Dan and then leaps to her feet. "Hooray," she shouts and begins to applaud.

It is as if the room had been waiting for permission to celebrate. Everyone in the room stands as one and begins to applaud. There are cheers and hoots of joy. Dan and Cheryl look at each other; Cheryl's eyes are brimming with tears and Dan pulls her to him for a long hug. He hears the applause and cheering grow even louder. He looks up at the three men on the stage, who have all turned to direct their applause at Dan and Cheryl. Dan realizes that there are tears on his own cheeks. He looks from John to Bill to Sifu. "Thank you," Dan says softly. He reaches for Sifu and Sifu is immediately at his side, putting an arm around Dan's shoulders. Cheryl reaches for Sifu and the three embrace. "Sifu, you overwhelm me!" Dan says in his friend's ear.

Sifu pulls back to look at the Burtons, his face lit with sheer joy. "There is much more, Dan," Sifu says, chuckling delightedly. "John is just getting started!"

Dan looks up at John. John raises his hands, and the applause slowly subsides. "This purchase means that the People First philosophy that Sifu Li taught Dan Burton, and which Dan introduced here twelve years ago, will be our business model going forward. And who better to guide us in this philosophy? We have the man who originally devised it." Here, John gestures to Sifu. "We have the man who first initiated People First at Prestigious Products," as John gestures to Dan. "And we have the former chairman who oversaw the installation of People First.

"And I must add that these men are not acting as friendly advisors; they have both made significant financial investments in this venture. Sifu Li said to me this morning, 'I suppose it is time for me to put my money where my mouth is.'" Laughter erupts around the room, and John and Sifu grin at each other.

Again, John raises his hands for silence. "I must confess, however, that I am being presumptuous in saying that we have Dan Burton. It is my very sincere hope that he will want to continue to advise me as a friend and mentor. But many of you do not know that staying with us will be a very difficult decision for him." John pauses for a moment and looks at someone behind him. Out of the corner of his eye, Dan sees two people he does not know approaching the stage. One of them, a man in his mid-twenties, is carrying something that looks like a large poster board.

"The first afternoon I visited the Burton home," John continues, "Dan and Cheryl told me that before David Burton's death, the family had decided to open a foundation, a People First foundation, that would help families in distress, families who are struggling due to financial reversals, addiction, emotional distress." He looks at Dan and Cheryl apologetically. "I hope you will forgive me for sharing this information publicly, but the Burtons had already decided that they will make a significant investment in that foundation. They are putting *their* money where their mouth is by using their family nest egg to invest in people. Dan and Cheryl both told me that their son's death had only strengthened their commitment to making that investment. It was their commitment..."

John is interrupted by a burst of applause from the crowd. Dan looks down at his wife and pulls her close to him. "Sweetheart," Dan says softly, "I don't know that I've ever been so proud of you as I am today!"

John waits for the applause to subside. "It was the commitment that the Burton family has modeled for me, the commitment to do the right thing, the *best* thing, no matter what the personal cost, that stirred me to ensure that Prestigious Products remains a People First company. But I learned something else about commitment that day; I watched how Dan and Cheryl Burton, even in the midst of the most terrible trial, drew strength from each other and it made me realize how I had done nothing to make my wife and son strong. I was fortunate to be able to reach my wife and son and beg them for forgiveness. And they are here today. Please welcome my wife Peijing and my son Johnny."

There is warm applause. Dan turns to see a middle-aged Asian woman standing on the stage. Next to her is the young man with the poster board. He glances at Dan and Cheryl shyly and then his eyes drop to the floor, shuffling his feet nervously. Dan realizes that he is holding his breath; this is Johnny Kwan.

Dan hesitates for an instant, but Cheryl moves immediately to shake hands with Peijing and then turns to Johnny. She puts her hands on Johnny's shoulders and looks straight into his eyes. "Johnny, David would be so glad that you're here today. Thank you for coming."

Johnny looks up at Cheryl and then his eyes shift to Dan. Pain and grief are written clearly across his face. "Mr. and Mrs. Burton..." His voice is practically a whisper, and Dan strains to hear over the applause. "I'm so very sorry. I..."

Dan moves up next to his wife. "It's Dan and Cheryl, Johnny," Dan says in a warm voice. He includes Peijing in his smile. "I hope we'll get a chance to talk more when this is over, but know that we accept your apology and that we forgive you." He gives Johnny's shoulder a firm squeeze for emphasis.

Johnny looks at them both, not comprehending. "How can you possibly...?"

"We'll talk later," Cheryl says. She looks at Peijing with a genuine smile. "I think you'll both be surprised to find out how much our families have in common."

John has been watching anxiously. This was the one part of the day's proceedings that he was nervous about—surprising the Burtons with his son. As he watches the Burtons welcome Johnny so graciously, he feels a lump forming in his throat, and he approaches Dan and Cheryl.

"Dan...Cheryl...I hope you will allow my family to provide some seed money for your new venture." John smiles apologetically. "I'm afraid there wasn't a great deal left after the purchase of Prestigious Products, but Peijing and I both hope you will accept this gift to help with the startup of the People First Foundation. Johnny?"

Johnny clears his throat, and then, in a surprisingly strong, clear voice, he says, "Mr. and Mrs. Burton, the Kwan family would like to present you with a gift of one million dollars for your new foundation. We make this gift of love in memory of your son David." He turns the poster board around and holds it up for everyone in the room to see; it is an enlarged facsimile of a check for one million dollars!

Cheryl gasps. This Dan did not see coming. He realizes that his mouth is hanging open comically. Once again, the room erupts with cheers and applause. Sifu and Bill Newell are both grinning from ear to ear. Cheryl practically leaps at John Kwan to hug him. Dan accepts the check from Johnny and grips his arm. "Thank you, son," Dan says in a hoarse voice. "Thank you very much." He extends a hand to Peijing. "I don't know how to thank you," Dan says.

Peijing smiles, and her entire face lights with joy. "No, thank *you*, Dan. We have so much to thank you and your wife for!" At that moment Cheryl Burton, tears streaming down her face, engulfs Peijing in a crushing embrace. Then it is Johnny's turn. Peijing reaches in a pocket of her light jacket and hands Cheryl a tissue. "I thought you might want one," she whispers to Cheryl.

Cheryl gives a choked laugh of thanks.

"Ladies and gentlemen," John says to the room at large, "I have one more announcement and a request, and then we will dismiss.

"There is another reason why I introduced you to Sifu Li and Bill Newell. I originally approached Sifu Li to ask him for help in funding the purchase of Prestigious Products. I thought he might be able to introduce me to investors; I must confess I did not expect that he would become one of those investors!" John's voice softens slightly. "He told me that he has never had a friend whom he admired as much as Dan Burton, and that was the primary reason he made this investment."

Dan turns his head for a moment to look at Sifu. A long look passes between the two men, a look of love and trust and understanding that only a very few men will ever experience in a lifetime.

Dan refocuses. "As Sifu and I discussed leadership and the People First philosophy," John is saying, "I realized that the leadership principles Sifu was explaining are concepts that thousands of managers and executives have never heard! I have worked with a great many companies and dozens of executives throughout my career; it might surprise you to know how many of them are putting profits first and people last, just as I did when I first came here.

"I asked Sifu if we could meet with Bill Newell to discuss these leadership concepts, and the upshot of these conversations is that the People First Leadership Group is more than an investment group. Sifu told me that his work with Dan and other executives around the country has fueled his desire to teach more than the martial arts; he wants to bring his leadership philosophy to the world. And so the People First Leadership group will be working to build the very best blend of business systems *and* human systems here at Prestigious Products, and we plan to hold training programs and leadership summits here in this facility and throughout the country to help other leaders master this way of living."

John turns and smiles at Sifu. "Sifu Li told me that he wants to change the world with this People First philosophy. He wants to raise up an entire generation of David Burtons. He wants to mentor young men and women in the importance of honoring the dignity and worth of people and teach them about the power of building trust."

John pauses for a moment and looks out at the room. Dan sees a great many smiling faces; several women are dabbing at their eyes with tissues.

John's voice is suddenly husky. "That was the announcement; this is my request. I have asked my family to forgive me for my terrible negligence; I have asked the Burtons to forgive me for the devastation I have brought to their lives. But I must also humbly ask all of you for forgiveness as well. I did not lead you well. I did nothing that would cause you to trust me or the way I was leading this organization. I recognize now that trust is not something that is lightly given; once trust has been broken, it takes a great deal of time and effort to rebuild it.

"I have made that commitment to my wife and son. I will work every day to earn their trust, and I have asked them to call me to account immediately if I give any indication that I am beginning to slip back into my old ways. I also have three of the best mentors that any man could hope to have. They are here on this stage with me. I have asked them to continue to show me my blind spots and to teach me how to make People First an everyday reality here at Prestigious Products. I intend to be living proof that the leopard *can* change his spots, and I hope to begin that process by proving it to my family, to the Burtons, to my teachers, and to each of you. I ask you to give me a chance to do that. I firmly believe that if we work together, we can make Prestigious Products the shining star of our industry once again."

John nods his head with finality. "That's all." He smiles at the assembled group. "Thank you for your kindness and for your genuine celebration of these remarkable people. I look forward to meeting you all in the weeks ahead. And I commit to doing everything I can to rebuild trust and put People First at Prestigious Products." John's smile widens with genuine warmth. "Make it a People First day today."

Dan raises his hands to begin to applaud John, but the crowd beats him to it. It is as if the home team had just scored the winning touchdown; they rise to their feet as one and roar their approval.

Postscript

THIS BOOK IS A MIXTURE of fact, fiction, and vision. I know no one named Dan Burton, Sifu Li, or John Kwan. But I've met men and women just like them during my career. I've known young people who are mired in despair, just like Marcy Burton and Johnny Kwan. Some of them are members of my own family and, just as Dan did for Marcy, I pray for them every day. I've met genuine heroes like David Burton; some made the ultimate sacrifice in Iraq and Afghanistan, laying down their lives for a shining ideal of freedom for people whom they had never met. And I've sat with grieving families, like that of Claudia Barnes, and shed tears of pain and loss with them.

But, of course, the seven business leaders you met in this book are entirely real, and they have far more than a classroom understanding of concepts like trust and sustainable profitability; they have amassed decades of rich experience applying their knowledge to real-world challenges. When I was a young man, I sat under a number of professors who taught business and psychology; I could have saved a great deal of money and learned a *lot* more by interviewing these men!

The final chapter of this book gives you a glimpse of my vision for the People First Effect. The vision statement for my company is to change the world through the People First philosophy. But that won't happen just because I want it to; it will take *your* vision and *your* passion to make it a reality. I invite you and exhort you, Dear Reader, to make my vision for The People First Effect *your* vision.

Immerse yourself in this philosophy and create the People First Effect, first and foremost, in your home. Practice People First with your loved ones and develop a similar accountability system so that you have trusted people in your life who will speak the truth in love to you when you wander off this proven path of personal and professional excellence. If I am weak in one of the keys of trust, I want to know about it! So should you.

Once you've embraced the People First philosophy in your personal life, bring it into your community. Look for ways to Sincerely, Specifically, Immediately, and Personally (SSIP) honor the dignity and worth of every man, woman, and child you meet. Practice the principles of People First at your church or synagogue or civic organization; celebrate the dignity and worth of people you meet in the drugstore, the grocery store, your dry cleaners, in airports, in movie theatres…everywhere you go!

And then take this philosophy into the workplace. You may be the CEO of your organization; perhaps you are a senior executive, a middle manager, or a line supervisor. Trust me when I tell you—and trust the leaders you've met in this book when they tell you—the men and women who work with you and for you will be transformed into passionate, powerful Purpose Partners when you bring this philosophy into your business.

But perhaps you are the worker on the line; perhaps you are the newest hire in an entry-level position; perhaps you only work part-time. You might think that your job title means you can't play a role in instituting the People First Effect at your company. Nothing could be further from the truth!

My dear friend Tom Manenti often asks his MiTek Purpose Partners, "Who is leadership at MiTek?" The answer Tom wants is an enthusiastic "I am!" from everyone in the room. One of

MiTek's seven core values is "Empowered Purpose Partners," and Tom is committed to making that value a palpable part of the MiTek culture.

Wherever you work, let me encourage you to borrow a page from the MiTek manual and see yourself as a leader at your organization. If you haven't read the first *People First* book, buy it—you can read it (or listen to the audio version) in an afternoon—and begin to practice the principles expressed by the Pyramid of People Power right away. Begin to build a People First culture right where you are.

And please remember this: your supervisors, managers, and executives need celebration too! I'm afraid many people wrongly believe that the People First philosophy only cascades downward. They think that the responsibility for generating the momentum of a People First culture lies squarely on the backs of senior leaders, who are tasked with cascading the spirit of recognition and celebration throughout the organization.

I heartily encourage all leaders at every level of their organizations to practice People First. But it doesn't have to start there! No matter what your position in an organization, *you* can initiate a People First culture in your department. *You* can create a virtual hotbed of recognition and celebration in your organization. Again, you'll want to read (or reread) *People First* and immerse yourself in the concept of making deliberate, daily efforts to catch people doing things right and celebrating them.

Be sure to tell your supervisor what you're doing. Now, I am *not* suggesting that you tell your boss, "You're really *bad* at providing positive reinforcement, so I'm going to take matters into my own hands!" That approach will not yield good results.

You *could,* however, tell your supervisor, "I just read a book about positive reinforcement and I realized that I haven't done a good job of recognizing and celebrating all that you do for our department. For example, I'm so impressed by the way you..." and then sincerely, specifically bring out something that your supervisor does that brings out the best in you and your Purpose Partners. Perhaps your boss is consistently strong in one or more of the seven keys of trust explained in this book. That would certainly be something to celebrate!

Let me emphasize the importance of being *sincere.* You're not doing this because you're trying to elevate your standing; you're doing it because you want to make deposits in another person's human spirit. After you've celebrated your supervisor, launch out into your department! Be on the lookout for things your Purpose Partners do that make your department better. Think about the seven keys that are laid out in this book; which of these keys do they embody? When you've decided on a point you can sincerely and specifically celebrate, do it!

When we first brought our *People First Leadership* program to MiTek Industries, the stories we heard from the people who work there were extremely heartening. One man told us that groups of MiTek Purpose Partners were spontaneously forming "celebration flash mobs" to let Purpose Partners know how much they appreciated them. Was CEO Tom Manenti practicing the People

First philosophy also? Of course he was! But his Purpose Partners didn't sit on their hands, waiting to see if the CEO was going to live it. They took *ownership* of the philosophy. They brought People First to life at MiTek.

I'd love to see you start People First chapters within your organization. One chapter might be working through the Pyramid of People Power, which is contained in the first book, and a second group could practice how to live out the seven keys of trust.

When you and I wake up every morning, as Sifu said to Dan, *committed* to running to represent the People First brand, remarkable things will happen! I was recently contacted by the mayor of one of our South Florida communities, who was asked about becoming the world's first People

First community. And at this writing, there is a major city in South Carolina that is actively working to beat Florida to the punch!

But why must we wait for our civic leaders? Why can't you and I take the lead on bringing People First into our towns? I cannot remember a time when the American people were as bitterly divided as we are today; rather than dividing over things like our politics, our skin color, our education, or our income, why not seek out those things we can unite around? And what could be more unifying than agreeing to make a conscious commitment to celebrate the dignity and worth of everyone we meet?

Tom Manenti said that he embraces the truth that united our founders, "that all men are created equal and that they are endowed by their Creator with certain unalienable rights, that among these are life, liberty, and the pursuit of happiness." These are principles that we can all embrace and celebrate together.

Let's do it! Let's partner together to start putting people first in every aspect of our personal and professional lives.

Will you join me? Let's put people first!

Breakthrough Business Growth Opportunity

I WANT TO COMMEND YOU and congratulate you for finishing *The People First Effect, 7 Keys for Mastering High Trust in a Low Trust World*. If you like the ideas that you learned in my book, I want to extend to you a breakthrough business opportunity to apply the 7 Keys of Trust as a comprehensive change management system for your organization.

Here is my offer to serious-minded business owners that are looking for a proven, time-tested organizational development system to take their organizations to a new level of sustainable profitability—I want to give you a two-day, People First® Effect Seminar for *free* to qualified business owners. If you own your business or are considering starting your own business all you have to do is go to www.peoplefirsteffectseminar.com and fill out the application form.

Now, you may be wondering, if the seminar is free why do I have to qualify in order to attend? The answer to this question is simple. First of all, I am only interested in teaching people who have a deep hunger and an unquenchable passion for the truth about personal and organizational development. Moreover, we only allow three hundred people to attend our two-day People First Effect Seminars. Therefore, the application process enables my team to more intelligently discern who will benefit the most from this People First Effect business growth opportunity.

As an added bonus to qualified business owners, I will allow you to bring an additional person with you for the two-day People First Effect Seminar at no additional charge. However, each person who qualifies to attend will be responsible for their own transportation to and from the event, lodging, and meals over the two-day People First Effect Seminar.

I am willing to invest two days of my life in you that will change your life and the life of your organization forever. If you are willing to invest in yourself and in a right-hand person whom you choose to attend with you, then with our combined investment of time and passion for human betterment, I believe that you will experience one of the greatest personal and professional breakthroughs in your life.

The personal and organizational breakthrough truths that you will be learning over these two extraordinary days are the same human systems and business systems that I have taught to the greatest organizations in the world for over four decades. My People First® Leadership and Organizational Development systems and strategies have helped organizations win national awards, make millions of dollars in profits, and transformed the personal lives of their employees.

Please go to peoplefirsteffectseminar.com to learn more about the personal and business growth systems that will enable you to unlock your potential at the People First Effect Seminar.

To Your Transformation,
Jack Lannom
Chief Belief Officer
People First International

www.ThinkPeopleFirst.com
People First is a Registered Trademark of People First International

Acknowledgements

This book would have never become a reality without the belief, love, and support of my darling wife, Debbie. I can't say enough about the grace and patience she showed me when I would take time away from her to work on the manuscript while we were on vacation. Debbie is truly the wind beneath my wings. I am eternally grateful for how she has unreservedly invested all of her time, talent, and treasure to make me into the man that I am today.

I also want to thank Yolanda Harris, president of The Keynote Group, for all of her effort in finding a quality publisher. This book would not have been published without Yolanda introducing me to Austin Miller and Nena Madonia Oshman.

I am deeply grateful to Austin and Nena for believing in me and the transformational value of *The People First Effect*. They were an absolute delight to work with as they helped me through the rigorous process of bringing the manuscript to life in excellence.

I want to give a very special thanks to Dan Philips. I am deeply indebted to Dan for his brilliance with respect to bringing every character in the book to life with his masterful ability to create compelling dialogue that keeps readers completely captivated as they vicariously experience the gut-wrenching tragedies and transformational triumphs of each character. Dan is truly one of the most gifted writers I have met in my life.

In addition, I want to thank my seven friends—Tom Manenti, James Donnelly, Ray Aschenbach, Keith Guller, Noel Fogarty, Richard Thorne and Keith Koenig—who allowed me to capture their organizational experience and wisdom regarding how to accelerate trust-based relationships so that organizations can more effectively achieve their bottom-line results.

Finally, I celebrate Jorge Rendon for his incredible design ability. Jorge took my ideas for a book cover and transformed my crude drawings into a beautiful piece of art. Jorge is a creative genius, and it is has always been my honor and joy to collaborate with such a loving, humble, and talented man.